SOUTH INDIA AND HER MUHAMMADAN INVADERS

SOUTH INDIA AND HER MUHAMMADAN INVADERS

BY

S. KRISHNASWAMI AIYANGAR

GYAN

Published by

Gyan Publishing House
5, Ansari Road
Daryaganj, New Delhi-110002
Phone: 011-47034999, 9811692060
E-mail: books@gyanbooks.com

Distribution Network
gyanbooks.com
India, USA, Canada, UK, Australia

ISBN: 978-93-6208-830-7 (HB)
First Published, 1921

2nd Impression 2024

Printed at: Gyan Press, Delhi.

SOUTH INDIA AND HER MUHAMMADAN INVADERS
Author: S. KRISHNASWAMI AIYANGAR

SOUTH INDIA AND HER MUHAMMADAN INVADERS

SOUTH INDIA AND HER MUHAMMADAN INVADERS

BY

S. KRISHNASWAMI AIYANGAR, M.A.,

Professor of Indian History and Archæology, University of Madras

Fellow of the University of Madras;
Member of the Royal Asiatic Society
of Great Britain and Ireland;
Fellow of the Royal Historical Society;
Professor and Fellow of the Mysore University;
Reader, Calcutta University.

Author of '*Ancient India*,' '*Beginnings of South Indian History*', etc.

HUMPHREY MILFORD

OXFORD UNIVERSITY PRESS

LONDON BOMBAY CALCUTTA MADRAS

1921

INSCRIBED

BY GRACIOUS PERMISSION

TO

HIS HIGHNESS

SRĪ KRISHNARĀJĒNDRA WODAIYER BAHADUR,

G.C.S.I., G.C.B.

MAHĀRĀJA OF MYSORE,

IN TOKEN OF THE AUTHOR'S HIGH AND SINCERE ESTEEM FOR

HIS HIGHNESS

AS THE OCCUPANT OF THE THRONE OF THE PATRIOTIC SOVEREIGN

VĪRA BALLĀLA III

WHO DEVOTED HIS LIFE TO THE CAUSE OF HINDUISM

AND

MADE IT POSSIBLE FOR THE SOUTH INDIAN HINDUS TO BE

THE HINDUS THEY ARE TO-DAY

CONTENTS

APPENDIX A

APPENDIX B

ILLUSTRATIONS

PREFACE

In the course of writing the introductory chapter to my forthcoming history of the Empire of Vijayanagar, I was led to an investigation of the actual circumstances under which that Empire came into being, and, as a consequence, the condition of South India on the eve of the Muhammadan invasions. The result of this investigation is set forth in the following six lectures delivered as 'the Third Course of Special Lectures in the Department of Indian History and Archæology' at the University of Madras. The first lecture traces the decadence of the Chola Empire, and shows how it split up into a number of chieftaincies. The disruption is traced to the pressure of the Pāṇḍyas from the South, the natural tendency to independence of the feudatories within, and a fratricidal war arising among the members of the Chola ruling family itself. The next traces the revival of the Pāṇḍya power which had been reduced to subordination by the Cholas very early in their imperial career. The re-assertion of their independence began with the weakening of the Chola power about the middle of the twelfth century, and culminated in the establishment of the Pāṇḍyas as one of only two South Indian Powers in the middle of the thirteenth. The third lecture concerns itself with the first invasions of the Dakhan by Alau-d-din and Malik Kafur. In the fourth it is pointed out that there is satisfactory evidence of Malik Kafur's invasion having reached as far south as Madura and Ramēśvaram, and that the character of the invasions had nothing of conquest or occupation of territory in it. The fifth lecture bears upon the career of Muhammad Tughlak and the character of the invasions of South India sent by him. Muhammad's policy was conquest and extension of his empire, and was thus opposed to that of Alau-d-din. Muhammad's empire was, it is pointed out, the largest that the Muhammadan empire ever reached in India and carried in it the seed of dismemberment. An attempt is made to arrange the chronology of Muhammad's reign on rational lines on the basis of the History of the Sultanate of Madura founded in his reign. The sixth contains a somewhat detailed exposition of the foundation and further history of the Sultanate of Madura, and its wars against the Hoysalas who, under their last great ruler, Vīra Baḷḷāḷa III made a patriotic effort to dislodge the Muhammadans from the South. The Hoysala King fell in the effort, and brought his dynasty to an end in carrying on this great national war of the Hindus. Some of the more prominent officers of his empire discharged their debt to cause and country by ultimately succeeding where their master had failed, and giving visible embodiment to their success in elevating to the dignity of 'Capital of the Empire' a new foundation of the last great Hoysala, Vīra Baḷḷāḷa III.

> Vijitya Viśvam Vijayābhidhānām
> Viśvōttaram yō nagarīm vyadatta.

This was Vijayanagar. The credit of this achievement is due to five brothers who all held positions of responsibility along the northern frontier when the critical moment had arrived. If one among them could be marked out, as peculiarly deserving of this honour, it was Bukka, his son Kumāra Kampana coming in for an honourable share.

We have the high authority of Lord Morley for the dictum, 'we have no business to seek more from the past than the very past itself.' I have striven hard to keep to the high level of this historical dictum, and trust I have kept out all bias one way or another. I have had occasion to lament with Freeman, 'I am beginning to think, that there is not, and never was such a thing as truth in the world. At least I do not believe that any two people ever give exactly the same account of anything, even when they have seen it with their own eyes, except when they copy from one another.' I have endeavoured to get at the truth despite this difficulty, and leave it to my readers to judge how far my effort has attained success.

The work embodies a considerable volume of information the collection of which was made possible by the liberal permission accorded by the Syndicate of the University of Madras to my making a tour in the parts of the country involved in the course of this history. I acknowledge my obligation to them for their sympathy. Even so it would have been impossible to have got together all the local information I have, but for the good offices of several of my friends, among whom I must mention prominently Rao Sahib M. Ct. Muthia Chettiar, M.L.C., Sheriff of Madras, Diwan Bahadur T. Desikachariar, B.A., B.L., M.L.C., and his assistant Mr. N. P. Swaminatha Ayyar, B.A., Archæologist of the Pudukotta State, and my late lamented friend Mr. C. S. Anantarama Ayyar, B.A., Revenue Divisional Officer at Devakotta, carried off in the prime of a very useful and unostentatious life to the detriment alike of the service of which he was an ornament, and all real Oriental Scholarship for which he had always had genuine sympathy, and, what is more, in which he could and did take active interest. I must not omit mention of M.R.Ry. V. Ramalinga Mudaliar, Tahsildar of Sivaganga, for much valuable assistance. I acknowledge my indebtedness to these gentlemen with the most sincere pleasure. I acknowledge with equal pleasure my obligation to Principal Tait, late of the Central College, Bangalore, who read through the manuscript for me and offered valuable advice adding to his many kindnesses to me through a long period of close on thirty years during which he was successively my professor, colleague and Principal, but all along a friend. I am grateful to His

Exalted Highness the Nizam's Government, Rao Bahadur R. Narasimhachariar, Prāktanavimarśa Vichakṣaṇa, Director of Archæological Researches in Mysore, Mr. A. H. Longhurst, Superintendent of Archæology, Madras, and Messrs. Wiele and Klein, Photographers, Madras, for having permitted the use of their excellent photographs for the illustrations.

Messrs. C. K. Ramadorai, B.A. (Hons.) and R. Gopalan, B.A. (Hons.), University Research Students, helped me in verifying references and preparing the index. My nephew S. Raju Aiyangar drew the map which forms the frontispiece. I acknowledge with pleasure my obligations to these.

In its final form, the substance of the book was delivered, by invitation of the Mysore University, as a course of Extension Lectures in Mysore, and one part under the name 'The Foundation of Vijayanagar' was similarly delivered as a lecture before the Mythic Society, Bangalore.

It is a matter of particular gratification to me that His Highness the Maharaja of Mysore was graciously pleased to accept the dedication of this work. It is peculiarly appropriate as it is this work that exhibits, for the first time, the glorious part played by the last great Hoysala of Mysore in saving South India and Indian culture for the Hindus. His Highness has but added one more to the many gracious acts of kindness for which I am debtor without hope of repaying the kindness except by gratitude. I hope, however, it will be given to me to repay this kindness by further work which may deserve well of His Highness.

S. KRISHNASWAMI AIYANGAR.

UNIVERSITY OF MADRAS,
February 22, 1921.

Other works and publications by the Author

ANCIENT INDIA.
(Messrs. Luzac & Co., London and S.P.C.K., Madras).

THE BEGINNINGS OF SOUTH INDIAN HISTORY.
(Modern Printing Works, Madras).

A LITTLE KNOWN CHAPTER OF VIJAYANAGAR HISTORY.
(S.P.C.K., Madras).

KRISHNADEVA RAYA OF VIJAYANAGAR.

SOCIAL LEGISLATION UNDER HINDU GOVERNMENTS.
(S.P.C.K., Madras).

SOURCE BOOK OF HINDU INDIA, 2 Parts
(Messrs. K. & J. Cooper, Bombay).

A SHORT HISTORY OF HINDU INDIA.
(Messrs. K. & J. Cooper, Bombay).

A HISTORY OF THE HINDU EMPIRE OF VIJAYANAGAR.
(in active preparation).

SOURCES OF VIJAYANAGAR HISTORY.
(Editor, published by the Madras University).

M. JOUVEAU-DUBREUIL'S INDIAN ARCHITECTURE.
(Editor, English Version, S.P.C.K., Madras).

SOUTH INDIA

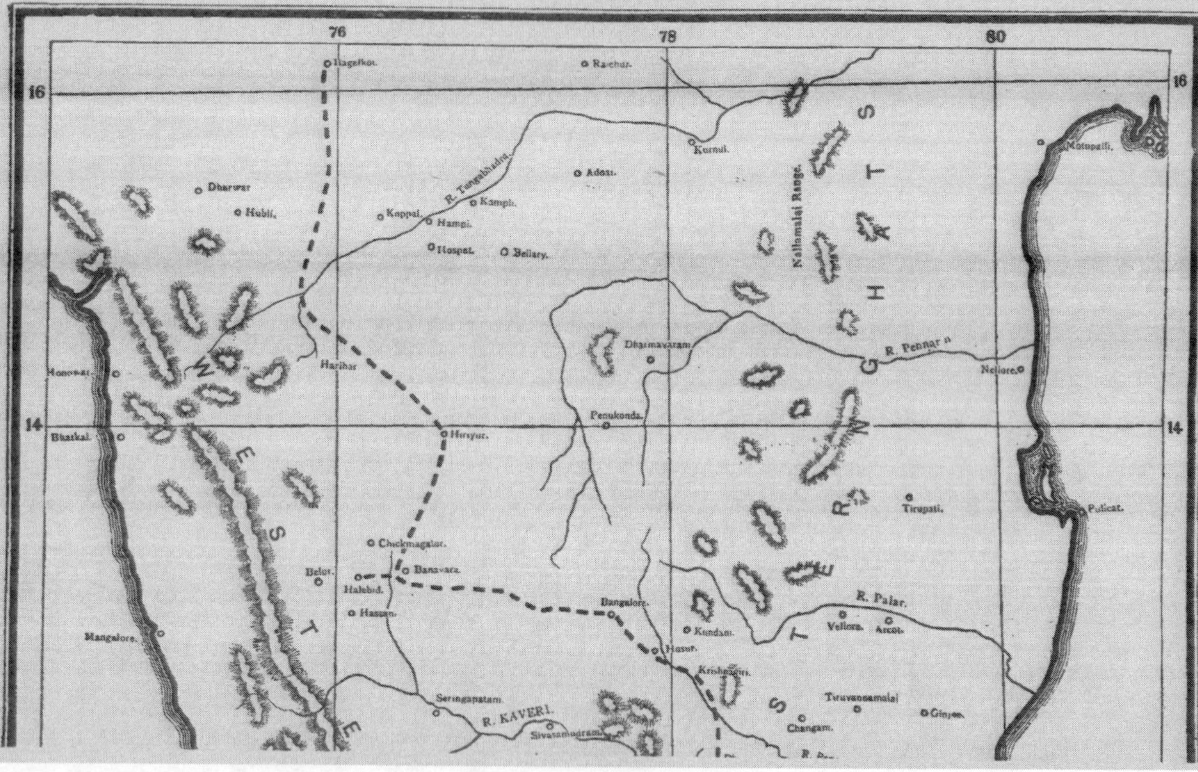

76
78
80
16
14
Raichur.
Kurnul.
Motupalli.
Dharwar
Hubli.
Kappal.
Hampi.
Kampli.
R. Tungabhadra.
Adoni.
Hospet.
Bellary.
Nallamalai Range.
Dharmavaram
R. Pennar
Nellore.
Honawar.
Harihar
Penukonda.
Bhatkal.
Hiriyur.
Tirupati.
Pulicat.
Chickmagalur.
Belur.
Halebid.
Banavara.
Hassan.
Bangalore.
Kundani.
Hosur.
R. Palar.
Vellore.
Arcot.
Mangalore.
Krishnagiri.
Seringapatam.
R. KAVERI.
Sivasamudram.
Tiruvannamalai
Ginjee.
Changam.

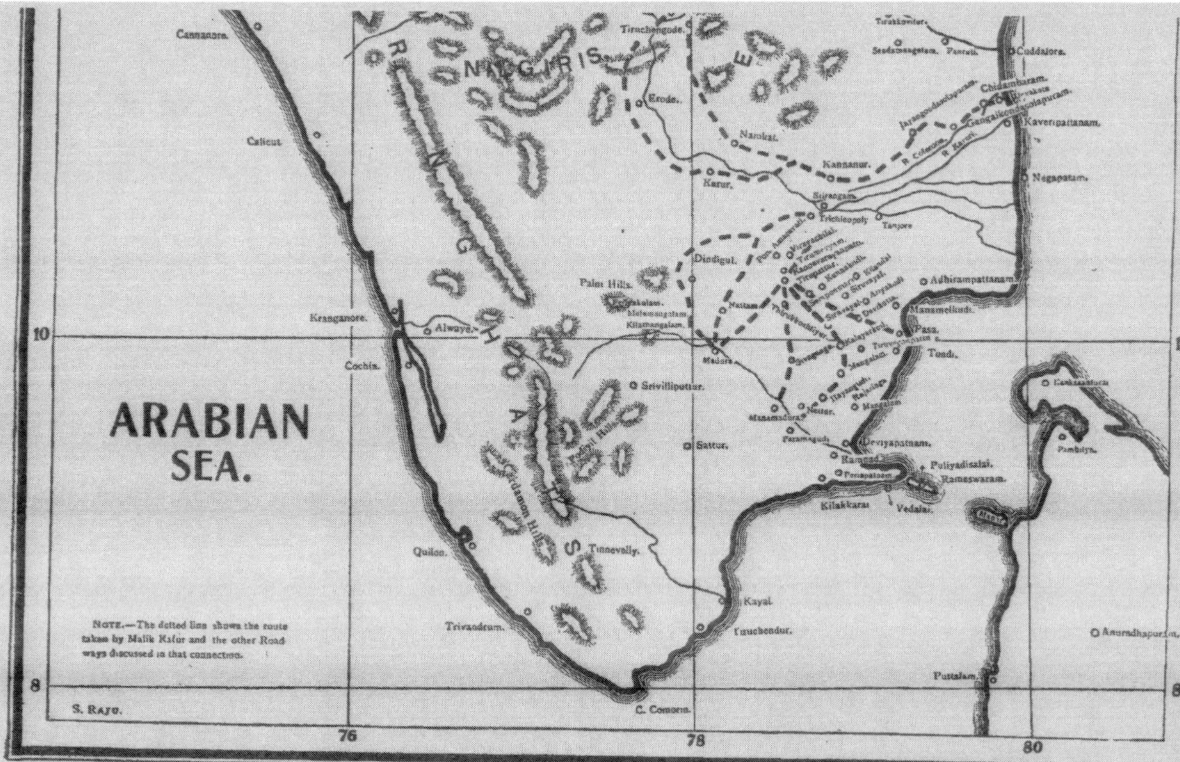

Frontispiece to South India and her Muhammadan Invaders

ERRATA

PAGE	LINE	ERROR	CORRECTION
88	8		omit , after Deogir
128	1	Jazia	Jizia
144	6	Dekhan	Dakhan
172	12	Same Virupaksha Paṭṭanam	Same as Virupaksha paṭṭanam
194	3	Calld	Called
203	33	Margossa	Margosa

South India and Her Muhammadan Invaders

LECTURE I

THE BREAK UP OF THE CHOLA EMPIRE

DURING the period of Chola ascendancy, beginning from the days of the great Parāntaka, early in the tenth century, the Pāṇḍyas may be regarded as subordinate to the Chola power. This subordinate position was not habitually acknowledged, and punitive wars had to be undertaken in consequence. At one time under Rājarāja the Great, or his son Rājēndra I, the imperial Cholas adopted the practice of appointing members of their family as viceroys of the Pāṇḍya and other kingdoms, with special designations indicating authority over the Pāṇḍya, Kongu and other kingdoms of old. This hardening of the authority of the Cholas reduced the Pāṇḍyas still further in importance so that it might justifiably be said that their power was extinct in the period of the 'Chola Ascendancy.' Members of the Pāṇḍya royal family, however, remained active in various places of importance in the Pāṇḍya territory and were causing considerable trouble to the administration. It was in all probability this state of things that led to the planting of military colonies by Kulottunga I, in agricultural tracts in the Pāṇḍya country along the road to Koṭṭāru throughout the whole length of the territory. The Pāṇḍyas often became fugitives in Ceylon from their own country. There are records of several wars waged by the Cholas against the Ceylon rulers for having given asylum to the Pāṇḍyas. Up to the middle of the twelfth century, the

Cholas continued to be victorious and successfully asserted their authority over the Pāṇḍyan kingdom, and, to a modified extent, over parts of Ceylon also. In the latter half of the twelfth century however, those that occupied the Chola throne degenerated both in power and personal ability, and, as a consequence the tendency in the border kingdoms, was to throw off the imperial yoke. It was in this state of affairs, when the Pāṇḍya kingdom was already breaking up into a number of principalities, that a disputed succession in Madura brought on an invasion from Ceylon.

The Ceylonese Invasion.—In A.D. 1170 or 1171 there were two rival claimants to the throne of Madura. One of them Parākrama Pāṇḍya was besieged in Madura by another named Kulaśēkhara. In this war Kulaśēkhara seems to have had the advantage to begin with, and Parākrama in distress appealed for assistance to Parākrama Bāhu of Ceylon who had just then emerged successfully out of a series of wars in his own country. During a period of sixteen years, according to the Mahāvamśa, he was engaged in constant wars against his rivals to bring all Ceylon under one ruler. If the statement of the Mahāvamśa is to be given full credit, he had succeeded in achieving this object of his ambition. On receiving the ambassadors from Parākrama Pāṇḍya, Parākrama Bāhu resolved to fit out and send a great army of invasion to place Parākrama Pāṇḍya on the throne. In the meanwhile Parākrama Pāṇḍya was captured and put to death with his wives and children, and Kulaśēkhara placed himself on the throne of Madura. The invasion started under the famous Ceylon general Lankāpura Daṇḍanātha as he is called. The army set out from the capital and reached Mahātittha (Manthot of the maps) in Ceylon. Information was by then received that Kulaśēkhara had taken possession of Madura and had put to death his rival and all his family. Parākrama Bāhu ordered the continuation of the march so that the kingdom might be

Gandamādavaparvata—Rāmēsvaram
(by permission of the Madras Archæological Department)

taken from Kulaśēkhara and given over to one of the children of his friend. From Mahātittha, the army proceeded to a harbour 'Talabbilla,' in Ceylon. After a voyage lasting a day and night they sighted the coast on the other side, and effected a landing in spite of opposition, at another haven called Talabbilla on the Pāṇḍyan side of the country.[1]

The chief command of the army was given, as was already noted, to the greatest Ceylon general of the time Lankāpura Daṇḍanātha. He attacked Rāmēśvaram and, after a number of battles, took possession of the place. He marched further forward to almost where Pamban is at present and took possession of a very convenient haven called Kundukāla[2] 'midway between the two seas and four leagues distant from Ramissaram.' Passing over minor

[1] Talabbilla on the Ceylon side was apparently the haven forming part of, or perhaps some little way from, Manthote. Talabbilla on the Pāṇḍyan side seems meant for the haven which is nowadays called Puḷiyaḍiśālai, two to three miles straight east from what is called Gandamādana Parvata, itself two miles north by east of the town of Rāmēśvaram. I make this identification, as in the locality there is current the tradition regarding a Kandyan monarch who built the sanctum of the temple at Rāmēśvaram. This is confirmed by certain inscriptions in the sanctum itself. This monarch got all the stones for the building dressed and fitted in Kandy, and brought them over to be landed at a convenient port thence to be carried over to Rāmēśvaram for the building, the island itself offering no stone quarry for the purpose. Some of these were brought in duplicates, the unused among which are said still to lie in the harbour Puḷiyaḍiśālai. The Gandamādana Parvata itself carries two foot-prints. These are pointed out as Rama's foot-prints there. But the character of the structure and the footprints themselves seem to indicate that the structure was intended to be a Buddhist shrine which the Ceylon General himself may have built during the occupation of the island. I am not aware of any worship of Rama's feet except the worship of the sandals which he left behind with his brother Bharata according to the Rāmāyaṇa when he went into exile, as a memento of his during his absence in the forests. The distance from there to Parākramapaṭṭaṇa, the fortified camp of Lankāpura would work out correctly on this basis.

[2] This is what is called Kundugāl just a mile and a half or two south of Pamban. This locality is made use of by the South Indian Railway authorities as both the dry and wet docks for the repair or refit of their steam-launches. I have not been able to trace any sign of the fortifications with the 'three circuits of walls and twelve gates,' but there is no doubt that it is the place referred to as Kundukāla. There is no memory of its having been called Parākramapura in the locality at all.

details, Lankāpura defeated the Pāndyan forces in a number of villages and towns. On his way back to his camp, he attacked the chieftain Āḷavanda Perumāḷ who was encamped at the 'village Vadali,'[1] and killed him. It was after this that Kulaśēkhara made a great effort by leading his forces personally. He is said to have collected his armies from all over the Pāndyan kingdom, including auxiliaries from the two Kongus and Tinnevelly. From his headquarters at the fortified villages of Erukoṭṭa and Iḍagalissara (which places I am not able to identify yet) he sent 'a great army by land[2] and many soldiers by sea and ships, to assault the fortress of Parākramapura.' There was a hotly contested battle, Kulaśēkhara having his horse shot under him, and the Ceylon General got so much the better of his enemy that the very camp of the Pāndya was burnt down. The Ceylonese then marched and occupied Vadali (Vēdāḷai). He made a further dash northwards from Vēdāḷai as the base, surprised Dēviyāpaṭṭaṇam (Dēvīpaṭṭaṇam, as it is now called) and marched further forwards to Śiriyavala.[3] He returned therefrom apparently by way of Kāḷaiyārkoil-Paramaguḍi road and took the two places Aṇivalakkoṭṭa (sometimes called Aṇivaḷakki in the narrative) and the fortress of Neṭṭūr.[4] These became afterwards the headquarters of the Ceylon army. While here, information reached the general that one of the sons of Parākrama

[1] This is apparently the Vēdāḷai of to-day about two miles south by west of the Manḍapam Camp Railway station.

[2] The tradition is even now current that there was no channel here between Manḍapam and Pamban. The name Manḍapam is said to have been given to the place as it did contain a Manḍapa to which the God of Rāmēś-varam used to be carried on occasions of certain annual festivals. Of course that could not be done across the sea.

[3] This is apparently Śiruvayal. There are two places of the name in the Ramnad-district one on the north by west of Tiruvāḍānai, and another one much farther north along the road from Paramaguḍi to Tiruppattūr ultimately. The former is apparently what is meant here.

[4] Neṭṭūr is about five miles west of Iḷaiyānguḍi and may be about seven or eight miles north-west of Paramaguḍi railway station on the South Indian Railway. This is the place where Kulottunga III defeated and cut off the head of Vīra Pāndya. Aṇivaḷakki must have been very near that.

Pāṇḍya was a fugitive in the Malayāḷam country. This was Vīra Pāṇḍya. Lankāpura sent him a message asking him to come over and join him. Sending intimation of this discovery to his master, he marched across, apparently at the instance of Vīra Pāṇḍya to Periyakuḷam in the ghats, and gained possession of Mĕlamangalam and Kīḻamangalam. He thought it better to hand these over on terms to the chieftain from whom he took them, and returned to his head-quarters at Aṇivaḷakkoṭṭa. Proceeding from there to Neṭṭūr he made a dash against another place not very far, which is called Mānavīramadura, apparently Manamadura, now a railway station. He defeated the chieftains who held the place, and brought the place under his authority. He then found a number of chieftains collected together at Pātapathā (a place I am not yet able to identify), assaulted the place and took it. He found it necessary now to march north-eastwards to Anjukoṭṭai near Tiruvāḍānai. He took the place and the two ports in the vicinity of Toṇḍi and Pāśa (Pāśipaṭṭaṇa, as it is now called), marched further forwards to Kurundanguḍi first, and thence to Tiruvēkambama, probably the place now called Tiruvēganpaṭṭu. As the chieftain, apparently of that locality, Māḷava Chakravarti, would not submit and retired to a place called Śemponmāri (on the borders of the Pudukoṭṭa State) in the Tiruppattūr Taluk, the Ceylon general advanced upon the place. The place was considered a great stronghold and the Cholas are said to have failed to take the place after a two years' siege. The Ceylonese are said to have taken it in less than half a day.[1] The Ceylonese in their turn were besieged in the fortress and the siege of the famous stronghold was raised by the heroic deeds of Lankāpura and his lieutenants. Apart from this fortress the Pāṇḍyan territory up to the boundary of the Chola country came under the

[1] Śemponmāri is said to belong to Talaiyūrnāḍu in the Tiruppatūr Taluk. Ep. Coll. 128 of 1908.

control of the Ceylonese. What is perhaps of greater importance the Vaiśyas (Vessas) and the Muhammadans (Yavanas) of this locality brought presents to him. He restored Śemponmāri however to Māḷava Chakravarti, and retired to Aṇivaḷakki, by way of Tiruvēgambama and Kurundanguḍi. While here he heard that another Tamil chieftain had taken Śiriyavala (Śiruvayal) having defeated Māḷava Chakravarti, whose head-quarters of Śemponmāri also fell into his hands. Lankāpura intervened between Māḷava Chakravarti and this new chieftain his enemy, and after effecting a reconciliation between the two, retired to Neṭṭūr. He then set about restoring the two tanks that were destroyed at Rājasīha Mahala (Rājasingamangalam) and Vālugama (Vālugrāma, Vālandaravaiḷ).

At this stage, Kulaśēkhara reappeared at the head of a vast army with auxiliaries from the Kongus and Tinnevelly. It was then that Parākrama Bāhu himself sent another army under the command of Jagad Vijaya, which arrived at Aṇivaḷakki. The two generals established themselves at Neṭṭūr and Aṇivaḷakki respectively. Lankāpura advanced from Neṭṭūr and fought a battle in Mangalam.[1]

He pushed forward from there to Śiriyavala (Śiruvayal) again.[2] Here he defeated the chiefs Puṇkonḍa Nāḍāḷvār and his allies, and burnt down the two storeyed palace of this chief. He then retired to Tirikkānupper (Kāḷaiyārkoil). In the meanwhile his colleague Jagad Vijaya marched west towards Manamadura and took a number of places, returning to Neṭṭūr. The two Ceylon armies now joined together and marched upon Tiruppālūr or Tiruppāli apparently against Kulaśēkhara. Kulaśēkhara in the meanwhile had

[1] This is the Mangalam otherwise called Vaḷudi Vāḷmangalam about eight miles south from Kāḷaiyārkoil on the road from Tiruppattūr to Paramaguḍi. The town is in ruins and an extensive raised plot of ground is pointed out as the site of the old city.

[2] Apparently the place on the road from Tiruppattūr to Paramaguḍi a little to the north of where the Śarugaṇi river cuts the road.

come to the city of Rajina (not identified yet). Here a great battle took place between Kulaśēkhara and the combined Ceylon armies. Kulaśēkhara was ultimately defeated and the city of Rajina was taken by the Ceylonese. This brings the first part of the campaign to a close. Kulaśēkhara retired from the Pāṇḍya country and found shelter in the country of the Toṇḍamān and sought assistance of the Cholas from there.

Having heard of the flight of Kulaśēkhara, the Ceylon general marched upon Madura and set Vīra Pāṇḍya in charge of the place. The chiefs that supported Kulaśēkhara and submitted to the Ceylonese after Kulaśēkhara's defeat, were restored to their places. Having done so much to secure the capital and the territory round it, the Ceylon general went in pursuit of Kulaśēkhara to Tiruppattūr along the main road from Madura. He took possession of Tiruppattūr and chased the garrison from there along 'the highway' till they reached Pon-Amarāvati, 'a space of three leagues.' He ultimately entered Pon-Amarāvati, and burnt down the three storeyed palace there, and 'many other houses and barns that were full of paddy they burnt down.' 'This valiant commander, that he might calm the fears of the inhabitants of the country, made a proclamation by beat of drums (assuring them that he would protect them).' He then returned to Madura.

In Madura he received orders from head-quarters to set about the celebration of the festival of the coronation of Vīra Pāṇḍya. The General Lankāpura made ready for the coronation and 'appointed Māḷava Chakkavatti (Māḷava Chakravarti) and Māḷavarāyar and Talaiyūr Nāḍāḷvār, men of the Lambakanna race to perform the duties of the office of Lambakanna.[1] He then caused a proclamation to issue

[1] 'Lambakannadhuram' the office is called. This could only mean the chiefship of the Lambakannas. This term means those that have pendent-ear-lobes, and seems to refer to the Nāṭṭukoṭṭai chetties who claim a right to a similar high function at the courts of Tamil kings.

inviting all the chieftains of the Pāṇḍya kingdom to assemble for this ceremony. ' He caused the prince to be anointed duly in the temple which stood at the northern gate of the palace of the former kings, and which aforetime had been honoured with the sound of the drums of victory. The famous general then caused the prince to go round the city in state.'

Kulaśēkhara meanwhile had obtained the assistance of the Toṇḍamān[1] and others, and he issued from the mountain fastnesses and took the stronghold of Mangalam. Among the number of Mangalams about Madura it is difficult to settle which this is. From the circumstances of the narration it seems to be the Mangalam in Śāttūr Taluk. Fortifying himself near the place he fought against the allies and relations of the Toṇḍamān chief and took the fortress; he followed up his victory by capturing Sivaliputtur (Śrīvilliputtūr) in the Tinnevelly district. Kulaśēkhara then made a supreme effort by collecting the forces from Tirinaveli (Tinnevelly), and sought and obtained the assistance of the two Kongus. Collecting his armies he took his stand at the fortress Santaneri.[2] The two Ceylon generals, Laṅkāpura and Jagad Vijaya, made a joint attack upon Kulaśēkhara who cut open the bund of a tank to prevent the enemy from making use of it. The generals however repaired the breach and set forward against Kulaśēkhara defeating him in battle and took two villages called Sirimalakka and Kattala (Kuttalam). The former Lankāpura ordered to be burnt down as that was the place where Parākrama Pāṇḍya was slain. He marched further forward from there and occupied the village Colakulāntaka (Śoḻakulāntaka). He now received a large accession of strength from the chieftains of the Chola country. Among those that brought

[1] Perhaps the chieftains of Arantāngi who had this title in the period immediately following and before the rise of the Pudukkoṭṭa Toṇḍamāns.

[2] This seems meant for a place called ' Sattalēri in inscriptions, in the Ramnad Taluk (*vide* No. 1 of 1912).

him reinforcements, we find the name Pallava Rāyar of the inscriptions, as also several other Nāḍāḷvārs who were all chieftains of fortresses in what is now the state of Pudukoṭṭa and its southern frontier. With these allies Kulaśēkhara fixed his camp in Pāṇḍu Naḍukoṭṭa and Ūriyēri. Outmanœuvring Kulaśēkhara's forces from there the two Ceylon generals marched upon Palamcotta, drove Kulaśēkhara out of it and took the fortress. While there they heard Kulaśēkhara had marched towards Madura. They marched immediately on Madura and Kulaśēkhara again sought refuge in the Chola country.

Leaving Jagad Vijaya at Paṭṭanallūr, Lankāpura marched forward to Tirukkānappēr. About this time Kulaśēkhara applied to the Chola king actually for assistance and obtained from him an army commanded by Pallava Rāyar, and other chiefs. He sent the army including the auxiliaries to the ports of Tonḍi and Pāśa, possibly by sea. When Lankāpura heard of this he ordered his colleague to keep watch in Madura while he himself marched further from Tirukkānappēr upon the frontier fortress of Kīḻānilaya (Kīḻānilai in the Tiruppattur Taluk and on the utmost northern border of Madura). The battle here seems to have taken the form of a running fight all along the road from Kīḻānilai to the two ports of Vaḍa Maṇamēkkuḍi and Maṇamekkuḍi (Maṇamēlkuḍi at the mouth of the Veḷḷār, and the town and suburb north of it). Having defeated the Tamil chiefs, Lankāpura burnt down these two ports and another Manjakkuḍi. As a punishment for this interference of the Cholas, he burnt the Chola country, for a distance of seven leagues. He then marched across the road to the village called Vēlankuḍi [1] that belonged to the chief Nigaladha Rāyar, who had gone over to Kulaśēkhara. This

[1] There are two Vēlankuḍis in the vicinity. The one is a temple-town near Kānāḍukāttān ; but the Vēlankuḍi referred to here is the village of the name, a few miles from Tiruppattūr on the old high road leading from

chief had succeeded in enlisting the co-operation of various other chieftains and the armies had swollen in size by various contingents including those of Tinnevelly. Kulaśēkhara took his stand in Pon-Amarāvati. Lankāpura marched from Vēlankuḍi. Having been defeated again at Pon-Amarāvati, Kulaśēkhara fled from the place. Lankāpura then felt that he had rid the Pāṇḍya country of the enemies of Vīra Pāṇḍya and returned to his headquarters. He then ordered the use of the Ceylon coin *Kahapana* bearing the superscription of Parākrama throughout the Pāṇḍya country of his ally. Sending forward, the men, horses and elephants captured in war, he himself returned to Ceylon, handing over the Pāṇḍya kingdom to Vīra Pāṇḍya. Parākrama Bāhu received him as became a victorious general, and in memory of this great victory founded the village of Pāṇḍu Vijayaka, the lands of which he distributed in charity among the Brahmans. Thus ended the great Ceylon war.

The Ceylon account is certainly one sided, and describes the war in true epic fashion. The victory is all in favour of the Ceylonese generals, and yet we find ultimately Vīra Pāṇḍya does not find himself settled upon his throne firmly, ruling over the country subjugated to his authority. The Mahāvamśa itself admits that Kulaśēkhara had obtained assistance from his cousins in the two Kongus.[1] The Chola inscriptions that describe this war make it appear that the Chola intervention under Pallava Rāyar, the son of Edirilīsōḷa Śambuvarāyan, was effective, and was the deciding factor in the retirement of the[2] Ceylonese. Kulaśēkhara was able, after the departure of the Ceylon army, to main-

Madura to Pon-Amarāvati by Tiruppattūr, and thence to Trichinopoly. It is also on the road, across this, along the frontier between the Chola country and the Pāṇḍya from Paṭṭukoṭṭa to Tiruppattūr.

[1] See Mahāvamśa by Turnour and Wijesimha chapters 76–77, and Venkayya. Epi. Rep. for 1899.

[2] Ārpākkam and Tiruvālangāḍu Inss. Ep. Coll. 20 of 1899 and 465 of 1905.

tain the campaign, and ultimately victory seems to have turned in his favour. The war continued against Vīra Pāṇḍya even after the retirement of the Singhalese. Kulaśēkhara died in the course of the war or soon after. The last great Chola Kulottunga III, as heir-apparent, took up the cause of his son Vikrama Pāṇḍya vigorously, and, according to the Chola record at Tirukkollambūdūr of the fourth year of Kulottunga III (A.D. 1182) 'the Singhalese soldiers had their noses cut off and rushed into the sea. Vīra Pāṇḍya himself was compelled to retreat. The town of Madura was captured and made over to Vikrama Pāṇḍya.'[1] The war thus ended in favour of the Cholas, sometime in the seventies of the twelfth century.

In regard to the date of the whole war, inscriptions of the fifth year of Rājādhiraja II, who ascended the throne in A.D. 1171–2[2] describe it and therefore the war must have taken place before A.D. 1175 which is the date of the Arpākkam grant. According to the Mahāvamśa it commenced some time after the sixteenth year of Parākrama Bāhu.

The Results of the Chola Intervention.—The Chola intervention in this Pāṇḍya war restored the Pāṇḍyas to some little of their power. At the same time it contributed largely to the weakening of the Chola hold upon the Pāṇḍya country. Soon after the war however, the Chola throne was occupied by the last great Chola Kulottunga III who, as crown prince, had already rendered distinguished service in the war against the Ceylonese in favour of Kulaśēkhara Pāṇḍya, and after his death, in favour of his son Vikrama Pāṇḍya. He succeeded to the throne in A.D. 1178 and his rule lasted till A.D. 1216.

Kulottunga (with titles Parakēsari, Tribhuvana Chola, Vīrarājēndra and Konērinmaikoṇḍān) was in all probability

[1] No. 1 of 1899. *vide* Ep. Rep. for 1899, Section 38; K.V.S. Iyer, Historical Sketches of Ancient Dekhan, p. 161.

[2] Epi. Rep., 1904, p. 12, Section 21; and pp. 206 and 7 S. I. Ins. iii.

the son of Rājarāja II, and came to the throne in succession to Rājādhirāja, an uncle. He took an honourable share in turning back the Ceylonese from the southern frontier of the Pudukoṭṭa State, making them beat an inglorious retreat from what promised to be a glorious invasion of conquest. Records of this ruler are available from his fifth to the fortieth year. The first eight years of his reign seem to have been uneventful. Records of his ninth year state that he assisted Vikrama Pāṇḍya against the son of Vīra Pāṇḍya, defeated the Māras (Pāṇḍya's) army, drove the Simhala (Ceylon) army into the sea, took Madura from Vīra Pāṇḍya and bestowed it on Vikrama Pāṇḍya.[1] This means that the civil war in the Pāṇḍya country was renewed after the death of Kulaśēkhara, the ally of the Cholas. The Ceylonese still helped Vīra Pāṇḍya, and Kulottunga had to intervene in favour of Vikrama, the son of his father's ally. A record of his eleventh year states that Kulottunga defeated and cut off the nose of Vīra Pāṇḍya's son, bestowed the crown of Madura upon Vikrama Pāṇḍya; and, when Vīra Pāṇḍya took up arms to wipe off this disgrace, 'took his crowned head at Neṭṭūr',[2] and 'carried his queen into servitude'. It was apparently on this occasion that both the Pāṇḍya and Kēraḷa rulers took their seats some way from the throne, and received from him their kingdoms and new dignities.

In his nineteenth year he undertook a successful invasion northwards and entered Kānchi. He did not stop short there, but went farther north as far as Nellore where there are inscriptions of Kulottunga III. Three or four years later he brought the two Kongus again under his authority, and by this act perhaps extended his sphere of authority well within the modern state of Mysore. His Hoysala contemporary, Baḷḷāḷa II, had his authority recognized in

[1] S. I. Ins. iii, p. 207. [2] For what this means see below.

the Anantapur District. The two apparently came to an understanding on this frontier and maintained themselves at peace cemented by a marriage alliance. One of the queens of Baḷḷāḷa II was known by the title Chola Mahādēvi. As long as peace was preserved on this frontier the Pāṇḍyas could not stir. It was only when the Hoysalas attempted an extension of territory on this side that the Pāṇḍyas could find the occasion to rise on their side.[1]

The Chola Empire in the beginning of the thirteenth century.—At the beginning of the thirteenth century A.D. the Chola empire stood restored so far to its former ascendency in South India under this 'Great Chola' Kulottunga III that one would hardly have expected its fall to come in the course of the next half century. The causes that ultimately brought about this decadence were discernible even then. The Pāṇḍya country, reduced to subordination after such expenditure of blood and treasure by Kulottunga, could but have rendered a sullen obedience. This had been rendered all the more galling after what Kulottunga had done to make a demonstration of his power. Having finally defeated the rebel Vīra Pāṇḍya, Kulottunga entered Madura and had himself anointed both as a hero-warrior and victor-overlord of the Pāṇḍya. In order that this might be the better impressed upon his enemies and feudatories, he arranged that both his Pāṇḍya and Kēraḷa feudatories be seated, apparently without thrones, a little away from him on one side. Seating himself upon the throne with his queen he placed his feet upon 'the crowned head of the vanquished Vīra Pāṇḍya', which had been out off on the field of battle according to the inscription, as if to say that that was to be the fate of those who would not acknowledge his authority. After this he conferred special honours upon both the friendly Pāṇḍya and the Kēraḷa rulers, and even

[1] Epi. Rep., 1912, Sections 30 and 45.

treated the latter to a banquet along with him to show the honours that awaited loyal allegiance.[1]

Such a treatment could not but leave the feudatories smarting under the disgrace, and would inevitably lead to an effort to re-assert their own dignity and to be on the look out for opportunities to inflict similar humiliation in their turn. That seems to have been the frame of mind of the Pāṇḍyan feudatories and instances of retaliation will appear in the history of their restoration.

The Principal Feudatories of the Cholas.—At about this period the following chieftains appear as Kulottunga's vassals in the records of his reign, as the records acknowledge the Chola suzerainty :—

(1) The chieftain of Nellore (Vikramasimhapura) took the title Madhurāntaka Pottappi Chola ; the first member of this title was perhaps in compliment to his overlord, Madhurāntaka, 'the death of Madura', having been an old and a very common title among the Cholas. Nellore is defined in one of these records to have belonged to the Peḍai Nāḍu sub-division, of the district Śēdikulamāṇikka vaḷanāḍu of the province, Jayangonḍaśoḻamanḍalam. Two chieftains are mentioned with this title and their personal

1 There are three points upon which I differ regarding the interpretation of the Śrīrangam Epigraph of Kulottunga III. (S. I. Ins. iii. 88).

(1) In line 3, there is the statement that Vīra Pāṇḍya's son had his nose cut off as a mark of disgrace—Vīra Pāṇḍya, to wipe off this disgrace, raised an army and fought the battle of Neṭṭūr.

(2) In line 4 occurs the expression வீரபாண்டியன் முடித்தலையுங் கொண்டமர் முடித்து, i.e., bringing the war to a close by taking off the crowned-head of Vīra Pāṇḍya (No. 370 of 1915); then follows அவன்மடக் கொடியை வெளமேற்றி. The word 'Veḷam' is read 'Vēḷam,' and interpreted as 'the Pāṇḍya queen having been sent into the harem' (in concubinage apparently). The correct word is Veḷam with the short *e* meaning service as in Veḷḷāṭṭi. Cf. வெளத்துப் பெண்டாட்டி கள்ளிச்சி in Pudukoṭṭa No. 82 in course of publication. The Pāṇḍya queen was reduced to servitude in the Chola harem (see note 4, p. 215 and note 5, p. 218, S. I. Ins. iii. 88, and the inscriptions printed below 2 and 3.

(3) Line 5 கொடிவழங்கும் வில்லவர்க்கு means, I submit, 'to the Villavan (Kēraḷa) on whose flag is usually seen the bow,' whose ensign was the bow. To him Kulottunga gave wealth that kings never obtain. The whole point of the record is that Kulottunga was as great in war as he was liberal in gifts, to justify *his hoisting of 'the banners of generosity and valour.'*

names are given as Tammasiddhi-araiśan with date the twenty-sixth year of Kulottunga III (A.D. 1203-4), and Nallasiddhi araiśar, an uncle of the former with date the thirty-first year of the same emperor (A.D. 1208-9). Two other records of Tammusiddhi are dated A.D. 1205-6 and A.D. 1207-8.[1]

(2) The next one is a Ganga chief Amarābharaṇa Śīya Gangan, otherwise Tiruvēgambamuḍaiyān. There are two records of this chief, one at Kānchīpuram, dated the twenty-seventh year of Kulottunga III, according to which the chief made a gift of a lamp; and the other of the thirty-fourth year according to which his queen Ariapiḷḷai made a gift of two lamps to the temple at Tiruvallam.

(3) There comes a class of chieftains who may be referred to as belonging to the Śengēṇi family and associated with Tiruvallam. The earliest known member is Śengēṇi Minḍan Attimallan Śambuvarāyan with a date in the eighth year of Kulottunga III. The next one in order of time is Śengēṇi Ammaiyappan Kaṇṇuḍaiperumān, otherwise Vikramaśoḻa Sambuvarāyan with a date in the eleventh year of Kulottunga III. Then follows his son Cholappiḷḷai, otherwise Aḻagiyaśoḻan, otherwise Edirili Śoḻa Śambuvarāyan, son of Śengēṇi Ammaiyappan, probably the one above. This last refers himself to the twenty-seventh and thirty-third years of Kulottunga III.

(4) Two other chiefs are mentioned along with Śīyagangan, and one of the Śengēṇi chiefs mentioned above in two records of the years twenty and twenty-one of Kulottunga III at Śengaṇma (Chengama). These are Viḍukādaḻagiyaperumāl of Dharmapuri, Tagaḍūr in the Salem district, and Malayan Vinayai Venṛān, otherwise Karikāla Chola Aḍaiyūrnāḍaḷvān. The former of these figures prominently in the records of Kulottunga's successor.

[1] S. I. Ins. iii. 207.

(5) Another family of chiefs comes into notice from the Śengaṇma record of the twenty-first year. Two of them are mentioned, namely, Tirukkāḷattidēva and his son Vīra Narasimhadēva. The father's name occurs in records of the sixteenth and seventeenth years of Kulottunga, while that of the son is available in those of the thirty-sixth and thirty-seventh years of Rājarāja III, the successor of Kulottunga. This Vīra Narasimha seems the chief referred to in a record of the fifteenth year of Kulottunga where he is described as 'Prince Simha, *alias* Vīrarākshasa Yādavarāja, the son of Yādavarāja *alias* Tirukkāḷattidēva.' Both father and son gave themselves the title (*biruda*) 'Vengivallabha,' and claimed the 'Śaśikula-Chāḷukya' lineage. The Venkaṭēśapperumāḷ temple at Tirupati contains a number of inscriptions of this family. One of them refers itself to the thirty-fourth year of Tribhuvana Chakravartin Vīra-Narasimhadēva Yādavarāya. According to another of his fortieth year the temple was rebuilt. Another chief Tribhuvana Chakravartin Tiruvēngaḍanātha Yādavarāya has a record of his eighth year, and belonged in all probability to the same family.

Geographical and Political Relations of these Chieftains.—This analysis of Kulottunga's records indicates that the Telugu Chola feudatories had their territory in the north with capital at Nellore. Then south of them was the family of Yādavarāyas with capital at Kāḷahasti, and claiming descent from the family of the Eastern Chāḷukyas. Then there was the Ganga chief associated with Tiruvallam, his territory lying along the Pālār basin. Then came the Śengēṇi chiefs connected also with Tiruvallam, and possibly having their territory extending westwards to Tiruvaṇṇāmalai and Śengaṇma; up the Ghats and in the Salem district were the chieftains of Tagaḍūr (Dharmapuri). Besides these figure two or three others prominently. The first that is mentioned is the Edirili Śoḷa Śambuvarāyan, the father of Pallavarāyar at Śēndamangalam and Kūḍal (Cuddalore). This family is sometimes described as Kāḍava. Then west and north there were the Malayamān chiefs of Tirukkovilūr and Kiḷiyūr. Farther west and in the Āttūr division of the Salem district was the chiefship of Ponparappi taking in Magadaimanḍalam. There seems to have been another chiefship in this region under the Vāṇakkovaraiyars with head-quarters at Taḍāvūr. These were the divisions of the empire on its northern frontier. The political relationships between these chiefs and their connection with the head-quarters is exhibited in two compacts entered into by some of them. A record of the thirteenth year of Kulottunga gives the details of a compact between two neighbouring chieftains, Rājarājadēvan Ponparappinār, otherwise Kulottunga Chola Vāṇakkovarayan of Āragalūr, and Kiḷiyūr Malayamān of Tirukkovilūr. It was stipulated 'that in settling the extent of the country belonging to each, the dominion lying to the south of the river Āḷvinayāru must go to the former, and the country to the north of the same should be held by the latter; that they should not behave inimically towards one another as long as they live; *that they should act in conjunction in serving the king*; and that if any harm is done to one, the other must take it as done to himself and render the necessary military assistance by sending his chiefs, army and horse'. In another epigraph of the thirty-fifth year a similar compact is recorded between the Śengēṇi chief Ammaiyappan Aḷagiyaśoḷan, otherwise Ediriliśoḷa Śambuvarāyan on the one hand, and three other chiefs on the other, namely (1) Ponparappinān Vāṇakkovarayan, (2) Kulottungaśoḷa Vāṇakkovarayar and (3) the King's brother-in-law Kāḍavarāya. The stipulation was that the three should not be enemies but the friends of the first Śengēṇi chief, 'neither giving shelter to offenders against him nor setting up new offenders.' On his side the Śengēṇi chief agreed to observe a similar mode of conduct. If he did otherwise 'he would be the bearer of shoes and betel bags both to his kinsman and to his enemies. He would also be one not born to his father.'[1] The clear statement of united service to the emperor seems directly to negative the inference in the Epigraphist's Reports, that the government was unsettled. Kulottunga's power was growing stronger as he advanced in his reign. These compacts indicate the freedom that the feudatories enjoyed against common enemies and disturbers of the peace. These chieftains are located on the most vulnerable frontier of the Empire, and the time was such that invasions were possible. United action would be absolutely necessary having regard to the available means of communication. The very terms of the compact stamp them as extradition treaties against criminals and gangs of robbers who must have been harrying the border lands then as now. These chiefs came to an agreement for united action in regard to these, apparently under the countenance of the head-quarters. Other instances of such action even by the people are extant in regard to really anarchical times.

KULOTTUNGA, BUILDER OF THE ŚIVA TEMPLE AT TRIBHUVANAM

During a long reign of about forty years Kulottunga III was able to keep the empire intact and carry on extensive works of improvement at the same time. He was a Śaiva. There is a story current at Tiruviḍaimarudūr in the Tanjore district that he was guilty of having put to death a Brahman. This atrocity weighed on his mind, and the spirit of his victim haunted him day and night. As a measure of expiation the king visited all the famous Śaiva shrines of holy reputation. Failing everywhere else he

[1] Ep. Rep., 1914, Sec. 17, p. 91.

sought relief at Tiruviḍaimarudūr. As was usual when he entered the sacred precincts, the spirit awaited his return at the door. After fervent appeal to the God, the king received advice to elude pursuit by escaping from the sanctum by a manhole in the rear, and got out of the temple by the West Gate, opposite the East by which he entered. He rode hard till he reached a village a little over a mile from the temple, and turned round to see whether the ghost followed him. Much to his relief he did not see it, and in thanksgiving for this great boon he vowed to construct a temple to the 'God of his heart.' He called the place Tiruppuvanam (the forest where he turned first). Whatever the actual truth of the story, an image of the ghost is found placed at the east entrance of the Tiruviḍaimarudūr temple, and a hole in the wall of the sanctum is pointed out as the one by which he escaped. Inscriptions copied in the temple at Tribhuvanam show that the temple was consecrated to Śiva, called here Kampaharēśvara (the God that removed the quaking due to fear). The king is described by the names Kulottunga and Tribhuvana Vīra, and receives the title Pāṇḍyāri (the enemy of the Pāṇḍya), who conquered the ruler of Simhala and the lord of Kēraḷa, and killed Vīra Pāṇḍya. He performed the anointment of heroes after capturing Madura. These details make the builder of the Tiruppuvanam temple identical with Kulottunga III. The inscription is in duplicate, and contains a record of the building works of this great Chola in whose reign the Empire of the Cholas retained much of its glory undiminished.

His other building works.—He built the *mukhamaṇḍapa* of Sabhāpati at Chidambaram, the *gopura* of the goddess Girīndrajā and the enclosing verandah of the shrine. Having done so much it is no wonder that he is described as an *ēkabhakta*, the *bhakta* without a peer, of Śiva at Chidambaram. He built the great temple of Ekāmrēśvara (at Kānchīpuram); the temple of Hālahālāsya at Madura; the temple at Madhyārjuna (Tiruviḍaimarudūr); the temple of Śri Rājarājēśvara;[1] the temple of Valmīkēśvara at Tiruvārūr, the big *gopura* and the *sabhā manḍapa*, the audience hall, of the last temple specifically. Lastly the king built this Tribhuvanavīrēśvara, which accounts for the name of the place being Tribhuvana (Tam-Tiruppuvanam) whose brilliant, tall and excellent *vimāna* (tower over the sanctum) interrupts the sun (in his course). The temple was consecrated by the establishment of Śiva and Pārvatī in the temple, the officiating priest having been his own religious preceptor Somēśvara, the son of Śrīkanṭa Śambhu. He is known by the surname Īśvara Śiva. It was at the instance of this *Rājaguru* (royal chaplain) that the privilege of collecting a brokerage fee by the village made to a temple at Kuḷikkarai in the Tanjore district, in the fifth year of Kulottunga III, was registered on stone in his twenty-eighth year, (No. 82 of 1911). Kulottunga was personally a devoted Śaiva and made large benefactions to the 'God of his heart.'[2]

His religious policy.—There seems to have been a severe famine in the twenty-third year of his reign, i.e. the first year of the thirteenth century, when the distress was so great that a Veḷḷāḷan (an upper class agriculturist) sold himself and his two daughters for 110 *kāśu* to the temple. Devoted Śaiva as Kulottunga was, there is a reference in a record of his son to his twenty-second year (i.e. A.D. 1300), which states, according to the Epigraphist, that 'in the twenty-second year of Periyadēvar, the elder king, there was a general crusade against monasteries of this type (*kuhai*

[1] The identification of this Rājarājēśvara is not quite beyond a doubt yet. Tanjore is known by that name. The Epigraphist, Mr. Krishna Sastri, identifies it with the Airāvatesvara temple at Dārāsuram, as it is called, near Kumbakonam. This seems quite likely. If so the sculptures in the temple will throw a great deal of light upon Śaiva history. There are images of the several Aḍiyārs and devotees of Śiva each one with a label giving the name. Some of these latter remain written, but yet uncarved.

[2] Ep. Rep., 1908, Sections 64–7.

iḍikalaham) when all the property of the monastery under reference was confiscated '. The monastery under reference is one at Tirutturaippūndi where a Śaiva devotee, Tiruchchirrambala Mudaliar, came into residence at the request of the inhabitants of the locality, who built a monastery and provided for feeding strangers that might be there on a visit. It is not clear from the record, as published, whether this was due to an act of persecution by the state, or a mere outburst of popular fanaticism. It can hardly be the former, as it is called a 'kalaham' an outburst or a riot, and as the devotee continued there apparently till his death two years after. In his twenty-fourth year Kulottunga III made a grant for the worship of the Nāyanmārs (the sixty-three Śaiva devotees) according to No. 506 of the Epigraphists' collection for the year 1912. Again according to No. 466 of the same collection they suffered a paḷḷichchandam (a Jain temple) in the locality. It is not safe to infer from this with the epigraphists, that the *kuhai iḍikalaham*, which happened in the twenty-second year of Periyadēvar (i.e. Kulottunga III) 'must have been instigated by the Brahmans against the non-Brahmanical Śaiva *maṭhas*.' Such a general persecution is the more unlikely as we have reference to the prosperous existence of four of these non-Brahman monasteries in the reign of Rājarāja III, the successor of Kulottunga III.

His Administration.—In other respects Kulottunga's administration was carried on efficiently on the lines laid down by his great ancestors. There is a reference to one of the periodical revisions of distribution of the lands of the village among the Śāliya-nagarattār (the weaver-class) at Tiruppālatturai.[1]

A piece of land purchased for laying out a road for carrying in procession the image of Śirāḷa-Piḷḷaiyār (deified-infant

[1] No. 441 of Ep. Coll. for 1912.

that was cooked and served by his devoted parents Śiruttoṇḍa and his wife to God Śiva) from Tiruchaṅgāṭṭāṅguḍi to Marugal, was made tax-free and removed from 'the register' by royal order.[1]

The left-hand classes under Kulottunga III.—Before passing on to a consideration of the reign of Rājarāja III, one or two other special features of the reign of Kulottunga III require to be noted. A record of his fortieth year at Ūṟṟāttūr relates to a decision that the Śrutimāns recorded, after a meeting held in the hall Uttamaśoḻan of the Siddharatnēśvara temple on behalf of the ninety-eight sub-divisions of the Iḍangaiyār (left-hand classes). In the words of the record: 'While, in order to kill the demons that disturbed the sacrifices of the sage Kaśyapa, we were made to appear from the Agni Kuṇḍa (the sacrificial fire-pit) and, while we were thus protecting the said sacrifice, Chakravartin Arindama honoured the officiating sage-priests (*rishis*) by carrying them in a car and led them to a Brahmana colony (newly founded by himself). On this occasion we were made to take our seats on the hind part of the car, and to carry the slippers and umbrellas of these sages. Eventually with these Brahmaṇa sages we also were made to settle down in the villages of Tiruveḷḷarai, Pāchchil, Tiruvāśi, Tiruppiḍavūr, Ūṟṟattūr and Kāraikkuḍi of Śennivaḷakkūṟṟam (all of which are places now in the Trichinopoly district). We received the clan-name Iḍangai, because the sages (while they got down from their cars) were supported by us on their left side. The ancestors of our own sect having lost their credentials and their insignia in jungles and bushes we were ignorant of our origin. Having now once learnt it, we the members of the ninety-eight subsects enter into a compact, in the fortieth year of the king, that we shall hereafter behave like the sons of the

[1] No. 66 of Ep. Coll. for 1913.

same parents, and what good or evil may befall any one of us will be shared by all. If anything derogatory happens to the Iḍangai class, we will jointly assert our rights till we establish them. It is also understood that only those who, during their congregational meetings to settle communal disputes, display the *birudas* of horn, bugle and parasol, shall belong to our class. Those who have to recognize us now and hereafter in public, must do so from our distinguishing symbols, the feather of the crane and the loose hanging hair (?) The horn and the conch-shell shall also be sounded in front of us, and the bugle blown according to the fashion obtaining among the Iḍangai people. Those who act in contravention of these rules shall be treated as the enemies of our class. Those who behave differently from the rules (thus) prescribed for the conduct of the Iḍangai classes shall be excommunicated and shall not be recognized as Śrutimāns. They will be considered slaves of the classes who are opposed to us'.[1] There are a number of other documents relating to this particular class which go to indicate that their occupation was agriculture, perhaps not of the peasant proprietor variety. A somewhat later record from Āḍuturai[2] in the Trichinopoly district relates to an agreement arrived at among themselves between the 'right-hand' ninety-eight subsects and 'the left-hand' ninety-eight, of the Vaḻudilambaṭṭu Uśāvaḍi against the Brahmaṇa and Veḷḷāḷa land owners (kāṇiyāḷans) of the division. While these documents afford evidence of the hardships to which the agricultural labourers were occasionally subjected, these also indicate clearly that these classes were quite conscious of their rights, and were allowed the freedom to 'jointly assert our rights till we establish them'.

Communal Responsibility.—We may note here two other examples of communal responsibility in matters of

[1] Ep. Rep., 1913, p. 109, Sec. 39. [2] Ep. Coll, 34 of 1913.

administration, and take leave of Kulottunga III. The first has reference to an unusual impost by a governor who is described as Piḷḷaiyār (prince) Yādavarāyar. In the thirty-fourth year of the king[1] this officer levied the tax *pon-vari* upon the village Punnaivāyal, otherwise Rājanārāyaṇa Chatur-vēdimangalam, apparently a Brahman establishment. The tax was one-fourth *māḍai* upon every *vēli* of land, but this levy failed to make the usual exemption of uncultivated wastes in the village. The collection of this impost was entrusted to a special officer. He collected the utmost he could out of the landholders and held the village assembly responsible for the balance. In this predicament the Brahman members sold the eighty *vēlis*, constituting the village Kuḷattūr, to a certain Pichchan Duggai-āḷvān for 200 *kāśu*. These eighty *vēlis* were assigned by the purchaser to a Vishṇu temple, a Jain Paḷḷi, a Piḍāri (village deity) shrine, the Bhaṭṭas (Brahmans), etc., and sixty *vēlis* made over with the permission of the king for the upkeep of the Vyākaraṇamanḍapa in the Tiruvoṟṟiyūr temple. The whole village was later on made rent free by order of the king. The record, as it has come down to us, is hardly complete enough to warrant any positive inferences. It would be interesting to know whether the impost was a new levy or an old one; whether it was levied with the consent of the community or otherwise. It seems possible to infer that this uniform levy and its unusually strict collection were intended to compel the bringing into cultivation of lands unnecessarily left uncultivated.

Another record of the fortieth year of Kulottunga III from Tiruvaranguḷam in the Pudukoṭṭa State declares certain *dēvadāna* (gift to gods) lands given to the temple, rent-free. In the course of their deliberations regarding this question the assembly came to some other items of

[1] Ep. Coll. 202 of 1912, and Ep. Rep. 1913, p. 109, Sec. 39.

understanding among themselves. The assembled people of Vallanāḍu (one of the five divisions of the present state of Pudukoṭṭa), 'declared that thenceforward they would afford protection to the cultivators (*kuḍimakkaḷ*) residing within the four boundaries of the sacred village of Tiruvaranguḷam and its *dēvadāna* village. In the course of their protection if any one of the assembly was found to rob, capture the cows of, or do other mischief to the cultivators, the assembly agreed to assign two *mā* (one-twentieth of the unit of about six acres) of wet land to the temple by way of fine for the offence committed. Also the seṭṭis, the kaikkoḷars, dancing girls (temple-servants would be better for *dēvaraḍiyār*), smiths, shepherds, and others inhabiting this sacred village who had acquired lands wet or dry from the assembly (*nāḍu*) were allowed to enjoy them on permanent lease and pay their dues direct to the temple.' This certainly means the placing of the charities to the temple, and its full appurtenances, under the protection of the particular community; but as to how far it can be held to indicate slackening of the central authority, it would be hazardous to venture an opinion, unless we could be certain what exactly was the distribution of powers between the central and the local authorities. From what we know of this division of functions, the arrangement described in the document cannot be held to indicate lessening of the central authority. Such agreements seem to have been of frequent occurrence in this part of the country.

Having gone into so much detail, we might state in conclusion that Kulottunga handed down to his successor Rājarāja III the central part of the vast empire of the Cholas intact. The forces of disintegration were already visible under the surface, in the sullen discontent of the Pāṇḍyas in the south, the aggressive ambition of the neighbouring powers in the north and the smothered restiveness of the ambitious chieftains within.

The last condition is indicated by the transfer of an officer from the Pāṇḍya country to the Toṇḍamaṇḍalam (the two Arcots and Chingleput) against some traitors (*rājadrohins*).[1]

There were powerful rulers of the Kākatīya dynasty in the north, and of the Hoysala dynasty in the north-west. These latter, however, were related by blood and were as yet within their own borders, showing no visible signs of inclination to expansion on this side.

Rājarāja III.—Rājarāja III (with titles Rājakēsari and Parakēsarivarman) ascended the throne nominally in the year A.D. 1216, but actually perhaps two years later as we have records of Kulottunga's fortieth year. The date of his accession is put beyond doubt by No. 268 of 1910 which equates his twenty-sixth year with Śaka 1165. The Hoysala Vīra Baḷḷāḷa II died in A.D. 1220, and his son Vīra Narasimha II's accession took place in A.D. 1218. The enterprising Pāṇḍya ruler of the time, Māravarman Sundara Pāṇḍya I ascended the throne of his father in A.D. 1216. During the first few years of Rājarāja III everything seems to have gone on smoothly, and the records of these years give one the impression that he became ruler to a quiet patrimony which required no extraordinary ability to maintain unimpaired. Appearances are often, if not always, deceptive. The Pāṇḍya contemporary was a young aspiring ruler, and Kulottunga's treatment of his predecessor was apparently rankling in his breast. Revenge was not possible under Kulottunga himself. Why not under his successor? Inscriptions of the ninth year of Māravarmaṇ Sundara Pāṇḍya I claim for him various achievements, among them the burning of Tanjore and Uraiyūr. He brought a victorious campaign to a close by driving the Chola out of his patrimony, and

[1] Ep. Coll. 120 of 1912 and Ep. Rep. 1913, p. 110, Sec. 40.

anointing himself in the hall at Muḍikoṇḍaśoḻapuram. That was not all. He marched into Chidambaram and had his anointment as a hero-victor in the great temple there. More than this, he exhibited his magnanimity to the fallen enemy by returning him his kingdom on terms. This gives a clear indication where the danger to the Chola Empire lay. There is one other particular in this Pāṇḍya record of Māravarman Sundara I's nineteenth year (A.D. 1225), which throws light upon contemporary history. The two rulers of Kongu came to the Pāṇḍya for the settlement of a dispute. He took them to Madura, gave them apparently a satisfactory award and sent them back. This was perhaps responsible for bringing down Vīra Narasimha II into the Chola country for the first time. Records of the Hoysalas show that Narasimha II's intervention in the affairs of the Chola-kingdom had been called for, and we find that this intervention took place in the region round Śrīrangam between the years A.D. 1222 and 1225-6. [1]

Rājarāja's Reign.—Before proceeding to reconstruct the story of this intervention and how it came about, it will be just as well to pass in review some few details of recent discovery regarding the earlier years of Rājarāja III. A record of his fourth year (A.D. 1220) in Muniyūr states that the earlier grants to the temple in the place were re-engraved on stone either because they had decayed by age or new works were undertaken. This was a common practice of the Chola sovereigns, and the particular instance would indicate the prevalence of peace and order. In the seventh year the king ratified the action of a woman who collected subscriptions and provided an image of the goddess for the 'bed-room' (Paḻḻiyarai) of the temple at Tirumaṇanjēri. [2]

[1] Epig. Indica, vii. p. 160 ff. [2] Ep. Coll. 28 of 1914.

In the same year the king sanctioned the removal of Tiruvoṟṟiyūr and dependent villages from the register of tax-paying villages. Tiruvoṟṟiyūr and the villages included in the group (*dēvadānamanḍalam*) had gradually been transformed into temple lands (*dēvadāna*). The point was raised whether the taxes should be paid into the royal treasury or the temple treasury. The matter had to be brought to the notice of the king who declared that these villages ought to be treated as *nīngal* (i.e. villages which ought to be removed from the state-register of tax-paying lands). Accordingly, some *puravuvari* (taxes) which had been uncollected for a time, viz. veṭṭi, puḍavai-mudal, tiraikkāśu, āśuvigal-kāśu, kuḍi-kāśu, fee levied on uvachchars (drummers) and on looms, inavari-kāśu, kāttigai-kāśu, vēlichchinnam, veṭṭi-kāśu and śiru-pāḍikkāval on lands growing gingelly and cotton, grain for supervision (kaṇkāṇi), kuṟṟa-danḍam, paṭṭi-danḍam, kārtigai-kāśu on oilmongers, fee on dyes and ariśi-kāśu on salt-pans were collected. [1] This order was issued through the royal officer Vīra-Narasimhadēva Yādavarāyan, Governor of Puḻarkkōṭṭam, otherwise Vikrama-śoḻavaḷanāḍu formerly known Rājēndra-śoḻavaḷanāḍu. It looks as though these taxes were held in abeyance because of the dispute as to the party to whom payment had to be made; but whether it would have made any change if the king's order were otherwise is more than can be stated from the record as it is available to us at present. [2]

A record of his fourteenth year, A.D. 1230 (at Valivalam near Tiruvālūr, Tanjore District) states that at the *dēvadāna* village of Kulottungaśoḻanallūr the lands of certain traitors (*rājadrohins*) were put up for sale by public auction (*Rājarāja-peruvilai*) and were sold for 33,000 *kāśu*.[3] This

[1] The exact significance of several of the taxes is not clear. A mere translation would be useless even were it possible.

[2] Ep. Coll. 199 of 1912, section 42 of Ep. Rep. for 1913.

[3] Ep. Coll. 112 of 1911 and Rep. for 1911, section 30.

may be held to indicate weakening of the central authority, the civil disorder being perhaps the result of hostile movement by enemies of the empire.

Like their predecessor Kulottunga III, Rājarāja and his successor Rājēndra III were Śaivas by conviction, and often exhibited their personal devotion to their religious persuasion in many ways. Notwithstanding the attempt at the destruction of some of the Śaiva monasteries in the twenty-second year of 'Periyadēvar' Kulottunga already adverted to, four of these non-Brahman Śaiva *maṭhas* received considerable patronage under Rājarāja and his successor. The Śaiva teacher Īśānadēva of the lineage of the Māligaimaḍam at Tiruviḍaimarudūr near Kumbhakonam, settled at the time at Nālūr, received a gift of land from a lady disciple who made the gift in carrying out the wishes of her husband at his death.[1] The Tirugñāna Sambandhamaḍam on the south-side of Tiruvagattīśvaram Uḍaiyar temple at Muniyūr in the Tanjore district is referred to in another epigraph.[2] A third establishment of the kind is the Tirumurai Tēvārachchelvan Maḍam at Tirukkaḻumalam (Shiyāḻi) and comes in for a grant from the inhabitants of Muniyūr.[3] The fourth institution was the Tavapperumāl Tirumaḍam in the first circuit round the temple (Tirumaḍaivalāgam) of Manattuḷ Nāyanār at Valivalam again in the Tanjore district. This was presided over by Somanāthadēva Mudaliar with the sacerdotal title Ediroppilādar (the unparalleled holy one)of the lineage of Tiruch-chattimuttam.[4] There are two records of Rājēndra registering gifts to this institution, according to one of which the lessees agreed to pay all the taxes due on the lands themselves, and made this condition also applicable 'to those who purchased the

[1] Ep. Coll. 49 of 1911. [2] Ep. Coll. 156 of 1911.
[3] Ep. Coll. 158 of 1911.
[4] Ep. Rep. 1909, section 53, p. 103; Ep. Coll. 108 and 109 of 1911.

land from them, to those who acquired them as *strīdana* (woman's property), and to those who inherited them by other means.'

In the nineteenth year (A.D. 1235)[1] we find Rājarāja III paying a visit to the Tiruvoṟṟiyūr temple on the occasion of the Āvaṇittirunāḷ (festival in August or September, each year). He was present at the musical rendering of the *Ahamārgam.*[2] This is apparently the singing, to the accompaniment of dancing, to exhibit the erotic sentiments embodied in the devotional works of the Śaiva saints. Some of these personal acts of the king would indicate that he had a reign of comparative peace, when he could take himself away from the more responsible duties of his high station. The apparent calm was but the precursor of the storm that was gathering from the hostility of the Pāṇḍyas on the south, the ambitions of the chief feudatories within, and the aggressions of his neighbours in the north. It is as against all this, and perhaps in an honest effort to help the Chola, that the Hoysala intervention took place.

The Political Condition of the Chola Empire.—The Chola empire under Rājarāja III comprised nominally at least both the Chola and Toṇḍa-maṇḍalams, and extended from the southern extremity of the Pudukoṭṭa state to almost as far north as the northern Pennar itself. But this empire at the time at which we have arrived was very much like a house divided against itself. The emperor had under him part of it round the capital, Śrīrangam, Tanjore, and Gangaikoṇḍaśoḷapuram being perhaps under him. The territory immediately north of it, that is the district of South Arcot, was under one family of chieftains, the most prominent member of which was the Pallava, or Kāḍava,

[1] Ep. Coll. 211 of 1912.

[2] There was a class of dancing women devoted to this particular art. They are known as Āḍal-Kūttiyar or Padiyilār, the latter term occurring often in inscriptions. Śilappadhikāram, v., l. 50 commentary thereon.

Kopperunjingadēva (Mahārājasimha of the Sanskrit inscriptions). The territory farther north, known generally as Toṇḍamaṇḍalam, but under the Chola empire as Jayangoṇḍa-Śoḻamaṇḍalam, was under the other family of chieftains, claiming to be of Pallava descent also, who called themselves Śambuvarāyans. In this unhappy condition, the territory of the Cholas was alike exposed to attacks from the south from the rising power of the Pāṇḍyas of Madura, and in the north from the Telugu-Chola chieftains of Nellore and the Kākatīyas beyond. Each one of these sought opportunity for intervention, perhaps as friends of the Chola, but the intervention usually resulted in the appropriation of a part of the empire, or the creation of the chieftaincies whose political interests made them more loyal to the foreigner than to their own liege lord. In this condition of the Chola empire, there came about the Hoysala intervention, which was due to the family relationship between the Cholas and the Hoysalas, and the aggressive activity of the contemporary Pāṇḍyan ruler Māravarman Sundara Pāṇḍya I.

Hoysala Intervention.—The Hoysalas were a dynasty of feudatories of the great Chāḷukya emperor Vikramāditya, called by historians Vikramāditya VI, and, in literature, Vikramānka Dēva. He was contemporary with the Chola emperor Kulottunga I. His empire marched with that of Kulottunga along the Krishna-Tungabhadra frontier, and from their junction, in a slanting line north-eastwards till it touched the frontiers of Orissa. Vikramāditya therefore had for his territory proper most of the Bombay Presidency south of the Vindhyas, the greater half of the Nizam's Dominions and the hilly portions at any rate of the Mysore plateau. When Vikramāditya passed away at the commencement of the second quarter of the twelfth century the empire passed into the hands of feeble successors. When two more rulers followed, the empire had become so weak, and the more powerful feudatories had grown so powerful, that a usurpation under Bijjala came in, which preserved the empire intact for another generation. A usurpation is never a stable cure for keeping the disorderly elements in an empire permanently in hand. When the powerful usurper Bijjala passed away, the greater feudatories on the distant frontiers from the head-quarters were quite ready to throw off the yoke of imperial authority. The semblance of empire was however kept up while each frontier chieftain did his best to make his power more real and his territory more compact. When the last emperor passed out of existence, the frontier chieftains openly threw off the imperial yoke and made themselves independent. Out of this dismembered empire, which in its days held together more than a dozen subordinate governments, there stood out in the last decade of the twelfth century three dynasties possessing compact states, and, in touch with each other on the frontiers warring incessantly for supremacy. The southern block of territory which belonged to this Chāḷukya empire was somewhat extended at the expense of the Cholas since the death of Kulottunga I, and this formed the territory of the Hoysalas, who, in the early stages of the imperial career of Vikramāditya, were the pillars of his empire. The territory of the Hoysalas was separated from that of the Yādavas of Dēvagiri, by the river Krishna in its upper course, and a somewhat uncertain line beginning from somewhere opposite to Adoni and going north along almost the middle of the present day Nizam's Dominions, separated the territory of the Yādavas from that of the Kākatīyas, a new dynasty that had sprung into importance from the ashes of the eastern Chāḷukyas. The southern power of the Hoysalas it was that kept itself in touch with the Cholas, and, when the Chola empire got into a helpless condition under Rājarāja III intervened effectively, and, for a time, restored Rājarāja to his former position.

The real founder of the Hoysala power was Biṭṭi Dēva or Vishṇuvardhana. His grandson Vīra Baḷḷāḷa however extended the territory permanently to the frontier of the Krishna and incorporated within it the eastern and north-eastern parts of Mysore. It was in the middle of his reign, in the year A.D. 1193, when the imperial power had become extinct, that he declared himself independent. He continued to reign till A.D. 1220, just four years after the commencement of the reign of Rājarāja III. In that year he was succeeded by his son Narasimha or Vīra Narasimha, the second of the name in this dynasty whose reign extended down to A.D. 1235. In the first years of Narasimha's reign his intervention in the affairs of the Chola empire was called for.

We have already pointed out that the last great Chola Kulottunga III ruled from A.D. 1178 to A.D. 1216. He was succeeded by Rājarāja III. The great war against the Ceylonese took place early in the life of Kulottunga III. When these foreigners were driven out of India, the civil war continued in the Pāṇḍya country. The Cholas upheld the claims of Kulaśēkhara Pāṇḍya and so long as Kulottunga lived Kulaśēkhara's successful rival found it impossible to retaliate upon the Chola. When Kulottunga died and was succeeded by Rājarāja, the Pāṇḍyas found the opportunity. About the same year as the accession of Rājarāja III there came to the Pāṇḍya throne a Māravarman Sundara Pāṇḍya. In some of the records of his ninth year he claims to have burnt down Tanjore and Uraiyūr, probably as the result of a Pāṇḍya invasion from the south. It is this invasion from the south that called for the active intervention of Hoysala Narasimha. He placed himself between the Pāṇḍya and Chola capitals, in the region round Śrīrangam, and for the time deterred the Pāṇḍya from advancing further. It was possibly then that Tammusidhi advanced upon Kānchi.[1]

[1] For details see the next lecture.

This move diverted Narasimha's attention, and the Pāṇḍya carried his conquests so far as to turn the Chola a fugitive from his capital and have himself anointed at Muḍikonḍaśoḷapuram, and as hero-victor at Chidambaram in obvious retaliation of the performance of Kulottunga III in Madura. These events must have taken place before the nineteenth year of Māravarman Sundara I (A.D. 1235).

During the reign of Kulottunga a family of Telugu chieftains had raised themselves to importance in the region round Nellore, which was otherwise known as Vikramasimhapura. They took advantage of suitable occasions to extend their power southwards and at one time they seem to have advanced as far as Kānchi on their own account, and when at last they were reduced to subjection by the Kākatīyas farther north. these latter essayed to keep their hold upon the northern part of the Chola dominions. In this state of affairs across the frontiers the subordinate chiefs of the Chola empire themselves proved troublesome; for, about the year A.D. 1331, the chief of Śendamangalam, Kopperunjinga, who called himself a Kāḍava, and also gave himself titles like Avaniyāḷappirandan (he that was born to rule the world) attacked Rājarāja III and kept him prisoner. Rājarāja was related to the Hoysala monarch, Narasimha II, who, on hearing the news of his captivity at Śendamangalam started from Dvārasamudra, seized the Magara kingdom on his way, and marched upon Kānchi. As there appears to have been a Yādava invasion on his northern frontier, he sent in advance to the relief of Rājarāja the Chola, two generals of his by name Appaṇa and Samudra Gopaiya. These generals carried the war successfully against the Kāḍava chieftain to Śendamangalam marching northwards from the region of Chidambaram. In the course of these campaigns they killed four Ceylon generals, among whom was Parākrama Bāhu 'the king of Ceylon' (probably a prince), compelled Kopperunjinga to release the Chola monarch, from Śendamangalam and restored Rājarāja to his position in the empire. Thus the first intervention against Māravarman Sundara I was at least temporarily effective, as it actually saved the empire from immediate destruction. The Pāṇḍya menace still continued real, and Kopperunjinga prudently allied himself with the Pāṇḍya against the Chola and the Hoysala.

Narasimha was succeeded in the year 1233 by his son Sōmēśvara, who apparently was associated with his father in the government of the kingdom and took an active part in the Hoysala intervention in the South. There are very few records of his in the south between the years five and twenty-one of his reign. About A.D. 1244 there seems to have been some disturbance in the Chola empire, apparently a civil war between the reigning ruler Rājarāja and his brother, who afterwards become Rājēndra III. Exactly ten years after his father's intervention, the son Somēśvara found it necessary to interfere. He completely defeated Rājēndra Chola on the field of battle; but seems to have restored him afterwards to his position.[1] While therefore Narasimha's intervention was on behalf of his relative Rājarāja, the intervention of Vīra Somēśvara on the other hand, seems to have been first against Rājēndra, and ostensibly in favour of Rājarāja III, ending ultimately in favour of Rājēndra himself. Rājēndra's inscriptions exhibit him as a hostile rod of death to the Kannaḍiga king, the 'hero anklets' of whose feet were put on by the hands of Vīra Somēśvara.[2] The explanation of these apparently contradictory statements seems to be that Somēśvara's intervention was first in favour of Rājarāja, and either because of his death, or something else that happened, he entered into a treaty with his successor Rājēndra. Thereafter

[1] Ep. Car. v. Ak. 123.
[2] No. 64 of 1892 and No. 420 of 1911. Also sec. 32 Ep. Rep. for 1912

Somēśvara did not leave the country of the Cholas, but established himself there with a capital built by himself at Kaṇṇanūr about five miles north of Śrīrangam, where he appears to have resided till his death about A.D. 1262, except for a short period in A.D. 1252 when he was in Dvārasamudra. Both Narasimha the father and Somēśvara the son assumed the title 'Chola-Rājya-Pratishṭāpanāchārya,' meaning thereby that both of them established the Chola in his position.

Hoysala occupation of Kaṇṇanūr against the Pāṇḍya

In the course of these wars, Kopperunjinga, the chieftain of Śendamangalam, was apparently in active alliance with the Pāṇḍyas, and therefore Pāṇḍya intervention was regarded as imminent. The conquest of the Magaras in the north by the Hoysala, and the absence of mention of the Śambuvarāya chieftain go to show that the northern frontier was left to their charge and looked after by them. Thus for the time being we find the Hoysalas established firmly in the Chola country, though at the same time we find Rājēndra III ruling as the Chola sovereign. The establishment of the Hoysala near Śrīrangam seems definitely to have been intended against the rising power of the Pāṇḍyas, (whose history we shall study in the next lecture), and to prevent their junction with their active ally Kopperunjinga at Śendamangalam.

Rājēndra Chola III.—About the year A.D. 1243 there arose in the family of the Cholas a new aspirant to the Chola throne with the title Rājēndra Chola, the third of the designation. He claims in a record of his seventh year at Śrīrangam to be 'the very Rama (in destroying) the northern Lanka which was renowned to be the abode of Vīra Rākshasas (great-heroes), the elevator of the race of Manu, the terror of his enemies in the battlefield, the chastiser of

Kaṇṇanūr : the Hoysala capital of the south ; the Bhojāśvara Temple
(cor. of Hoysalēśvara Temple)
(by permission of the Madras Archæological Department)

those who despised the Chola family, the cunning hero who killed Rājarāja after making him wear the double crown for three years, the subduer of the Pāṇḍyas and the Chēras, the plunderer of the Pāṇḍya country, (the hero) whose sword was clever in cutting off the crowned head of the Pāṇḍya king, he who placed his feet on the jewelled crown of the Pāṇḍya, who was death itself to the Karnāṭa king, who drowned the figure of the Kali Age in the ocean, and on whose leg Vīra Somēśvara, 'the wrestler of hill forts (the capturer of hill forts is better for *giridurga-malla*) placed (with his own hands) the anklet of heroes.' He also lays claim in another record where he styles himself Mahārājādhirāja Tirubhuvana Chakravartin Rājēndra Choladēva, 'who took the crowned heads of two Pāṇḍya kings, and was entitled Konērimaikoṇḍān, to have made a gift to the temple of Tiruchiṟṟambalam *Uḍāiyar* in the village of Nenpākam (modern Lepaka) in Pottappi Nāḍu, a sub-division of Rājēndraśoḷa-Manḍalam.[1] The recital of his deeds contained in the above extracts makes his position clear. He was a distinguished member of the Chola family (race of Manu). His conquest of the Vīra Rākshasas does not from their location, refer to any conquest of Ceylon. It seems clearly to refer to the northern portion of the Chola dominions extending northwards into the territory of the Kākatīyas. The 'northern Lanka' here seems to be a variant of the old Tamil Māvilangai territory which at the time of Rājēndra III was under the Śambuvarāyans, and further north of them the Telugu-Cholas of Nellore, who were feudatories of the Kākatīyas. The reigning chief of Nellore, contemporary with Rājēndra was Manmasiddha, the patron of the Telugu poet Tikkana-Somayāji, the author of the Telugu *Bhāratam* and *Nirvachanōttararāmāyaṇam.* The latter work states of Manmasiddha that he was turned out

[1] Ep. Rep. 1912, sec. 32.

of his kingdom by his cousins, but was restored by the Kākatīya king, Gaṇapati, through the poet's intervention.[1] He calls himself the ally of Rājēndra Chola III, and the existence of the latter's records so far out as Cuddapah confirms this. It is likely that in the northern exploits of Rājēndra III he got into alliance with the Nellore chief. The next following statement that he allowed Rājarāja to wear the double crown for three years and killed him afterwards is clearly a reference to his having helped Rājarāja to regain a considerable portion of his territory from the rebel chieftains within, the Pāṇḍya without, and it may be even Vīra Somēśvara in alliance with the latter. That seems the condition reflected in the next following statement that Vīra Somēśvara was at first hostile to him and then submitted to the Chola, according to the Chola records; whereas apparently the same incident is referred to in Hoysala records that Vīra Somēśvara 'uprooted' Rājēndra Chola in battle and reinstated him when he begged for protection. Thus then it is clear that during the last three years of the reign of Rājarāja III there was a civil war between Rājarāja III and Rājēndra III, in which the Śambuvarāyans on the one side, the Pallava Kopperunjinga on the other within the Chola dominions, the Telugu-Chola Tikka, the father of Manmasiddha and later, Kākatīya Gaṇapati from the north, and Māravarman Sundara I, and later his successor Sundara II, and Vīra Somēśvara from the southern side, played each one his part and succeeded ultimately in crippling the power of the Cholas. Rājēndra III's initial date falls in A.D. 1246, and he continued to rule for at least twenty-one years. He gave himself the title *Manukulameḍuttaperumāḷ* (the king who raised the fame of the family of Manu, the ancient Chola) apparently in consequence of his efforts to maintain the power and prestige of the imperial Chola family.[2]

[1] Ep. Rep. 1908, sec. 75.

[2] Ep. Rep. 1911, p. 33, sec. 75.

Divisions in the Chola Kingdom.—At the stage at which we have now arrived, we find the kingdom of the Cholas proper divided into three parts with a variety of political interests. The first is the territory extending south-wards from Chidambaram and the Veḷḷār to well into the interior of the present day district of Ramnad. This still continued to be nominally under the Cholas, constantly struggling to keep out the Pāṇḍya with the assistance of the Hoysala. The capital was still at Gangaikoṇḍaśoḷapuram, and the northern frontier seems to have extended along the Uḍaiyārpālayam road to Kaṇṇanūr, north of Śrīrangam, which was the head-quarters of the Hoysala Somēśvara. This last ruler was still in occupation of Kaṇṇanūr. The Chola for the time being was Rājēndra III, after the death of Rājarāja III, but Rājēndra's territory to begin with seems to have lain farther north in the Chola country, and beyond that, into the territory of the Telugu-Choḍas of Nellore. He was the successful rival for the Chola throne and was in occupation of it about the year A.D. 1250.

The second was the territory nominally included in the Chola kingdom, but just outside of its boundary. It comprised the South Arcot district and was in the occupation of a family of Pallava chieftains of whom at the time Kopperunjinga was the actual representative. He assumed titles such as *Sakalalokachakravarti* and *Avaniyāḷappirandān*, which indicate great power. He seems to have been a constant source of trouble to the Cholas, and to have allied himself with their enemies as occasion offered. On one occasion he was in alliance with Somēśvara, but the latter was generally in alliance with Rājarāja III, to save whom from imprisonment by Kopperunjinga he actually came into the Chola country. We find this Pallava chieftain in alliance with the Pāṇḍya ruler for the time being, Māravarman Sundara Pāṇḍya II, and later even with Jaṭāvarman Sundara I.

The third was the territory to the north embracing within it North Arcot and Chingleput, with an extension perhaps even into the farther north. This was the territory which probably was the actual sphere of Rājēndra III, but in which we find both Rājēndra III and the Śambuvarāyans at considerable conflict of interests. About the time that the Hoysalas intervened on behalf of the Cholas, the Telugu chieftain Tikka of Nellore entered the Chola country from the north, ostensibly in the interests of the Cholas, and apparently against the Pāṇḍyas and the Pallava chieftain of South Arcot. But having come, he showed no more inclination to retire to his territory than his contemporary, the Hoysala monarch. Rājēndra III therefore had first of all to struggle against the Śambuvarāyans, during which struggle he obtained assistance from Tikka, but later on he had to war against Tikka and his son Manmasiddha, and carry the war into their own territory into the districts of Nellore and Cuddapah. In this enterprise Rājēndra was on the whole successful. It was this success that ultimately paved his way to the Chola throne, and that is perhaps what is meant when his inscriptions state that he helped the Chola Rājarāja III to wear the double crown, and killed him at last. What exactly were the actual circumstances that led to the killing, we are not able to see. It is probable that Rājarāja's subserviency to the Hoysala was objectionable to Rājēndra III, and finding it impossible to persuade him into a more vigorous policy he managed to get rid of him and ascend the throne in his stead. This act of his naturally put him at once into hostility with Somēśvara. Rājēndra's records claim that he defeated Somēśvara, and compelled him to put the anklet of heroes on the Chola's feet. On the other hand, the records of the Hoysala claim that Somēśvara defeated Rājēndra and bestowed upon him the Chola kingdom when he submitted. These apparently contradictory versions mean the same ultimately, that Rājēndra III and Somēśvara, the Hoysala, first of all fought against each other and afterwards came to an understanding between themselves. The cause of his unexpected peace perhaps was the advance of Māravarman Sundara Pāṇḍya II through the Chola territory in the Pudukoṭṭa State on which about this time the Pāṇḍya had established his hold, and the likelihood of his proceeding further north in alliance with the Pallava chieftain Kopperunjinga of Śendamangalam. We must now go back to consider the position of the Pāṇḍyas to whom we have had to make so many references in the course of our study of the history of the Cholas.

SPECIAL NOTE

THE DATE OF THE CEYLON INVASION

According to the Mahāvaṁśa Parākramabāhu the Great ascended the throne in A.D. 1164 (Wijesimha's list). This list makes a correction by subtracting eleven years on the authority of the Polonnorua Inscription which gives his date of accession as A.B. 1743 with the equivalent Christian date August 23, A.D. 1200. Subtracting from this the total of forty-seven years for the reigns from Parākrama to Līlāvatī, the immediate predecessors of Sāhasamalla, Parākramabāhu's accession would fall in A.D. 1153. This date for the accession of Parākrama is in accordance with the dates ascribed to that event both in the *Rajaratnākari* (Upham. ii. 86), and the *Nikāyasangraha* (Epi. Zey. i, p. 123). So Parākrama's accession took place in A.D. 1153.

According to the Mahāvaṁśa Parākrama had ruled for sixteen years before he thought of sending an expedition to Ramañña (Pegu) against its king Arimardhana. This invasion proved a protracted affair and when at last news of its ultimate success reached Parākrama. Parākrama Pāṇḍya's appeal for help reached him also. He made arrangements and fitted out a large expedition. We may not be far wrong if we assume that the expedition set forward in the year 20 of Parākramabāhu, i.e. that Lankāpura started in A.D. 1173, it may be a little earlier.

The date of accession of Rājādhirāja II according to the late Dr. Kielhorn is March A.D. 1163 on the basis of his examination of astronomical details in five of his records. According to the same authority the date of accession of Rājarāja II is A.D. 1146. (*Epi. Indica*, ix. 219). The Ekāmbranātha temple inscription (No. 7 of 1893) of Rājādhirāja II states that his eighth year was fifteen years from the nineteenth year of Rājarāja II (*S. Indica Ins.* iii. 207). This will give the latter a reign of twenty-six years at least, and the accession of his successor must have taken place in his twenty-sixth year, i.e. in the year *A.D. 1172* (initial year 1146 + regnal year 26). As a matter of fact there is a record of his twenty-seventh year, and this notwithstanding, the date of *accession of Rājādhirāja must now be accepted as the year A.D. 1171-2.* (*Ep. Rep.* 1904, Sec. 21).

The Arpākkam grant of his fifth year (*Ep. Rep.*, 1899, pp. 8-9) and the Tiruvālangāḍu inscription of his twelfth year (465 of 1905) refer to this invasion in some detail. The former of these two refer to the war as of almost contemporary occurrence, describing in particular the circumstances that brought about the Chola intervention in the war. Hence the lower and the upper limits of the war have to be A.D. 1175 and A.D. 1171, respectively.

The lower limit of A.D. 1167 as actually fixed by Dr. Hultzsch in *J.R.A.S.*, 1913, p. 519 and quoted by the late Dr. Vincent Smith in his Oxford History of India will have to be given up. The doubts that are discernible in *Ep. Rep.* 1910, Sec. 28 and 1913 Sec. 37, obviously on the assumption of A.D. 1163, Kielhorn's initial date for Rājādhirāja II, seem inconsistent with *Ep. Rep.* 1904, Sec. 21.

LECTURE II

SOUTH INDIA IN THE THIRTEENTH CENTURY

The Revival of Pāṇḍyan Greatness.—We have already stated in the previous lecture that the power of the Pāṇḍyas suffered considerable eclipse in the civil war which brought on the intervention of both the king of Ceylon and the reigning Chola Rājādhirāja II and his heir-apparent, who became after him Kulottunga III. It is clear that the position of the Ceylonese as the arbiters of the destinies of the Pāṇḍya kingdom was made impossible by the active intervention of the Chola prince Kulottunga and the Chola feudatory Pallavarāyar. The campaign was continued so successfully by these latter that in the eleventh year of his reign, Rājādhirāja called himself conqueror of Īḻam and Madura. It seems to be that the war continued into the reign of Kulottunga III, as inscriptions of Kulottunga III describe him as 'having taken Madurai (Madura), Īḻam (Ceylon), Karuvūr (Karur) and the crowned head of the Pāṇḍya' and being pleased 'to perform the anointment of heroes and the anointment of victors at Madura.'[1] This achievement was regarded as of such consequence that a grant of tax was made to a temple in the Pudukoṭṭa State for the merit of the king during his stay at Madura,[2] and memory of this seems to be preserved in the name of the South-Western parts of Pudukoṭṭa, Kaḍalaḍayādilangai konḍa Vaḷanāḍu (the division of him that took Ceylon without building a dam across the sea). This division was

[1] Ep.Rep. for 1915, Sec. 27. [2] Ep. Coll. No. 339 of 1914.

otherwise known Virudarājabhayankaravaḷanāḍu. Kulottunga III's achievement therefore amounts to a reassertion of the authority of the Cholas over the Pāṇḍya country. All the same during the period of his reign there were a number of Pāṇḍyas ruling simultaneously, among whom at least one name stands prominent; that of Jaṭāvarman Kulaśēkhara I, whose reign extended from A.D. 1190 to A.D. 1216, the last year of Kulottunga III himself. It is just possible that this Kulaśēkhara was the son of Vikrama and grandson of the Kulaśēkhara whose cause the Cholas supported in the war of succession.

Māravarman Sundara Pāṇḍya I.—The succeeding Pāṇḍyan, Māravarman Sundara Pāṇḍya, whose reign began in 1216 and continued to 1239, and his successor Māravarman Sundara Pāṇḍya II, whose reign commenced in A.D. 1238 and lasted on to A.D. 1255, take up the period of rule of Kulottunga III's successors Rājarāja III and Rājēndra III and of the life time of the Hoysala Vīra Somēśvara who ruled from Kaṇṇanūr, near Śrīrangam, the whole of the Hoysala empire.[1] During this period, the Pāṇḍyas recovered much of their lost power and prestige. Māravarman Sundara I seems to have carried on a successful invasion of the Chola territory capturing the country round Tanjore and Uraiyūr. He claims to have defeated the Cholas taken their country and made 'a present of it' again. He then proceeded to Chidambaram, and after worshipping God Naṭarāja there, performed the anointment of heroes at Muḍikoṇḍaśoḻapuram.[2] So much is clearly stated in an inscription from Tirukkōḷūr in the Tinnevelly

[1] Kielhorn's list of Pāṇḍya kings. Ep. Indica, ix. pp. 226–8.

[2] Ep. Rep. for 1915, Sec. 32. This Muḍikoṇḍaśoḻapuram seems apparently another name for Gangaikoṇḍaśoḻapuram, as Muḍikoṇda and Gangaikoṇḍa are titles of Rājēndra I; Ep. Rep. sec. 24 of 1910 and 200 of 1912. Rājēndra I issued the orders conveyed in the Tiruvālangāḍu plates from his palace at Muḍigoṇḍaśoḻapuram. This fact may be held to be conclusive in regard to the identity.

South entrance, Bṛhadīśvara temple Gangaikoṇḍaśoḷapuram

South-east view of bastion : Siva temple, Gangaikoṇḍaśoḷapuram

district where this Sundara Pāṇḍya is said to have lowered 'the tiger and the bow flag', burnt down Tanjore and Uraiyūr and having turned out the Chola into the forest, anointed himself in the 'thousand-pillared hall', of the Cholas. He then proceeded further north putting an end to the other kings, till he reached Chidambaram, when the Chola came with his wives and children begging for his protection. On his submission, the Pāṇḍya bestowed upon the Chola his crown. Then there came to him the ruler of the north and south Kongus with whom he returned to Madura. He settled the boundary dispute between them and sent them back contented. The ungrateful Chola now undertook an invasion against the Pāṇḍya. Defeating the army of the Cholas and killing their chief, he again performed the anointment of heroes at Muḍikoṇḍaśoḻapuram. This is a free translation of the preamble of the inscription of the year 20 of Māravarma Sundara Pāṇḍya [1] published in the *Sen-Tamil*, volume xii, pages 346 to 350. This date would correspond to the year A.D. 1236–37.

This claim is well attested by the existence of his inscriptions in the Trichinopoly and the Tanjore districts and in the Pudukoṭṭa State, in addition to Madura and Tinnevelly. He also assumed the title Śoṉāḍu-Vaḻangiyaruḷiya (who was graciously pleased to present the Chola country).

Māravarman Sundara Pāṇḍya II.—His successor of the name who ruled from A.D. 1238 to 1255 does not appear to have done much. There are a few records of his however, which give us an interesting insight into the political condition of the Chola country. A record of his fourteenth year refers to the construction of a temple by a person called Tirupullāṉi Dāsar at Kiḻachevval [2] for which the required land was given by a lady Pammiyakkan. The

[1] Ep. Rep. for 1912, 520 of App. B, Sec. 32 of Rep. See appendix below for the record and its translation.

[2] Ep. Rep. for 1912, Sec. 34; also Nos. 522–5 of 1911.

name sounds Kanarese, and the lady that bore the name may have been a member of the Hoysala family, which had entered into marriage relations with the Cholas and the Pāṇḍyas. One of the queens of Vīra Baḷḷāḷa II went by the name Chola Mahādēvi as was already stated. It seems likely that Rājarāja had married either a sister or a daughter of Baḷḷāḷa's son Narasimha who first intervened in the affairs of the Chola country. Hoysala Somēśvara is referred to in a record of Māravarman Sundara Pāṇḍya as Māmiḍi, meaning uncle. [1] At the request of this uncle, Māravarman Sundara made a grant of the village to a Brahman, and called the village Vīra Somi Chatur-vēdimangalam after the name of the uncle. This fact is found recorded in a grant of the eleventh year of Sundara Pāṇḍya, which would correspond to A.D. 1250. Apart from these references we find a general of the Hoysala king by name Appana Daṇḍanāyaka settling disputes at Tirumeyyam in the Pudukoṭṭa State,[2] a clear indication of the grip that Vīra Somēśvara had over the Chola country proper extending down to the frontier of the Pāṇḍyas.

Jaṭāvarman Sundara Pāṇḍya I.—It was in this state of political affairs in the Chola kingdom that there came to the Pāṇḍya throne a ruler, apparently one among a number, 3, 4, or 5, according to the particular period under reference, who claims to have reduced the whole of the Chola Empire to subjection under him; and this was Jaṭāvarman Sundara Pāṇḍya, whose accession is dated in the year A.D. 1251, and whose rule perhaps lasted on to his twenty-third or twenty-fourth regnal year. He assumed the title 'who took all countries'. There are numbers of his records all through the Chola country up to Nellore,[3] which clearly indicate the extension of his authority all through this region. His

[1] No. 156 of 1894 at Murappu-Nāḍu (Tinnevelly District); also Ep. Rp. 1912, Sec. 34.

[2] No. 387 of 1906. Ep. Rep., Sec. 47 of 1901 and Sec. 26 of 1907.

[3] Ep. Rep. of 1911, Sec. 40.

inscriptions, such as they are, recite all his great deeds, but do not give us exactly to understand the order of occurrence of various of his achievements. As recorded in these inscriptions he entered the Malaya country (Malabar), defeated and destroyed the army of the Chera, killing the latter in battle.[1] He then put another ruler on the throne, possibly a counter claimant, or a member of the royal family. He then entered the Chola country apparently by way of Pudukoṭṭa. He placed the Chola under tribute and marched against the Hoysala. He destroyed the army of the Hoysala killing several of his generals, among whom was Śingaṇa Danḍanāyaka given over to an elephant.[2] He did not pursue the Hoysala who was then in full flight. He, however, ordered the death of the Chēra who played the traitor by pretending to be his ally while working in the interest of his enemies.[3] He then attacked *Kaṇṇanūr-koppam*, the capital of the Hoysalas in the Chola country, and brought the Chola country as much under his authority as the Pānḍya country itself was before. He then levied tribute of elephants upon the Hoysala who had retired behind the first line of his outposts in the Tamil country.[4] It was apparently at this time that he mastered possession of Magadai country (the Āttūr division of the Salem district) and the neighbouring parts of South Arcot, and further

[1] See appendix, ll. 21–22 also

மீளாவழிச் செல்லவேணாடர் தங்களை வென்றதடந்

தோளான் மதுரைமன் சுந்தரபாண்டியன் சூழ்ந்திரைஞ்சி

யாளான மன்னவர்தன் னேவல்செய்ய வவனிமுட்ட

வாளால் வழிதிறந்தான் *வடவேந்தரை மார்திறந்தே.*

Ins. on the North Wall of the East Gopura at Chidambaram. Śen-Tamiḻ, iv. 492.

[2] Ājau Simhaṇamunmadasya kariṇōdatvāparāgaṁtatō, Driṣṭvā Rāmamahīpatēḥ praśamitakṣēmābhiṣangōbhuvaḥ. Śrīrangam Pillar Ins. Śen-Tamiḻ iv. 496.

[3] Appendix quoted above, ll. 38–9.

[4] Ibid. ll. 40–45.

west of this the Kongu country. It was then that he received tribute in jewels and elephants sent by the ruler of Ceylon. Apparently Vīra Pāṇḍya his co-regent, who claims the conquest of Ceylon, sent from the king the tribute.[1] Without accepting the tribute sent by the Pallava Chief, Sundara Pāṇḍya marched upon Śendamangalam the citadel of Kopperunjinga (Kāṭakadurgam of the Sanskrit records) and laid siege to it. He took the fortress and bestowed it again upon the Pallava.[2] He then visited Chidambaram where he paid his worship at the shrine of Naṭarāja, covered the roofing with gold and anointed himself ruler of the Pāṇḍya and Chola kingdoms, after performing a tulābhāra ceromony (weighment, against gold and pearls).[3]

Then he went to Śrīrangam and after making some of his benefactions had himself crowned in the temple with the crown *Nagarōdaya*.[4] He then marched further north; turned the Bāṇas into the forests and came into occupation

[1] Appendix quoted above, ll. 42–44.

கொங்க ருடல்கிழியக் குத்தியிரு கோட்டெடுத்த
வெங்க ணழலில் வெதுப்புமே—மங்கையர்கண்
சூழத்தா மம்புனையுஞ் சுந்தரத்தோள் மீனவனுக்
கீழத்தானிட்ட இறை.

Chidambaram Ins. East Gate, south side. Śen Tamiḻ, iv. 493.

[2] Ibid. ll. 50–55.

[3] Ibid. ll. 55–65; also

இனவஸ்ரீ சிம்புரிவெண் பிறைக்கோட்டி கல்வெங் கடுங்கட்
சினமத்த வெங்கிரிச் சுந்தரத் தென்னவன் றில்லைமன்றில்
வனசத் திருவுடன் செஞ்சொற்றிருவை மணந்த தொக்கும்
கனகத் துலையுடன் முத்துத் துலை(யுங்) கலந்ததுவே.

Ṣen Tamiḻ, iv. 491.

Rājasūryassamāruhyattulāḥ kanaka mauktikaiḥ. Ibid. 495. Ins. at Chidambaram.

[4] The Tamiḻ Praśasti in the appendix; ll. 78–80. The record is probably in the temple at Śrīrangam.

Tulābhāra Ceremony, sculptural representation, Mahāmakham Tank, Kumbakonam
(by permission of the Archæological Department, Madras)

of Kānchi having killed Gandagopāla in battle.[1] When his brothers threw themselves upon his mercy, he restored the kingdom to them. He then continued his advance apparently inflicting a terrible defeat upon the Telungas and their allies the Āriyas at Mudugūr, and drove them up to the Pērāru (Krishna).[2] It is in this state of his campaign that he is described as a tiger to the antelope, Gaṇapati, a ***kūṭapākala*** fever to the elephant Kāṭaka, the slayer of Gaṇḍagopāla, etc. The reference to the Āriyas seems to be to the Yādavas of Dēvagiri. If the Rāma Mahīpati[3] in one of the Śrīrangam epigraphs could be held to refer to Rāmachandra or Rāmadēva, the Āriyas would undoubtedly be the Maharattas. Such an inference seems warranted as the Āriyas are referred to in close association with the Hoysalas in all the three references to them we have.[4] The only other possibility seems to be that this Rāma Mahīpati was the Chēra ruler who was put to death for treacherous conduct as an ally. The Kākatīya king Gaṇapati, must have died some time before this if the order adopted above

[1] வாக்கியல் செந்தமிழ்ச் சுந்தரபாண்டியன் வாளமரில்
வீக்கிய வன்கழற் கண்டகோபாலனை விண்ணுலகிற்
போக்கிய பின்னவன்றம்பியர் போற்றப்புரந் தரசி
லாக்கிய வார்த்தை பதினாலுலகமு மானதுவே.

Chid. Ins. East Gate, south side, vii. 3. Śen Tamiḻ, iv. 493.

[2] Ep. Rep. 1914, sec. 18.

[3] See note on p. 63 ; also,
காரேற்ற தண்டலைக்கா விரிநாடனைக் காணுலவுந்
தேரேற்றி விட்டசெழுந் தமிழ்த்தென்னவன் சென்றெதிர்ந்து
தாரேற்ற வெம்படையா ரியந்கண்டு படத்தனியே
போரேற்றுநின்ற பெருவார்த்தை யின்னும்புது வார்த்தையே.

Chidambaram East Gate, north side. Śen Tamiḻ, iv. 491.

[4] A certain class of local chiefs in Pudukoṭṭa and the neighbourhood called themselves Araiyars. It does not seem likely these are under reference here as the Tamil word used in the verse is ' Āriyam.'

7

is correct (on this point see the Tirupputtkuḻi[1] Ins.) though there is the possibility that the Hoysala Somēśvara was killed in a campaign on Sundara Pāṇḍya's return journey, a contingency which seems very highly probable as the Hoysala monarch is definitely stated to have fled when Kaṇṇanūr fell, and Sundara held it unwarlike to press on a flying enemy and fight with him again. The Kāṭaka apparently has nothing to do with Kaṭak in Orissa as a record of Sundara's co-regent Bhuvanēkavīra Vikrama Pāṇḍya states explicitly that he did not go upon his campaign farther north, as he ceased to be angry because of the two fishes, the eyes of Gaṇapati, and since he heard that the ruler there was a woman.[2] This is decisively against any assumption of his war having reached farther north than the Krishna.

[1] Jitvā Kēraḷamudgamayya Magadān nirjitya Lankādipa(m)'s
Chitvā, Kshēmimudasya Hoysalapatim Vidrāvya Chōḷēśvaram,
Bhaṅktva Kāṭakadurgam Āndranṛpatim hatvādhirūḍastulām,
Kānchyām Sundaṛa Pāṇḍya bhūbhṛdaśisha (t) Vīrābhishiktō mahīm.
Tirupputkuḻi Ep. Śen-Tamiḻ iv. 513.

[2] Chidambaram ix. Śen Tamiḻ, iv. 493–94.

புயலுந்தருவும் பொருகைப் பு[வ]நேக வீரபுனல்
வயலுந்தரளந் தருகோற் கைகா வலவாரணப்போர்
முயலுங்கணபதி மொய்த்தசெஞ் சோதிமுகத் திரண்டு
கயலுண் டெனுமது வோமுனிவாறிய காரணமே.

வெங்கண் மதயானை விக்கிரம பாண்டியனே
பொங்கி வடதிசையிற் போகாதே—யங்கிருப்பாள்
பெண்ணென்று மீண்ட பெருமானே பேரிசையாழ்ப்
பண்ணென்றும் வெய்வாய் பகை.

Similar sentiments are ascribed to the Yādava King, Mahādēva. *Bom. Gazetteer*, I. ii. 246.

Yastasyaiva raṇē jahāra kariṇastat pancha śabdādikām
Yastatyāja vadhūvadhā duparatastad bhūbhujām *Rudramām*.
Praśasti, i. 52.

Ayam śiśu strī śaraṇāgatānām hantā *Mahādēva* nṛpōnajātu
Ittam viniśchitya tatōzti bhītair *Āndhraiḥ* purandhrī nihitānṛpatvē.
Praś. I. 14.

Hēmādri's Intrd. to Vṛata Khaṇḍa. Bhandarkar's Dekhan. *Bom. Gazetteer*, I. ii. 273–74.

Śrīrangam, town and temple from the south
(by permission of Messrs. Wiele & Klein, Madras)

In regard to the dating of the campaign, it began apparently soon after Sundara's accession in A.D. 1251. The march from the frontiers of Travancore to the banks of the Krishna with all the campaigning might well have occupied ten years. When he came to the northern end of his progress the Kākatīya Gaṇapati had died and his daughter had just come to the throne in A.D. 1260. After a coronation at Nellore, he set forward upon his return march, and reached Kaṇṇanūr and Śrīrangam in the next two years or so. There was probably another war in which the Hoysala Somēśvara fell, and Sundara entered Śrīrangam and made his great donations to the temple. A record [1] of his fourteenth year (A.D. 1264–65) which he issued from Kaṇṇanūr gives us the limit of date for his campaigns. The Ranganātha inscription of Sundara Pāṇḍya published by Dr. Hultzsch in Vol. III of the *Epigraphia Indica* gives in minute detail all his benefactions to the temple, and hints broadly for the first time of the death of the Hoysala Somēśvara. This death is referred to as a recent event in the first verse of the inscription. 'Having caused to long for the other world (to set or die) the moon of the Karnāṭa (country)'.[2]

The account of his benefactions to this temple which we find recorded in the Tamil work called Koyiloḻuhu seems apparently to be based upon the inscriptions, but adds a few more details. It is hardly necessary to give in detail all the repairs he made, or new structures and extensions that he constructed, which took on the character of extensions of colonnades and halls, providing connecting passages roofed over, and paving the circuits round the main temple. He seems to have added vastly to the

[1] Ep. Coll. 702 of 1904.

[2] Yēnāsau Karuṇāmaniyata daśām Śrīrangapadmākaraḥ, Kritvā tam bhuvānantara praṇayinam Karnāṭa doshākaram.

See also Ep. Rep., sec. 47 of 1911.

thousand-pillared hall, and another hall, in the same yard. It was also he that constructed the various buildings, the *Yāgaśāla* (building for the celebration of Vedic sacrifices) and those adjoining. But what is of some interest here is that these and various other things such as cars, gold and jewel fittings for the car, jewels of various kinds for the God and Goddess, all these amounted to eighteen lacs of pieces of gold of the current coin. This vast amount he set apart for these various purposes by a peculiar kind of *tulābhāra* (weighment against gold). He got two boats of the same size and weight constructed, and had them afloat on the river in the bathing ghat which goes by the name Makha (the asterism in the full moon of February-March of each year under which a festival takes place). He probably connected them both, and on one of them placed an elephant seven cubits, 'of the carpenter's yard' high, and himself mounted on it in full panoply of war with all his warlike accoutrement; and on the other put in an equal weight of gold and pearls and gems of all sorts so mixed as to rise to the same height.[1] He then made it over to the temple for these miscellaneous items of expenditure. This magnificent gift had to lie over for two years as the temple authorities, in the name of God, would not accept it for some reason. Ultimately they were persuaded to accept it. His difficulties did not come to an end there. After making all the vast repairs and new constructions he cherished the ambition, natural to persons of the kind in such circumstances, of placing a statue of his and apparently that of his queen Chērakulavalli in some prominent place in the temple. These again the temple authorities would not have, perhaps on the ground that no statue of a human personality, however high, should defile the precincts of the

[1] The elephant feature at any rate is mentioned in the inscription on the pillars in the Mahāmanṭapa. Mukuṭachayair vijitya Yadu-Kērala-Chola nṛipāṁstaduphṛtaiḥ bhalāt *dviradhirūḍhatulābharitaiḥ* Śen Tamiḻ, iv. 512.

holy temple. The great Pāṇḍya had to content himself with merely making two statues in the form of a god and goddess, but bearing the respective names 'Ponvēynda Perumāl' or 'Hēmāchadanarāja', the great one that covered the roof with gold, and 'Chērakulavalli', as also a large sized statue of Garuḍa the Brahmani kite, 'the chief vehicle' (vāhana) of Vishṇu. These are yet shown in the temple. His munificence however, in spite of the want of a statue of *his*, is yet green in the memory of people, and the name of Sundara Pāṇḍya is familiar to those that know anything of the temple. His name is handed down in various forms on coins of his; 'Emmanḍalamumgonḍaruḷiya' (the conqueror of all kingdoms), 'Eḷḷāṁtalaiyānān (he that is first of all), being some. It is apparently this Sundara Pāṇḍya that enjoyed the special distinction of Vāḷālvaḻitirandān (he that opened the way by the sword).[1] He is also given the title Kōdanḍarāma, on some of his coins and inscriptions.

Jaṭāvarman Sundara's Co-regents.—Along with this great ruler, we have records of at least two others, it is possible that there were three, who ruled simultaneously. One of them went by the name Vikrama Pāṇḍya[2] and the

1 மீளாவழிச் செல்லவேணாடர் தங்களை வென்றகட[ந்
தோ]ளான் மதுரைமன் சுந்தரபாண்டியன் சூழ்ந்திறைஞ்சி
யானான மன்னவர்தன் னேவல்செய்ய வவனிமுட்ட
வாளால் வழிதிறந்தான் வடவேந்தரை மார்திறந்தே.

Chid: Ins. Śen Tamiḻ, p. 492.

2 Chidambaram Ins. ix. Śen Tamiḻ iv. 493. See also Sec. 20 Ep. Rep. for 1914. The first of these Tam. Inss. states that the Podiyil, Hill, the streams flowing down which send out sprays against the rising sun, is the hill of Vikrama Pāṇḍya, conqueror of Vēṇāḍu. This is misunderstood as implying a victory at Podiyil Hill for the Pāṇḍya in the Epigraphist's Report. The error is repeated in Mr. V. Rangachari's index. (Sec. 157 of South Arcot); the verse runs:

ஏந்து மருவியிரவி புரவியின் முன்
பூந்து வலைவீசும் பொதியிலே—காந்துசின
வேணாடனை வென்ற விக்கிரமபாண்டியன் மெய்ப்
பூணாரம் பூண்டான் பொருப்பு.

other Vīra Pāṇḍya ; both of them alike lay claim to conquests against the same enemies as Jaṭāvarman Sundara Pāṇḍya I. A record of Vīra Pāṇḍya (acc. A.D. 1253) states clearly that he 'took Īḻam (Ceylon), Kongu, and the Śoḻamaṇḍalam (the Chola country), and, having conquered the powerful Chola king, was pleased to perform the anointment of heroes and victors at Perumbaṟṟappuliyūr (Chidambaram). He must have come after Māravarman Sundra Pāṇḍya II, as one of his grants refers to Murappunāḍu as Vikrama Sōmi Chaturvēdimangalam, which received this name under Māravarman Sundara II.[1] This circumstance would indicate that in all probability they were not separate rulers, but lieutenants of the empire, who took an active part in the achievements of the chief ruler for the time being.[2] He is said to have instituted a Sundara Pāṇḍyan Sandi (an offering of food) in 197 of the Epigraphist's collection for 1906. This same record of the fifteenth year of Vīra Pāṇḍya mentions Kopperunjinga. These references would only confirm the conclusion. The actual number of Pāṇḍyas that held sway at a particular time, the relations between them, and in fact the history of the Pāṇḍyas generally of this period require to be worked up a great deal more, before it is possible to arrive at any definite conclusion regarding these matters. There are two more Pāṇḍyas that come in, Jaṭāvarman Sundara Pāṇḍya II and another one of the same name, whose reign began somewhat later.[3] Whether these were successors of the two others or whether they were additional rulers, it is not possible to say at present. So much, however, is clear that in this period, extending from about A.D. 1250 to 1275, there were as many as four Pāṇḍya rulers, it may even possibly be five.

Māravarman Kulaśēkhara.—The next great Pāṇḍya whose history is of sufficient importance to be dealt with

[1] Ep. Coll. 435 of 1906. [2] Ep. Rep., Sec. 37 of 1912.
[3] Ep. Rep. 1912, Sec. 36 ; Ep. Rep. 1913, Sec. 45.

is the last great one among them called Māravarman Kulaśēkhara I, whose accession took place in A.D. 1268 according to the late Professor Kielhorn, and of whose forty-fourth year [1] we have a record or two. His reign therefore would extend from A.D. 1268 to 1311 almost. This long reign was one of comparative peace and uniform prosperity, if the statements of Marco Polo and the Muhammadan historians are to be given full credit. This ruler is apparently the 'Khales Dewar' of the Muhammadan historians, and the 'Asciar' or 'Ashar' of Marco Polo. Of Khales Dewar, Wassaf says that he 'had ruled for forty years in prosperity and had accumulated in the treasury of Shahr-Mandi [2] 1200 crores in gold.' In his days, Kāyal a port of the Pāṇḍya country was in a very prosperous condition, and Marco Polo says of him that he was 'the eldest of the five brother kings.' Of Kāyal he says: 'it is at this city that all the ships touch that come from the west, as from Hormos [3] and from Kis [4] and from Aden, and all Arabia, laden with horses and with other things for sale. And this brings a great concourse of people from the country round about, and so there is great business done in this city of Cail.' [5] Reverting to his account of the king he continues 'the king possesses vast treasures, and wears upon his person great store of rich jewel. He maintains great state and administers his kingdom with great equity, and extends great favour to merchants and foreigners, so that they were very glad to visit his city.' According to a grant of this Kulaśēkhara he is described as in residence at his palace located 'in a grove south of the town of

1 No. 106 of 1916. Ep. Rep. 1916, Sec. 30.

2 Shahr Pāṇḍi, the city of Pāṇḍya, Elliott III, p. 52.

3 Not Myos Hormos—Mussel Harbour a port of the Ptolemies in the Red Sea. 27-12 N. and 33-13 E, but Ormuz in the Persian Gulf—Urimanjī of S. Indian writers.

4 Kis or Kais, an island in the Persian Gulf, the chief of which Maliku-l Islam Jamal-ud-din was the chief horse trader with the Pāṇḍya.

5 Marco Polo Edn. by Yule and Cordier II, p. 370.

Jayangoṇḍa-Śoḻapuram ' and the royal seat in the palace is called Kāḷingarāyan. This Māravarman Kulaśēkhara is also known by the other title Konērinmaikoṇḍān (the king who had no equal). His records are generally without introduction, although the Āḻvār Tirunagari record,[1] has one which recounts his achievements. The fact that the name of the officer Kāḷingarāyan figures in this document and in various others of a king Māravarman Kulaśēkhara goes to prove the identity of the ruler referred to. In one document of his seventeenth year, which would correspond to A.D. 1285, the king is said to have been in residence at Gangaikoṇḍa-paṭṭaṇam.[2] He is represented in the one grant with introduction as ruling over both the Chola and the Pāṇḍya countries. Of this particular period it can almost correctly be said that there were five Pāṇḍyas[3] at the time, as Marco Polo says.

But there is one point worth remarking in Marco Polo's account, and that is that the port of Kāyal was under 'Asciar' of Marsden, Ashar of Yule, in both cases alike a modification of Śēkharar, omitting the first part of the word, Kulaśēkhara. He is also described as ruling from Madura, and we have already noticed above he had his royal residence in Jayangoṇḍa-Śoḻapuram. These taken in combination would warrant the inference that he was the principal monarch, the eldest of the five brothers, as some of our authorities mention, while there were other Pāṇḍyas, members of the royal family, and, perhaps related even as brothers in a number of cases, subordinate to his authority,

1 No. 465 B. of 1910. Śen Tamiḻ, vol. ix, p. 357 *vide* Appendix for Text and Translation of part of the record.

2 71. C. of 1916. It is not certain whether this is the same as Gangaikoṇḍaśoḻapuram. The fact that the king is said to have been in residence at his palace at Jayangoṇḍaśoḻapuram, and the change in the name taken together might be interpreted to mean that the capital had been changed on account of the city having become over-crowded for the habitual residence of the ruler.

3 Ind. Antiq. vol. xlii. On some new dates of Pāṇḍya kings by Mr. L.D.S. Sec. iii.

though liable to be referred to as rulers of their respective territory by foreigners visiting their shores.

It is this Kulaśēkhara that is referred to in chapter 90 of the Mahāvamśa of Ceylon.[1] In recording the history of Parākrama Bāhu III, who ruled from A.D. 1288 to 1293 according to this authority, there is a reference made to a famine in Ceylon and to an invasion of the island by the Tamils. It is just in the years immediately preceding, that the predecessor of this Parākrama Bāhu, by name Bhuvanēka Bāhu, drove away from Ceylon 'all his Tamil foes, as Kāḷinga Rāyar, Choḍaganga, and the others who had landed from the opposite coast, and also removed the Singhalese Vannian princes Kadalivata, Mapana, Tipa, Himayanaka and others.' After a few years of pious effort to make the teachings of the Buddha spread through the island by getting copies of the 'three Piṭakas' made and placing them in every monastery in the island, he died and was succeeded by his nephew Parākrama Bāhu. It was then that there arose a famine in the land, 'then the five brethren who governed the Pāṇḍyan Kingdom, sent to this island at the head of an army, a great minister of much power, who was *chief among the Tamils* known as Āriya Chakravarti, albeit he was not an Āriya.[2]

'And when he had landed and laid waste the country on every side he entered the great and noble fortress, the city of Śubhagiri, and he took the venerable tooth-relic and all

[1] Translation by Turnour and Wijesimha, Edn. by the Ceylon Government Press, Colombo.

[2] The term Āriya Chakravarti has been taken to imply a Muhammadan general as there happened to be, at the time, a Muhammadan Customs Officer in high favour with the Pāṇḍya monarch. It is hardly necessary to point out that the existence of a Muhammadan in high position in the Pāṇḍya country will not warrant his identification with this Āriya Chakravarti when he is described by the chronicle as *chief among the Tamils*. He is said to be not an Āriya for the simple reason that he was a Tamil, a distinction that is maintained in the previous sections of the narrative as between the Tamils and the Singhalese. The term Āriya Chakravarti was a title, and many Tamil chieftains bore similar titles during this period.

the solid wealth that was there, and returned to the Pāṇḍyan country, and there he gave the tooth-relic unto the king Kulaśēkhara, who was even like unto a sun expanding the lotus-like race of the great Pāṇḍyan kings'. Parākrama Bāhu apparently did not find himself strong enough to undertake an invasion to recover the precious relic, but preferred to go there with a few determined friends of his and obtain the relic ultimately as a favour by pleasing the monarch Kulaśēkhara during his stay there. This is a clear indication of the power and prestige of the Pāṇḍya monarch in the estimation at least of the Ceylonese, and that is fully reflected in what little of information we are able to glean from Chinese sources. Among the kingdoms which sent tribute to Kublai in 1286 is mentioned Ma-pa-'rh (Ma'bar). There are references to diplomatic intercourse between China and Ma'bar from 1280 onwards. One of these mentions the 'five brothers who were Sultans (Suantan) referring apparently to the Pāṇḍyas of Marco Polo's time. There is the further mention of Chamalating (Jamalu-d-din) who had been sent from Ma'bar to the Mongol court.[1]

In regard to Sundara Pāṇḍya who had died recently when Marco Polo visited the country, he was in all probability the ruler, called by Kielhorn, Jaṭāvarman Sundara Pāṇḍya II, who ruled, according to the same authority, from A.D. 1276 to 1292. There were other Sundara Pāṇḍyas besides.

THE RIVAL BROTHERS—SUNDARA PANDYA AND VIRA PANDYA

Māravarman Kulaśēkhara had two sons, the elder of them is known to epigraphists as Jaṭāvarman Sundara Pāṇḍya III and his accession took place sometime in A.D. 1302-3.

[1] Pauthier quoted by Yule, Marco Polo, ii. 337.

There was also a 'natural son' who is described as Jaṭāvarman Vīra Pāṇḍya and whose date of accession is A.D. June-July 1296. Apparently the father thought better of Vīra Pāṇḍya, and actually designed hini for the succession as the Muhammadan historians have it. This is indicated by the fact that he is earlier associated with the father in the government, while the other rises to that honour six years after. The father's preference for the more gifted prince provoked the jealously of the less gifted son, and led him to turn parricide about A.D. 1311–12; and the disputed succession provided the occasion for the invasion of Malik-Kafur, which will be dealt with in a later lecture.

THE DISINTEGRATION OF THE CHOLA EMPIRE—ITS CAUSES

During much of this period, as has already been more or less clearly indicated in the course of the above history of the Pāṇḍyas, the Chola empire had reached a high degree of disintegration. The principal cause of this was the weakness and ineptitude of the Chola emperor Rājarāja III, 1316-1346, and at the end of his reign the civil war between himself and another prince, probably a brother, Rājēndra III. The Hoysala intervened to preserve for Rājarāja the Chola Empire, but succeeded only in securing to him the southern most part of the empire—the Chola country proper. This intervention from the north-west naturally provoked less friendly intervention from rising powers from the north, and did not effectually prevent aggression from the south. The history of the rising power of the Pāṇḍyas, as already indicated above, exhibits the results of Pāṇḍya intervention from the south.

The Telugu Choḍas.—The northern power whose records state in clear terms an intervention in behalf of the Chola was that of the Telugu Choḍa chieftains of Nellore, known in inscriptions as Simhavikramapura or Vikramasimhapura. Under five generations of rulers these had gained possession of the northern districts of the Chola empire and even held possession of the town of Kānchi, the head-quarters of the northern viceroyalty. Inscriptions of Manmasiddha and his brother Tammusiddha are available relating to early thirteenth century. The son of the former, Tikka by name, claims to have captured Kānchi and defeated Sōmēśa at Champāpuri, (Śambuvarāyanallūr, near Tiruvallam) in the district of North Arcot, the country primarily of the Śambuvarāyans. His son Manmasiddha, who seems otherwise called Gaṇḍagopāla, which had become more or less a family title, was active in that region and having been dispossessed, sought and obtained the help of the contemporary Kākatīya ruler Gaṇapati. With his assistance, he fastened his hold on Kānchī till the rival Chola Prince, Rājēndra Chola, rose to power and turned both Manmasiddha and Gaṇapati backwards perhaps as far as Nellore in the forties of the thirteenth century. He was followed by another ruler of that family usually known as Vijayagaṇḍagopāla, whose reign lasted from about A.D. 1250 to 1292. He was succeeded by a son of his Vīragaṇḍagopāla. These continued to be subordinate to the authority of the Cholas so long as the Chola power lasted, and afterwards perhaps to the Pāṇḍya, as we have already seen the great Pāṇḍya, Jaṭāvarman Sundara I, carried his arms successfully as far north as Nellore and performed there 'the anointment of the victorious warrior.'

The Śambuvarāyans.—The region immediately adjoining, that is the district of North Arcot, was under a family of hereditary chiefs generally known by the class title Śambuvarāyan (Sans. Champa) rulers, who figure for the first time as powerful feudatories in the reigns of Rājādhirāja and Kulottunga III. They rise into importance and are found fighting sometimes on the side of their liege lords, the

Cholas, and occasionally against them also. In the disturbed period extending from the end of the first quarter of the thirteenth century to the end of the Pāṇḍya ascendancy, they maintained the substance of real power though nominally subordinate to the Chola head-quarters, and later the Pāṇḍya. Except for figuring in the wars on the northern frontier, they do not appear to have played any very decisive part. They maintained their position intact along the Pālār. About the end of this period they rise into importance and we have inscriptions of Vīra Chola Śambuvarāyan, and Vīra Śambuvarāyan about the year A D. 1314–15. In the period immediately following we find two rulers who assumed high titles indicating independence. Of these the first is Sakalaloka Chakravartin Venṛu Maṇkoṇḍa Śambuvarāyan, whose date of accession is A.D. 1322–23, followed by Sakalaloka Chakravartin Rājanārāyaṇa Śambuvarāyan, whose date of accession is A.D. 1337-8, and whose reign extended to A.D. 1356-57.[1] It was apparently this latter ruler that was overcome by prince Kumārakampana of Vijayanagar, who put an end to the independent power of the Śambuvarāyans in the North Arcot District with Virinchipuram and Kānchī as their alternative capitals, and Paḍaivīḍu as their hill fortress. Along with these figure another class of minor chiefs who go by the designation Vāṇakkovaraiyar, the remnants perhaps of the Bāṇa dynasty.

The Kākatīyas : Gaṇapati and Rudrāmba.—During this period the Kākatīyas of Warangal made an effort at extending their territory southwards, and, on occasions, were in occupation of Kānchi. The first Kākatīya intervention comes along with the advance of the Telugu-Choḍa chieftains to the south. It is king Gaṇapati of the dynasty that made this advance towards the south, and we have an

[1] Ep. Rep. 1904, Sec. 27.
,, 1911 ,, 65.
,, 1913 ,, 67.

inscription of his in the Vishṇu temple at Kānchīpuram.[1] This advance seems to have been at a time when the throne of Rājāraja III had passed on to Rājēndra III, and Kopperunjinga dominated the whole of the northern division of the Chola empire. Kopperunjinga at any rate claims to have defeated the Kākatīyas, and we have already noted that Rājēndra Chola, the successful rival of Rājarāja, also lays claim to conquests in the Telugu country reaching at least as far as Cuddapah and Nellore. During the last years of the reign of Gaṇapati, the great Pāṇḍya ruler, Jaṭāvarman Sundara Pāṇḍya I, marched northwards, and his victorious advance up to Nellore and his coronation there made the Kākatīyas withdraw into their own territories. Gaṇapati's successor Rudrāmba, who ruled from A.D. 1260 to 1291 succeeding her *father* Gaṇapati, had apparently enough to do to keep her own kingdom without thinking of extending her territory. There is, however, a statement in one of her inscriptions that one of her officers, Amba Dēva by name, destroyed the Kāḍava Rāya. The same chief is also said to have established at Nellore, Manma Gaṇḍagopala who was dispossessed of his kingdom. These are all the glimpses that we get of Kākatīya activity in the south during the long reign of Gaṇapati and that of his daughter, which together practically cover the century, from A.D. 1200 to 1291-2, soon after which Marco Polo visited the Coromandal Coast of India.

Marco Polo.—Marco Polo calls the province that he first touched after leaving Ceylon Ma'bar, the usual Musalman designation of the Coromandal Coast extending from Kulam (Quilon) to Nilawar (Nellore). Marco Polo sailed westward from his port of embarkation for a distance of about sixty miles till he came to the province of Ma'bar, which he says was styled 'India the Greater.' According to him it is the

[1] No. 2, Ep. Coll. of 1893. Another in the *Ekāmranātha* temple no. 26 of 1890 both of A.D. 1250.

best of the Indies and is on the mainland. He refers to the coast wherein he landed as among the possessions of the Pāṇḍyas, and of whom at the time there were five brothers ruling. 'Sonder Bandi Dēvar' (Sundara Pāṇḍya Dēvar), was the crowned king. He undertook to give a detailed account of the five provinces of the kingdom ruled by these brothers, and forgot to fulfil his promise. But the province that he describes at some length is 'the finest and noblest in the world', and was the sphere of Sundara Pāṇḍya. He refers apparently to the fishery coast where pearl fishing was the principal industry. This must be borne in mind to understand his itinerary. The port he visited on this coast has much exercised the ingenuity of scholars, and from various considerations both Yule and Cordier would refer the port to Kaveripaṭam. [1] The lead is taken by all these authorities from the statement of the Muhammadan writer Wassaf that Fittan, Mali Fittan and Kabil constituted the famous ports of which Takhiud-din Abdur-Rahman was the Marzaban (Margrave). These three names are obviously Paṭṭaṇam, Mēlai Paṭṭaṇam, and Kāyal or Kāyal Paṭṭaṇam in the language of the locality. Kāyal, according to Marco Polo, was the premier port, whereto came all merchants from the east as well as the west, and from all over India, for purposes of trade. The other two

[1] Yule's Marco Polo: New Edn. by H. Cordier II. 332–8.
H. Cordier in his new work 'New Light on Ser Marco Polo' bas an additional note on this on p. 112. Quoting from Chau Jua Kua a passage extracted in Ma Tuan-lin and the Sung-shi, he states the Chola capital was five li distant from the sea, though the latter have 5,000 in place of five. He adopts Yule's suggestion that Kaveripaṭam, the 'Paṭṭaṇam' par excellence of the Coromandal Coast, and at one of the mouths of the Kaveri, was the then Chola capital. Kaveripaṭam is not mentioned in any of the large number of the inscriptions of the time known to me; nor have I come across any reference to it in the literature of the period. If 'all figures connected with Chu-lien in Chinese accounts are inexplicably exaggerated,' and if a 'Paṭṭaṇam' was the Chola capital, Gangaikoṇḍa-paṭṭaṇam, already referred to on p. 56 must be the city meant. There is a reference, in another Chinese authority (ibid p. 114) to Pa-tan where there was a *stūpa*. This undoubtedly refers to Negapatam, and would justify my conclusion that there were several ports referred to by this abbreviated designation.

stand in some geographical relation with this one. The words would stand, the port and the upper port, the term paṭṭinam meaning port. I believe the port on what is the island now is called Ramēśvara Paṭṭinam, sometimes also Paṭṭinam merely, but at the time of Marco Polo there was another great port on the inner side of the Gulf of Mannar, the ruins of which are now known as Periya Paṭṭaṇam. In the wars of Parākrama Bāhu in favour of one of the Pāṇḍyan princes, and against his brother, he is supposed to have taken on the mainland and in the peninsula, a village called Kundukāla and having fortified it with three circuits of walls and twelve gates, called it Parākrama-paṭṭaṇam, equi-distant from either sea. A little way to the south and on the coast lie the vast ruins of a city called Periya Paṭṭanam (large port or city) in the Ramnad Zamindari, already referred to above, where till recently people picked up coins and antiquities of sorts, and I am informed, a considerable portion of the ground plan of the city could still be traced at low water. Any one of these three places might do, and that is the place where one would expect a boat sailing from Ceylon to land, having regard in particular to the fact that the port of embarkation at the time seems to have been Puttalam (Bathelar) in Ceylon, the Bhattala of Ibn Batuta; and the distance would be perhaps about sixty miles, a little more or less. We are bound to look for Fitan in that locality as the Mali Fitan seems certainly to be Dēvi Paṭṭaṇam about ten miles north of the town of Ramnad, but on the northern side of the island of Ramēśvaram. A medieval map is said to mark Mali Fatan in or about the locality.[1] For the mere name Paṭṭaṇam there are any number along the coast, more than twenty along the Tanjore coast; of which, at the time to which we are referring, the very town of Topputturai,

[1] See *J.R.A.S.* IV. (N.S.) p. 345 ff.

as it is known at present, was called Vīraśoḻan Paṭṭaṇam; not far was a Kulottunga-śoḻa-paṭṭaṇam set over against Tirutturaippūṇḍi. A little way to the north of it was Negapatam; Kaveripatam at the mouth of the Kaveri; Jayangoṇḍapaṭṭaṇam near the mouth of the Coleroon and so on. In the Palk Strait itself south of Topputtorai, there is Adirāmpaṭṭanam to begin with, the name may be a later one; there is Ammāpaṭṭaṇam, there is Sundara Pāṇḍyan Paṭṭaṇam itself, and any number of paṭṭanams like that. Battelar, which according to Marco Polo is the place where the ships collect before going on a pearl fishing expedition seems much rather to refer to a port on the continent than to one in Ceylon. We have a port in the peninsula near Maṇḍapam which goes by the name Vēdāḷai now, and it is just on the southern shore of the peninsula, and at the head of the Gulf of Mannar, a convenient starting point for the fisher-folk. There is a harbour to the east of it that is called Toṇitturai even now, apparently the place where boats assembled on their fishing expeditions for pearls.

After describing the prosperity of the country under the rule of the Pāṇḍya, and referring to the horse trade of the locality he proceeds to describe Mailapūr and St. Thomas' Mount, and apparently proceeds further northwards as he says 'when you leave Ma'bar and go about a thousand miles in a northerly direction you come to the kingdom of Mutfili (or Mosul). This was formerly under the rule of a king, and since his death, some forty years before it had been under his queen, a lady of much discretion, who for the great love she bore to him never would marry another husband. And I can assure you during all that space of forty years she had administered her realm as well as ever her husband did, or better. And as she was a lover of justice, of equity, and of peace, she was more beloved by those of her kingdom than ever was lady or lord of theirs before.'[1] He then proceeds to describe the diamond mines and recounts the famous story and the fabulous ways in which diamonds were got. 'In this kingdom also are made', according to him, 'the best and most delicate buckrams, and those of the highest price; in sooth they look like tissue of spiders' web!! There is no king nor queen in the world but might be glad to wear them.'

We have referred above to his description of the Port of Kāyal, and quoted his statement that 'Asciar' was the eldest of the five brothers. This we have already stated was the Pāṇḍya king Kulaśēkhara who ruled from A.D. 1268 to 1312 almost. We have inscriptions of this monarch in the Chola capital Gangaigoṇḍaśoḻapuram, in the capital Madura itself, and in the Tinnevelly district as far south as Āḻvār Tirunagari, so that the statement that he is the supreme monarch is quite correct, and the Sundara Pāṇḍya that Marco Polo refers to must be the predecessor of the name who died in A.D. 1292, or the prince brother or nephew in charge of the coast district of Ramnad and the neighbourhood which Marco Polo must have touched in the course of his voyage.

The Coromandal Coast of Marco Polo.—From these various statements of Marco Polo we find that the Coromandal coast from the farthest south to the mouths of the Krishna, which were in some respects the limit of navigation, was ruled over by two dynasties of kings only; the Pāṇḍyas perhaps over the greater portion of the coast in the south, and the queen of the Kākatīyas in the north. At the time that Marco Polo was in this part of his voyage, queen Rudrāmba of the Kākatīyas must just have abdicated in favour of her grandson Pratāpa Rudra II, the last great king of the Kākatīya dynasty who came to the throne in A.D. 1291-2, and in whose reign Telingana, his kingdom,

[1] Marco Polo Opus Cit., pp. 359–60.

was reduced to subordination by the Muhammadans. The south was under a powerful king also, that is, Māravarman Kulaśēkhara I, who had a long reign of forty-four years, beginning with A.D. 1268 and reaching up to almost A.D. 1311. The territory of the former occupied the coast from almost the frontier of Ganjam up to the mouth of the northern Pennar and extended into the interior, north and south, across the middle of the present day Nizam's dominions. The region extending south from there to Cape Comorin and perhaps even farther west, was the territory of the Pāṇḍya, which at the time included the great bulk of the Chola kingdom. Its boundary was wide enough to include the district of Salem and part of Coimbatore extending south along the Western Ghats to the Cape. The northern frontier was uncertain. The conquests they made up to Nellore seem not to have been made permanently at all so that we might roughly demarcate the boundary between the Pāṇḍyas and the Hoysalas along a line drawn from Trichinopoly to Tiruvaṇṇāmalai and Villupuram along the road from Madura to Madras. On the other side of this line extended into the interior the territory of the Hoysalas, which under the greatest of their rulers Vīra Somēśvara, reached northwards as far as the frontiers of the Krishna, perhaps even a little beyond. The existence of a record of Somēśvara in Panḍharpur may, it is just possible, be held to indicate that his actual rule extended so far north.

The Hoysala Empire in the Period.—About the time to which we have come the Hoysala empire had for near forty years remained divided into two kingdoms. Somēśvara had associated with himself, since A.D. 1254-5 his son Vīra Rāmanātha, who succeeded him in the southern division of the empire. His alternative capitals were Kaṇṇanūr near Śrīrangam, and Kundāṇi in the northern frontier of the Salem district; the territory above the ghats was ruled by his half-brother Vīra Narasimha III. Vīra Rāmanātha died about A.D. 1293, and a son by name Vīra Viśvanātha ruled only for three years, perhaps four. Vīra Narasimha died almost about the same time as Rāmanātha, and was succeeded by his son Vīra Baḷḷāḷa III in whom, in the early years of the last decade of the thirteenth century, the Hoysala empire again united. He maintained the three capitals at the three strategic points of the empire, namely, Halebīḍ in the north or north-west, Kundāṇi in the middle keeping communication with the country below, and Kaṇṇanūr in the south, with Tiruvaṇṇamalai as an alternative. The country immediately north of the Hoysalas and west of the Kākatīyas on the southern side of the Vindhya mountains was under the dynasty of the Yādavas of Dēvagiri with their capital at Dēvagiri. This was the political division of the south when the Muhammadans made the first irruption into the Dekhan under Alau-d-din Khilji in A.D. 1296.

The four kingdoms of the Peninsula.—India south of the Vindhyas in the last decade of the thirteenth century and the first of the fourteenth was thus divided into four well-marked kingdoms. The first was, as was stated above, the Yādava kingdom of Dēvagiri with its Capital at Dēvagiri (Deogir). It was ruled by the last great Yādava, Rāmachandra, who ascended the throne in A.D. 1271 and ruled till some time in A.D. 1309-10. The eastern half of the Dekhan and the Telingana coast was under Queen Rudrāmba of the Kākatīya dynasty with Capital at Warangal in the Nizam's Dominions. Sometime in A.D. 1291 she raised her grandson Pratāpa Rudra to the throne and retired. Pratāpa Rudra ruled from A.D. 1291 to A.D. 1328. The frontier of these two kingdoms came to almost a line drawn from Goa, or a little north, to the mouth of the northern Peṇṇār, somewhere to the east of Nellore. The whole country south of this was divided along a diagonal line say from Chidambaram or Cuddalore, along the main roads of traffic to Tiruvaṇṇāmalai and Kundāṇi getting into the tableland a little way north of Hosur and from there to the Krishna, along eastern Mysore. The line proceeded further west along the mountains right down the Palghat gap to the sea. All north of the first line roughly belonged to the Hoysalas and all south to the Pāṇḍyas ; the more open country along the coast right up to Nellore on the great Madura-Madras road, was a debatable frontier between these two powers. The last great ruler of the united Hoysala empire was Vīra Baḷḷāḷa III who succeeded his father Narasimha III in A.D. 1291-2 and ruled till his death in A.D. 1342. He was succeeded by a son Baḷḷāḷa IV, who perhaps ruled for three years more. All through this period the kingdom of the Pāṇḍyas in the south was held by a remarkably gifted ruler who gave the country peace and prosperity. This was Māravarman Kulaśēkhara I, whose forty-fourth year we have records of. He ascended the throne in A.D. 1268 and ruled till sometime in A.D. 1311-2. The dissensions between his two sons brought in the Muhammadan intervention which took the form of the first Muhammadan invasion of the south.

Muhammadans in the Pāṇḍya country.—It was not the Muhammadan invasions from the north that brought the Muhammadans into this country for the first time. Muhammadan intercourse with the west coast of India seems to have begun much earlier ; and we have considerable evidence of pre-Mussalman trade of the Arabs and other people with it. Arab settlements, after the introduction of Muhammadanism, were made in several places on the coast whose principal object was merely trade, for which the Hindu states of the interior apparently gave all facilities. The piratical character of the West Coast appears to have made the coast of the Konkan except for the northern ports of Kambay and Broach, as far down as Bombay undesirable for these foreign traders, possibly along with the dangers of getting close to the shore in the monsoon weather. There was besides the peculiar custom of the land that vessels driven ashore by stress of weather became the property of the authorities of the port into which it happened to be driven.[1] The governments of the east coast on the contrary seem to have pursued a more enlightened policy as the charters to the oversea traders of the Kākatīya Gaṇapati and the Reḍḍi Chief Vēma indicate. Under these charters traders were not only relieved from this disability, but were also offered special advantages by way of excuse from all port dues excepting the customs duties (Kūpaśulka).[2] It is this that made the eastern ports such welcome places to foreign merchants from China and the east on the one side, and the western traders on the other. Hence the name Ma'bar (Arabic for passage) for the Coromandal coast. The same policy seems to have been adopted by the rulers of the Malabar coast also as far north as Canara. Hence at the time that we have come to, that is about A.D. 1290, there were a number of flourishing ports on the east coast, of which the principal ones were Moṭupalli in the Kākatīya dominions in the north near the mouth of the Krishna, and the well-sheltered port at the mouth of the Tamaraparani in the Gulf of Mannar in the south, called Kāyal, not far from the far famed Korkai (Kolkhoi of the classical geographers). Of a number of trade settlements, enjoying the special protection of the rulers, that probably were in existence in all these ports there was one in Kāyal which has come in for prominent mention. This was the agency established at Kāyal by an Arab chieftain who is described by the Muhammadan historians as Maliku-l-Islam Jamalu-d-din ruler of Kis, and later the farmer-general of Fars. Such an agency was required because of the vast trade in horses. According to Wassaff, about this time as many as

[1] Yule's Marco Polo : II. 386 and note 4 to the chapter. Ibn. Batutah : note below.
[2] Ep. Rep. 1910, Sécs. 45 and 61.

10,000 horses were imported into Kāyal and other ports of India of which 1,400 were to be of Jamalu-d-din's own breed. The average cost of each horse was 220 dinars of 'red gold'. The cost even of those that died on the way was paid by the Pāṇḍya king for whom they were imported. Jamalu-d-din's agent was a brother as it seems, Takiu-d-din Abdur-Rahman, son of Muhammadu-t-Thaibi described as Marzaban (Margrave). This agent had his head-quarters at Kāyal, and had the other ports of Fitan and Mali Fitan also under his control. This description means that he was the agent general for the import trade of the Arabs in this part of the country, as according to the same authority the trade of this region in those days was very great, both in volume and value. In the words of Wassaf, 'Ma'bar extends in length from Kulam to Nilawar (Nellore) nearly three hundred *parasangs* along the sea-coast, and in the language of that country the king is called *Dewar*, which signifies the lord of empire. The curiosities of Chin and Machin, and the products of Hind and Sind, laden on large ships (which they call junks) [1] sailing like mountains with the wings of winds on the surface of the water, always arrived there. The wealth of the islands of the Persian Gulf in particular and in part the beauty and adornments of other countries, from 'Irak and Khurasan as far as Rum and Europe, are derived from Ma'bar, which is so situated as to be the key of Hind.' [2] This description is supported in full by what Marco Polo has to say of the eastern ports

[1] At Surat they excel in the art of ship-building. Their bottoms and sides are composed of planks let into one another, in the nature, as I apprehend, of what is called rabbet-work, so that the beams are impenetrable. They have also a peculiar way of preserving their ships' bottoms, by occasionally rubbing into them an oil they call wood-oil, which the planks imbibe. 'There would be no exaggeration in asserting that they (the natives) build incomparably the best ships in the world for duration, and that of any size, even to a thousand tons and upwards. It is not uncommon for one of them to last a century.' Grose, *Voyage to the East Indies*, vol. i, pp. 107–8 (A.D. 1750–64).

[2] Elliot, iii. 32.

both of Kāyal and of Moṭupalli. It was from one of these ports that an embassy went to China sometime about A.D. 1297 under Fakhru-d-din Ahamad bin-Ibrahim-ut-Thaibi. This ambassador was the son of Jamalu-d-din. He returned after a stay of four years in China and died on board when two days distant from Ma'bar about the end of A.H. 704 (A.D. 1305). 'His tomb is in Ma'bar, near that of his uncle,' the Marzaban, who died two years before. It seems likely there were other settlements of these Muhammadans even in the interior of the country. In the course of his description of the campaign of Malik Kafur in the Tamil country, Amir Khusru says 'Thither (to Kandur) the Malik pursued the 'yellow-faced Bir', and at Kandur was joined by some Mussalmans who had been subjects of the Hindus, now no longer able to offer them protection. They were half Hindus, and were not strict in their religious observance, but, 'as they could repeat the *Kalima* (the Confession of Faith of the Muhammadans), the Malik of Islam spared their lives. Though they were worthy of death, yet as they were Mussalmans, they were pardoned.'[1] This shows that at Kandur, which I have identified with Kaṇṇanūr, near Śrīrangam, there was a settlement of Muhammadans quite different from the northern Mussalmans, who came along with the invaders. Ibn Batuta's statement that Vīra Baḷḷāḷa had a contingent of 20,000 Muhammadans in his army, though made up of slaves and prisoners of war, would seem quite probable as he had a number of Muhammadan settlements on the west coast under his government, among whom the leading one at Honawar owed allegiance to his Viceroy Hariyappa Oḍayar (Horaib), the Harihara I of Vijīanagar history. It seems thus clear that the Muhammadans of South India have a history anterior to the invasions from the north.

[1] Elliot, iii. 90.

Takiu-d-din Abdur Rahman, who is described as Wazir and Marzaban in Ma'bar and who died in A.D. 1303, was succeeded by his son Siraju-d-din and by his grandson Nizamu-d-din in succession in the same position as the principal farmers-general of the customs of the Pāṇḍyan coast. It must be remembered that these were Arabs by descent. The position of Wazir or Chief minister ascribed to these Arabs is not confirmed by any Indian evidence so far, though it is quite likely, from the important positions these occupied, that they exercised considerable influence in the councils of the Pāṇḍya rulers at the time. There is some confusion in Wassaf's account as copied by Rashidu-d-din, as he has introduced another Jamalu-d-din, his informant Shaik Jamalu-d-din. It is likely this was not the only family that was settled in official positions of importance in the courts. The probabilities are, on the contrary, that there were a larger number of these settlements in the various important ports of trade, and it is these that became the nuclei of various Muhammadan settlements of Arabic character in all the sea-port towns of this coast, as well as that of Malabar, giving rise to various communities of mixed descent. These had neither part nor lot with the Muhammadan invaders of the north who carried fire and sword through the country in the course of their first invasions of the south. These too stood on occasions to suffer quite as much as the other inhabitants of the country as we have an instance of such suffering on record in connection with Khusru Khan's invasion of this region.

LECTURE III

MUHAMMADAN INVASIONS OF THE DEKHAN

The First Invasion due to an accident.—Sometimes great revolutions happen in the history of empires by accident, and the first invasion of the Dekhan may well be brought under the category of accidents. During one of the Mameluk revolutions that took place in Delhi, *a Khilji* high official, one of the slaves of the masterful Ghiyasu-d-din Balban raised himself to the throne. He was an old man remarkable alike for bravery and clemency. He came to the throne with three grown-up sons, one of whom at least was a warrior of reputation like the father. He had two nephews, sons of a brother, of whom the elder was a daring unscrupulous man of high ambitions. These nephews had married, each of them a daughter of the Sultan. Of these two ladies, the elder one was apparently a proud and indiscreet person, and conducted herself in such a way as to make her ambitious husband feel his position intolerable. Her mother the Malika-i-Jahan had great influence over the king, and as our Muhammadan authorities state, encouraged her daughter in her proud bearing towards her husband. So long as the young man was at court, he kept his pride under control. A chance came early for him however, to go out to a governorship as the result of a rebellion which was successfully put down. He took the opportunity of the remoteness of his head-quarters from court to mature his plans to carry himself to a higher position than that of a governor, and to teach the proud princess, his wife, a lesson. Gratitude to an uncle who brought him up like a father, gave him one of his daughter's in marriage and promoted him to offices and positions of trust, did not come in the way of his ambition. The one essential required for the fulfilment of this was money. He had not much chance of raising it in his own province unobserved by the agents of the court and the sovereign himself. He therefore cast longing eyes across the mountains, and made use of an occasion when he conducted an expedition to Bhilsa, to make the requisite enquiries and satisfy himself as to the wealth that was to be got by an invasion of the Dekhan. That was how the first invasion came about.

The Khiljis.—The uncle monarch Jalau-d-din and his ambitious nephew Alau-d-din both alike belonged to the new dynasty of the Khiljis, which held away over Delhi and Hindustan during the last decade of the thirteenth and the first score of years of the following century. These were a people who were Turks; but having been long settled in Afghanistan, first round Herat and then further eastward, they became so assimilated to the populations of the locality that they were taken to be more Afghans than Turks. After the rule of Ghiyasu-d-din Balban, whose masterful rule left no man of dominant ability or position in the state, the feeble and dissolute character of his successor made orderly administration impossible. In the course of the struggle for power, a man of military ability with a distant governorship certainly came up, and this was Jalalu-d-din Feroz, the leader of the Khiljis, whose genius for war gave him a considerable following. The dissolute youth who nominally occupied the throne was literally 'kicked out of existence.' Jalalu-d-din Feroz succeeded to the throne in A.D. 1290. In the early distribution of the offices, which usually followed a new succession, the names of his three sons figure prominently as also his two nephews Alau-d-din and Almas Beg. For about a year Alau-d-din was at Court, but the rebellion, in Karra and Oudh, of Chajju, a nephew of Ghiyasu-d-din Balban gave the opportunity for the preferment of Alau-d-din. Alau-d-din was appointed Governor of Karra first of all, to which was later added Allahabad. In his new government he was joined by a number of the rebels whom Jalalu-d-din with great, perhaps unwise, clemency pardoned. Alau-d-din's government became thereafter the head-quarters of intrigue against the good monarch, his uncle. Any access of gratitude was made impossible by the constant irritation that he had from the conduct of his proud wife. He had, therefore, formed his plans for conducting an expedition against the Dekhan without the knowledge of his uncle.

Sinews of war needed to prosecute the higher ambitions of Alau-d-din.—It would be unusual for a man who cherished ambitions to occupy the throne of Delhi to complicate his position by a distant invasion at the same time. Alau-d-din's idea in the distant invasion was not exactly conquest or addition to the empire. In this instance there was absolutely nothing of either. His object was chiefly plunder, and plunder of a neighbouring Mussalman governor had no chance whatever of being overlooked at court. The invasion of a Hindu kingdom on the otherside of the Vindhya Mountains, where no Muhammadan had yet set foot appealed to the ambitions of the knight-errant, if there was any in him; but the chief motive was money to provide himself with the wherewithal for the purpose of carrying his ultimate ambition through, of occupying the throne at Delhi. This ambition seems to have been clearly formed in his mind and received considerable encouragement from those about him at the time. The court was not without some knowledge of his ambition, but the good Sultan could not be brought to think ill of his nephew son-in-law who had made effective use of his younger brother at court to counteract the honest efforts of the ministers to awaken the suspicions of the Sultan.

Deogir the objective.—While in Bhilsa conducting an expedition for the Sultan, Alau-d-din made enquiries, and found that across the mountains lay the powerful kingdom of Mahārāshṭra with its capital at Deogir. He also had definite information that the last ruler Rāmachandra had been on the throne for some considerable time already, and had accumulated vast wealth ; and, what was more important for his purpose, that at the time that he had made his plans, the main army of Rāmachandra, Ram Deo as the Muhammadan historians call him, had been led southwards towards the Hoysala frontier by his eldest son Shankar Deo. Alau-d-din therefore obtained permission of the court to undertake a punitive expedition against Chanderi, the Hindu chieftain of which, according to him, had grown proud of his wealth and declined submission to his government. The permission of course was easily granted and Alau-d-din went as far as Chanderi publicly, and therefrom made arrangements that no information of his movements should reach head-quarters. He marched at the head of 8,000 chosen horse and made a dash from Chanderi to Elichpur across the mountains and not far from the frontiers of the kingdom of Ram Deo.[1] After a much-needed halt for rest at Elichpur he proceeded to Ghati Lajura,[2] about twelve miles from Deogir, without meeting any opposition. He was cleverly giving it out on his march that he was going towards Rajamundri to take service with the Raja there as he was far from being satisfied with his uncle's treatment of him. Deogir happened to be denuded of its troops at the time as Shankar Deo had 'gone southwards at the head of his army on pilgrimage.' When information reached Deogir that Alau-d-din was at Ghati-Lajura, Ram Deo collected together such forces as he could and sent about two or three thousand men to oppose the further advance of the Muhammadan army. Alau-d-din overpowered this small force easily and sent it in hasty retreat into the

[1] Elliot, vol. iii, p. 149-50.

[2] Lasur as it is otherwise called.

capital, himself following in hot pursuit. The Raja threw himself into the citadel, which was then undefended even by a ditch. The garrison had not adequate provision to stand a siege. At this time a caravan of bags which merchants were bringing from the Konkan happened to be abandoned at the approach of the enemy, and these were laid hold of and put into the fort in the belief that they contained grain. Having received this welcome supply Ram Deo determined to stand a siege. In the meanwhile, Alau-d-din's troops entered the town, captured the Brahmans and the principal merchants of Deogir, and plundered the city. In the course of these operations Alau-d-din adopted the clever ruse of circulating a rumour that his was but the advance-guard of the main army of 20,000 horse following him. On hearing this Ram Deo considered it prudent to come to terms, and on his side commissioned agents to make Alau-d-din understand that it was time that his son should return at the head of the whole army of Deogir, and that it would be prudent for Alau-d-din to accept such terms as he offered. He also pointed out to him the dangers of a retreat in the face of a hostile force, as his retreat would lie through Khandesh, Malva and Gondwana, the Rajas of which would certainly cut off his retreat. Alau-d-din understood the dangers of his position better than Ram Deo, and agreed to depart from Deogir in a fortnight if Ram Deo guaranteed to him a 'ransom of fifty maunds of gold, seven maunds of pearls and some valuable stuffs in addition to forty elephants, some thousands of horses and the plunder which he had already collected from the city.' In the meantime Shankar Deo hearing of the approach of the Muhammadans returned to the city by forced marches. Ram Deo sent word to him of the conclusion of the treaty, ordering him at the same time not to attack 'the Turks.' The prince, however, finding that his army was twice as strong as that of the Muhammadans, disregarded the father's orders, threatened to annihilate the Muhammadan army unless Alau-d-din restored all the plunder that he had taken, and left the kingdom immediately. Alau-d-din disgraced the messengers by parading them through the camp with their faces blackened, and prepared to fight Shankar Deo. He detached one thousand of his men under Malik Nasrat, and left him to watch the fort. With the remainder he fell upon the forces of Shankar Deo. After a fierce contest the Muhammadans were hurled back, and were about to retire when Nasarat Khan left the fort without orders and joined the army. The arrival of this new force was mistaken by Shankar Deo's army for the main Muhammadan army of 20,000 which Alau-d-din gave out was approaching. In an alarm the army broke and fled. Alau-d-din now returned quietly and pressed on the siege of the citadel, putting a number of captives to death and parading the more respectable among them in chains before the fortress. Ram Deo resolved to stand the siege, but discovered, on opening the sacks of the new supply put in, that they contained salt not grain. Finding it impossible to stand the siege much longer he again opened negotiations. Alau-d-din took advantage of the situation as he inferred that the position of Ram Deo must be bad indeed to ask for terms again. Charging the Hindus with breach of faith he insisted upon far heavier terms, and, if Ferishta is to be believed, exacted from them a 'ransom of 600 maunds of gold, seven maunds of pearls, two maunds of other jewels, thousand maunds of silver, and an yearly tribute of the revenues of the Elichpur province.' With the wealth thus collected he returned to his own province of Karra. The invasion not only provided Alau-d-din with the much-needed sinews of war for the time, but it also opened the way to the Dekhan and South India for the Muhammadans.

The wealth of the Dekhan too tempting to an enterprising adventurer.—Ever since Alau-d-din reached Elichpur, the court at Delhi had no information about him, and it was not till Alau-d-din had completed his work in Deogir and was about to return that rumours reached head-quarters that he had had a victorious campaign in Deogir, and was about to return with enormous booty in the shape of gold and elephants. When information of this reached Jalalu-d-din, it naturally created suspicion which was only confirmed by successive arrivals of further news as to the movements of Alau-d-din.

Honest counsels were not wanting at court. Alau-d-din's ambition was known to several, who also understood that it was the want of gold that kept him from prosecuting his ambition. Ahmad Chap, the faithful Chamberlain of the Sultan, offered the piece of advice that 'Elephants and wealth when held in great abundance are the causes of much strife; whoever acquires them becomes so intoxicated that he does not know his hands from his feet. Alau-d-din is surrounded by many of the rebels and insurgents who supported Malik Chhaju. He has gone into a foreign land, without leave, has fought battles and won treasure. The wise have said "money and strife, strife and money", that is, the two things are allied to each other. My opinion is that we should march with all haste towards Chanderi to meet Alau-d-din and intercept his return. When he finds the Sultan's army in the way, he must necessarily present all his spoils to the throne whether he likes it or not. The Sultan then can take the silver and gold, the jewels and pearls, the elephants and horses, and leave the other booty to him and his soldiers. His territories also should be increased, and he should be carried in honour to Delhi.' Sounder advice in the circumstances, it would be hard to find; but the Sultan neglected it with the reflection 'what have I done to Alau-d-din that he should turn away from me, and not present the spoils?' He went much farther and accepted the treacherous counsel of a creature of Alau-d-din at court. Alau-d-din was able safely to return to his headquarters, and slowly worked the confiding Sultan to consent to pay him a visit at Karra, where, under circumstances of peculiar atrocity, the old Sultan was murdered under his very eyes without Alau-d-din raising his little finger to defend his guest; nor did he exhibit the slightest contrition when the deed had been done. The Sultan was Alau-d-din's guest having discarded all his attendants, and was practically murdered in the arms of Alau-d-din.

The murder of the good uncle did not make the way to the throne quite open to Alau-d-din. Jalalu-d-din's eldest son had died, and the second son was Arkali-Khan, who was then Governor of Multan. He was a soldier of great reputation at the time, and had already done splendid service under his father. Had he been put forward in succession to the late Sultan, Alau-d-din would have found his position difficult, nay impossible almost, but the evil genius of the late Sultan in the person of the queen Malika-i-Jahan put up the third son Ruknu-d-din Ibrahim in preference to his elder brother, and thus lost the support of the more powerful among the nobles who would gladly have supported the cause of Arkali Khan. Alau-d-din found his opportunity now, made the very best use of it, and applied the Dekhan gold to pave his way to the throne. ' He rejoiced over the absence of Arkali-Khan and set off for Delhi at once in the midst of the rains, although they were more heavy than any one could remember. Scattering gold and collecting followers, he reached the Jamna. He then won over the Maliks and Amirs by a large outlay of money, and those unworthy men greedy for the gold of the deceased and caring nothing for loyalty or treachery, deserted the Malika-i-Jahan and Ruknu-d-din and joined Alau-d-din.' . . . ' Five months after the death of Jalalu-d-din at Karra, Alau-d-din arrived at Delhi and ascended the throne. *He scattered so much gold about that the faithless people easily forgot the murder of the late Sultan and rejoiced over his accession.* His gold also induced the nobles to desert the sons of their benefactor and to support him.'[1] About the same transaction Ferishta makes similar reflections. 'He commenced his reign by splendid shows, and grand festivals, and encouraged every description of gaiety, which so pleased the unthinking rabble that they soon lost all memory of their former king, and of the horrid scene which had placed the present one on the throne. *He who ought to have been viewed with detestation, became the object of admiration to those who could not see the blackness of his deeds through the splendour of his munificence.*'

An essential need of Alau-d-din's reign to keep the Mughals out of India.—Having thus successfully paved his way to the throne with blood and gold, Alau-d-din naturally had to fear plots against him from those in positions similar to that which he occupied at his uncle's court. There was further the probability of trouble in the subordinate governments of the kingdom of Delhi particularly as the succession was irregular. To add to these two, the Mughals who began to appear on the north-western frontier early in the century kept hanging like a cloud over the frontier and had to be kept out of it at all costs. He proceeded therefore to suppress revolts in the interior, and put the frontier in a footing to oppose possible incursions of the Mughals. Having done this preliminary he was able to defeat the Mughals. A ruler of ordinary ability in his position would have given himself up to ease and pleasure having so far succeeded in putting down disturbances, but Alau-d-din was not a man of ordinary ability. He knew that defeating the Mughals for once did not mean the suppression of the Moghul trouble, and his work therefore lay in providing efficiently for the permanent defence of the north-western

[1] Elliott, vol. iii, p. 157.

frontier on the one side, and the maintenance of peace by suppressing rebellions and disturbances in the country as necessary thereto. To effect both these objects, the prime necessity was what would be called a standing army of sufficient strength in a high state of efficiency. Such a standing army, having regard to the numbers in which the Mughals invaded India, should of necessity have been large and we need not be surprised at the statement of Wassaf that he maintained in very efficient condition an army of 475,000 soldiers of all arms.[1]

His revenue system and the invasions of the Dekhan had the same object in view—money.—The maintenance of such a vast army implies an unfailing treasury, which could, according to the economics of those days, be kept well-filled only by heavy taxation supplemented by the plunder of other states. His revenue measures were so adopted as to make rebellion impossible either for the Musalman or for the Hindu, and the recognized principle of revenue assessment in his reign was that the actual ryot was left enough to carry him through till the next crop. Even so, the treasury could not meet the demands upon it. He therefore naturally had to look outside of his territory proper to eke out his revenues. There was a very good precedent in the invasion of Deogir. It was the plunder of Deogir that provided him with the resources to accomplish the ambition of occupying the throne at Delhi. Deogir itself could be made to pay more, and there were other kingdoms besides, equally rich if not richer. Two alternatives would have presented themselves to a man of daring ambition like Alau-d-din, to conquer the kingdoms south of the Vindhyas and annex them to his empire, or to

[1] 'At the present time the imperial army consists of 475,000 Muhammadan disciplined holy warriors, whose names are recorded by the imperial muster-master, and whose pay and rations are entered in the regulations of the deputy victualler,' Elliott, vol. iii, p. 50.

war against them to produce the impression of his power, and make them pay tribute to him so that he might draw from their well-filled treasury gold and treasure to the utmost of his need. It is to the credit of Alau-d-din that he considered it bad policy to go on extending his empire by adding territory at great distances, which would only mean so many distant centres for disturbance and rebellion. He therefore chose the other alternative of maintaining these states under the Hindus, who must have appeared to him, as in fact they were, capable of administering their kingdoms economically and keeping themselves well-provided with treasure for any emergency. We shall see that his instructions to the invading generals were explicitly on this understanding.

Conquest of Gujarat.—In the early years of the reign of Alau-d-din, among various other expeditions that he sent out either against the Mughals or against states situated in the interior that rebelled against him, he had to send one against Gujarat. This expedition went under the command of Ulugh Khan and Nasrat Khan. Rai Karan, the ruler of Gujarat, was besieged in Nahrwala and after a month's siege he escaped from the fortress which surrendered. Among the booty taken was Kamalā Dēvi, the beautiful wife of the Rai. They proceeded further into Gujarat laid siege to Kambay and in the plunder there, they took a beautiful slave by name Kafur. These two persons Kamalā Dēvi and Kafur attracted the fancy of Alau-d-din so much that he appropriated both of them to himself. He took the former 'who, for beauty, wit, and accomplishments was the flower of India' into his harem, where she rose to be his favourite. The other beautiful slave, Kafur, appealed to his fancy equally and began his official career with the king's favour, which in the next few years raised him to the highest position in the state. These two persons each exercised the highest influence upon the

Sultan. Kamalā Dēvi, the ill-fated wife of perhaps an iniquitous husband, was pining away for the surviving one of her two little daughters with whom Rai Karan escaped from Nahrwala into the territories of Deogir. A demand was made for the surrender of the little girl Dēval Dēvi, but the father declined to give her up. The mother would not take a refusal and an invasion was necessary to gain possession of her. But for this one necessity, Alau-d-din at the close of the first decade of his reign could look upon his administration as a success and the following words of Barni may be regarded as exhibiting the actual position of affairs in regard to the Sultan :—'Wherever Sultan Alau-d-din looked around upon his territories, peace and order prevailed. His mind was free from all anxiety. The building of the fort of Siri was completed, and it became a populous and flourishing place. Devoting his attention to political matters, he made ready his army for the destruction of the Rais and Zamindars of other lands, and for the acquisition of elephants and treasure from the princes of the south.'

Invasion of Deogir.—It was in these circumstances that the matter was brought home to the Sultan that Ram Deo of Deogir had neglected to pay his tribute for the last three years. Before the year A.D. 1300 Alau-d-din made two attempts to get into Telingana by the eastern route, but neither of them advanced beyond Jajnagar,[1] the capital of Orissa in those days. Ram Deo, of Deogir, who had been sending his yearly tribute regularly, took advantage of the disturbances in the first years of Alau-d-din's rule and withheld the tribute. An expedition to punish this remissness and exact the much-needed tribute was necessary. A great expedition was therefore sent out under Malik Kafur, the

[1] This is apparently the place referred to as Śādinagar or Ādinagar in inscriptions of Rājendra-Chola 1, and corresponds to Yayātinagar identified with Sirpur Binka on the Mahānadi by Pandit Hira Lal, Ep. Ind., ix. No. 19.

most esteemed Muhammadan general of the time, Kwaja Haji being made second in command. Ein-ul-Mulk, Governor of Malva, and Alaf Khan, Governor of Gujarat, sent their troops to reinforce the invading army. This expedition was commissioned to take Dēval Dēvi from Rai Karan, and send her over to Delhi. Rai Karan, who was paying the penalty for a bad act of his, had on a previous occasion declined to give his daughter in marriage to Shanker Deo, the son of Ram Deo of Deogir. Knowing the danger in which she was at the time and having had a renewal of that request from Shanker Deo, he agreed to send her over under an escort provided by Shanker Deo and commanded by his younger brother Bhim Deo. The expedition went into Gujarat defeated Rai Karan, but failed in the principal purpose of the expedition as Dēval Dēvi had been for sometime on the march to Deogir. By an unfortunate accident, a body of three or four hundred of the army who went out on a holiday in the region of the Ajanta caves, met the escort, took the princess and sent her over to Delhi, thus fulfilling the first object of the expedition. Kafur's expedition marched south to Deogir, laying waste the country on the way and round the city itself. Ram Deo sued for terms. Malik Kafur sent him to make his personal submission to Sultan Alau-d-din, who received him kindly and made him stay in Delhi for six months. At the end of this period he dismissed him with marks of honour, and gave him the title of 'Rai Raiyan' with 'a red-canopy.' According to Ferishta even the district of Nausari taken from Gujarat was given over to Ram Deo as a personal estate. Ram Deo continued to send his tribute regularly afterwards. This was in the year A.D. 1306 according to Ferishta, A.D. 1307 according to Amir Khusru, and A.D. 1308 according to Barni.

Invasion of Warangal.—The kind of treatment Alau-d-din accorded to Ram Deo would seem to be in strange

Ajanta Caves, Panoramic View
(by permission of the Government Archæological Department)

contrast to what perhaps would have been expected from Alau-d-din. Alau-d-din's object in these various invasions of the Dekhan and the farther south appears to have gone no farther than making them the milch-cow for the gold that he was often much in need of for the efficient maintenance of his army to keep Hindustan free from internal disturbance and invasion by the Mughals from outside. That this was actually his policy is clear from the instructions he gave to Malik Kafur on the occasion of the expedition against Warangal. In the words of Barni the Naib was to do his utmost to capture the fort of Warangal and overthrow Rai Rudra Deo (Laddar Deo). 'If the Rai consented to surrender his treasure and jewels, elephants and horses, and also to send treasure and elephants in the following year, Malik Naib Kafur was to accept these terms and not press the Rai too hard. He was to come to an arrangement and retire without pushing matters too far, lest Rai Laddar Deo should get the better of him. If he could not do this he was, for the sake of his own name and fame, to bring the Rai with him to Delhi.' The policy here adumbrated involves two essential conditions: (1) The ruler was to be defeated to make an impression of power, but the territory was not to be annexed as it would involve government from a distance, which would mean constant rebellion and war; (2) he was to be allowed to rule, but to be fairly fleeced of all his wealth and treasure, and even all the elephants, the most powerful arm of Indian armies in those days. These ought to be regarded very wise measures to attain the object he had in view. In the year A.D. 1309 Malik Kafur left with a force similar to that which he took with him in the previous year on an expedition to Deogir. Accompanied in this expedition 'by the royal red canopy, through the kindness of "the sun of sultans," he departed towards the sea and Ma'bar.' Marching through uninhabitable tracts, which in the graphic language of Amir Khusru are called 'the Razor-bridge of Hell' and crossing five rivers in the course of six days, the army arrived at last in Elichpur (Irijpur) called by the Muhammadans, Sultanpur. Proceeding from there they arrived at Kandahar where they spent the first fourteen days of the Ramzan. At *Nilkanth*[1] on the borders of Deogir which was the frontier town of Rai Rayan Ram Deo, the minister of Deogir, met the army and attended to their wants till they passed the frontiers of Deogir. Marching for sixteen days in what seems a south-eastern direction, they arrived at the fort of Sarbar (Sirpur), considered to be within the province of Telingana. The fort was set fire to and the inhabitants massacred. They marched further forward and in four more days arrived at a place called Kunarpal, very near Warangal. They took possession of Hanumakonda (An Makinda in Amir Khusru) wherefrom 'all the edifices and gardens of Warangal can be seen.' Warangal was a double fortress; the inner wall was built of stone and the outer made of mud 'but so strong that a spear of steel could not pierce it; and if a ball from a western catapult were to strike against it, it would rebound like a nut with which children play.' The fort was immediately laid siege to. Malik Kafur fixed his head-quarters a mile from the gate of Warangal and pitched his tents close together all round the fort. Every division of his army was allotted 1,200 yards of land round the fort, the entire circuit of the wall being according to the same authority 12,546 yards. Orders were issued also that every division of the army was to surround itself with a stockade wall. They were so well and so strongly constructed and entrenched 'that if fire had rained from Heaven their camp would have been unscathed.' A night attack upon the camp by Vinayak Deo (Banak Deo) was unsuccessful and

[1] Nalgund is too far east. Could this be Naldrug ?

Hanumakoṇḍa Temple, General View
(by permission of H.E.H the Nizam's Archæological Department)

was beaten back with great vigour, and ridges and redoubts were successfully built commanding the inside of the fort. They were able to effect a breach at last by battering down the walls over the length of about 100 cubits. A few other minor breaches also were made. As escalading was considered too laborious an operation, it was resolved to make an attempt at taking the fort by storm. By a night attack three bastions of the outer wall were taken and occupied by the Musalmans. By persistent effort during the next three days, the besieging army got possession of the whole of the outer wall. They then began a vigorous attack on the stone bastions of the inner fortress. Rudra Deo thought it prudent to offer terms and sent his messengers offering payment of annual tribute and sending a golden image of himself with a golden chain round its neck in acknowledgement of his submission. The Naib demanded in reply 'everything that the Rai's country produced from vegetables to mines and animals.' Rudra Deo agreed and surrendered the elephants, treasures and horses. 'The Malik took the entire wealth of the Rai, which was brought, and threatened a general massacre, if it should be found that the Rai has reserved anything for himself.' An engagement was then entered into that the Rai should send Jizya annually to Delhi. Malik Kafur left Warangal with all his booty, 'a thousand camels groaned under the weight of the treasure,' in March 1310. He returned to Delhi by way of Deogir, Dhar and Jhain.

From this it is clear that there were two convenient roads by which an army starting from Delhi could reach the Dekhan, one seems to be an eastern road coming down the western bank of the Jamna to Agra and possibly even Allahabad, proceeding by way of Chanderi along the main railway line from Allahabad to Hosangabad and breaking southwestwards from there across the Vindhya Mountains, which are much broken at the place southwestwards to

Elichpur. The actual convenience of this route seems to have been that in spite of its being in certain parts the 'razor-bridge of hell' according to Amir Khusru, it avoided the Narbada in its lower course; but when Malik Kafur returned he returned by another route equally well known and along another line of railway of the present day across the country of Malva, and through the less arid parts of Rajputana straight to Delhi. There was a high road leading from Deogir to Dhar and straight across from there, through the western margin of Rajputana to Delhi. Elichpur is a convenient centre from which to march southward upon Deogir or south and then south-east upon Warangal. As a matter of fact on the occasion that Malik Kafur invaded Warangal he did go to Kandahar, which is some way northwards of Bidar and proceeded to the frontier of the country of Telingana and thence to Kunarpal; therefrom he marched a short distance and came within sight of Warangal. This line of march has to be borne in mind in connection with another line that Malik Kafur took from Deogir on his invasion of the farther south.

LECTURE IV

INVASIONS OF SOUTH INDIA UNDER THE KHALJIS

Malik Kafur's project for an invasion of Ma'bar for the same object, plunder.—According to Amir Khusru 'the Malik represented that on the coast of Ma'bar were 500 elephants, larger than those which had been presented to the Sultan from Arangal, and *that when he was engaged in the conquest of that place he had thought of possessing himself of them* and that now, as the wise determination of the king, he combined the extirpation of the idolaters with this object, he was more than ever rejoiced to enter on this grand enterprise.' Amir Khusru makes it appear that having seen all the country from the hills of Ghazni to the mouths of the Ganges reduced to subjection and having effectively destroyed the prevalence of the 'Satanism' of the Hindus by the destruction of their temples and providing in their stead places for the criers to prayers in monques, Alau-d-din was consumed with the idea of spreading the light of the Muhammadan religion in the Dekhan and South India. According to the same authority Ma'bar was so distant from the city of Delhi 'that a man travelling with all expedition could only reach it after a journey of twelve months,' and there 'the arrow of any holy warrior had not yet reached.' Apart from this statement of Amir Khusru, the object of this expedition is made quite clear in what he puts in the mouth of Malik Kafur himself that what he actually coveted were the elephants of better breed, and, what went along with them of course, other items of wealth. Having in the two previous invasions brought both the Dekhan kingdoms, Deogir and Warangal under subjection there remained only two more in the farther south, the Hoysala kingdom of Dvārasamudra and the Pāṇḍya kingdom farther south again. The army left Delhi on the 24th of Jumada-l Akhir, A.H. 710 (November A.D. 1310), and marched by the bank of the Jamna and halted at Tankal for fourteen days. After taking the muster of the army at that place, they marched rapidly for twenty-one days when they arrived at Kanhun. A further march of seventeen days brought them to Gur-Ganw (Gurgam). During these seventeen days Amir Khusru says they had to pass through the ghats and the road lay across heights and depths, where even elephants became nearly invisible. That was not all, they had to pass three rivers of which the Narbada was the greatest, and the other two of about the same size but smaller than the Narbada. At the end of this march the Raja of Telingana sent twenty-three powerful elephants. They remained at Gurgam for about twenty days, taking a muster of the army and sending on the elephants in advance. According to Amir Khusru they marched on towards Gurgam and reached ultimately the river Tawi (Tapti). Having crossed it, they reached Deogir on the thirteenth of Ramzan, apparently the same year. There they halted for preparations 'for extirpating Billal Deo and other Deos (demons).' Here the Rai Raiyan, Ram Deo, true to his allegiance forwarded all the preparations necessary for the equipment of the army 'to render it available for the extermination of rebels and the destruction of Bir and Dhur Samundar.' That was not all. The Rai Raiyan, who had already sent ahead his Daḷavāy (Dalvi, Commander-in-Chief) Paras Deo (Parasuram Deo) 'to hold the gates of access to the Bir and Dhur Samundar' was directed by his master to see to the wants of the Muhammadan army. On the seventeenth of Ramzan, the army departed 'from Imanabad Deogir to the Kharababad of Paras Deo Dalvi, in five stages, in which three large rivers were crossed,' the three rivers being 'Sini, Godaveri and

Binhur (Bhima).' Then 'after five days the army arrived at Bandri, in the country (Ikta) of Paras Deo Dalvi, who rendered all the assistance for the ultimate conquest of "Bir Dhul and Bir Pandi."' At Bandri, Malik Kafur stayed sometime to obtain information of the state of things in Ma'bar. According to Amir Khusru he was informed that there were two rulers in Ma'bar, of whom the elder was Bir Pandya and the younger Sundara Pandya who till then were friendly, but had gone to war against each other at the time. 'Billal Deo, the Rai of Dhur Samundar (Dvārasamudra), had marched down upon their cities with the object of plundering, but returned on hearing that the Muhammadan army was on the march.'

Invasion of Dvārasamudra.—On Sunday, the 22nd of Ramzan, Malik Kafur held a council of war. Apparently as a result of a resolution he took with him a select body of cavalry, and appeared before the fort of Dhur Samundar on the fifth of Shawwal 'after a difficult march of twelve days over hills and valleys and thorny forests.' Seeing the destructive character of the invasion, the ruler Vīra Baḷḷāḷa III having ascertained the strength of the Muhammadan army sent agents to propose peace, though Vīra Pāṇḍya had despatched an army to assist him.[1] Malik Kafur is stated to have sent the reply 'that he was sent with the object of converting him to Muhammadanism, or of making him *zimmi* (one who could enjoy the same political privileges as the Muhammadans on payment of *Jiziya*) and subject to pay tax, or of slaying him, if neither of these terms were assented to.' The Rai agreed to surrender all his property 'except his sacred thread' and on Friday the sixth of Shawwal, six elephants were sent accompanied by three plenipotentiaries. The next day some horses followed and on the Sunday following he is himself said to have

[1] Wassaf on p. 50 Elliott iii.

paid a visit to the Commander-in-Chief and surrendered all his treasures, having spent a whole night in taking them out. Malik Kafur remained twelve days in that city, which, according to Amir Khusru, is four months distant from Delhi, to which he sent the captured elephants.

The Baḷḷāḷa Prince sent over to Delhi.—The final terms of the treaty, however, do not appear to have been settled by Malik Kafur himself. As he did in respect of Ram Deo at Deogir, he sent prince Baḷḷāḷa to Delhi along with the elephants and horses on this occasion also to obtain the ratification of the terms from Alau-d-din himself. Amir Khusru does not state this detail, but there are a few inscriptions of Vīra Baḷḷāḷa III, which do make a reference to it. Two records [1] dated A.D. 1310 refer to the Muhammadan invasion, another one is [2] not dated but the name of the year is given from which we can make out that it refers to A.D. 1313. This latter records a grant to a temple on the occasion of the entry into the capital of Prince Vīra Baḷḷāḷa Rāya returning from Delhi after the war against the 'Turukas' (Muhammadans). Having achieved this at Dvārasamudra and satisfactorily settled matters as far as the Hoysala kingdom went, Malik Kafur got ready for the invasion of Ma'bar which term then stood for the country of the Chola and the Pāṇḍya under Pāṇḍya rule for the time being.

Invasion of Ma'bar.—We have already detailed above the state of the country of Ma'bar. The occasion that called for intervention by the Muhammadans is given as the fratricidal war in the Pāṇḍya country between the two brothers Sundara Pāṇḍya and Vīra Pāṇḍya. Hence there is very little doubt left that the ultimate objective of the invasion was the Pāṇḍya kingdom wherever it be. The Chola kingdom which ought naturally to come between the

[1] *Epigraphia Carnāṭaka*, vol. v, Has. 51 and 52.
[2] *Epigraphia Çarnāṭaka*, vol. vii, Sh. 68.

Hoysala and the Pāṇḍya country had practically gone out of existence as a separate political entity. Although perhaps the incidents of the war did take place as much in the Chola country as in the Pāṇḍya, still the ruling power against whom Malik Kafur directed his invasion was that of Vīra Pāṇḍya, as he had sent an army to assist Vīra Baḷḷāḷa against Malik Kafur. In the words of Wassaf 'Rai Pāṇḍya (meaning apparently Baḷḷāḷa) offered opposition, and begged the assistance of an army from Ma'bar. At that time enmity prevailed between the two brothers, Sundar Pandi and Tira Pandi, after the murder of their father. *The latter sent to his assistance an army* of horse and foot.' It was probably in consequence of this state of disunion that 'in the month of Rajab of the year A.H. 710 (A.D. 1310) the appointed leaders, accompanied by a select army, were despatched to conquer Ma'bar, and some of the towns were obtained through the animosity which had lately arisen between the two brothers; when at last a large army, attended by numerous elephants of war, was sent out to oppose the Muhammadans. *Malik Nabu, who thought himself a very Saturn, was obliged to retreat, and bring back his army.*' This was apparently an invasion distinct from the one by Malik Kafur himself.

The Pāṇḍya Fratricidal War.—It was already pointed out in a previous lecture that the Pāṇḍya who ruled almost up to the time of this invasion was Māravarman Kulaśēkhara I. He had two sons known to history; one of them, a 'natural' son Vīra Pāṇḍya, he associated with himself in the Government from A.D. 1296. The other, the 'legitimate' son Sundara Pāṇḍya attained to that dignity sometime in A.D. 1302. Both these princes, Vīra Pāṇḍya and Sundara Pāṇḍya, take the prefix Jaṭāvarman in inscriptions, and should not be confounded with others of the name but with a different prefix. This difference of treatment between the two sons may have been due merely to a difference of age or ability. According to one authority Sundara Pāṇḍya was the elder; Amir Khusru makes him younger; but both of them Wassaf and Amir Khusru, agree that Sundara Pāṇḍya was 'the legitimate' and Vīra Pāṇḍya perhaps an 'illegitimate' son of the ruler for the time being. The preference given to Vīra Pāṇḍya either by advancing him to the position of co-regency, or because sometime about A.D. 1311 Kulaśēkhara, almost at the close of his life, actually ordered the succession in favour of Vīra Pāṇḍya, Sundara Pāṇḍya felt so far discontented as to assassinate his father and actually take possession of the throne. Vīra Pāṇḍya soon after attacked him and drove him out of Madura. Sundara Pāṇḍya thus driven from the throne looked out for help and sought the assistance of the Sultan of Delhi either at head-quarters directly, or with the Naib of the Sultan, Malik Kafur, who was then in the South. Sundara's appeal gave the occasion for interference, if such an occasion were necessary for Malik Kafur at all. This is the trend of events described by Wassaf in relation to the fratricidal war in the Pāṇḍya country. Kales Dewar, Kulaśēkhara Dēva, was a highly prosperous monarch whose rule extended over 'forty and odd' years, 'during which time neither any foreign enemy entered his country, nor any severe malady confined him to bed.' He had accumulated much wealth during this long reign so that he had in the 'treasury of the city of Mardi' (Madura) 1,200 crores of gold not counting the accumulation of precious stones 'such as pearls, rubies, turquoises, and emeralds.' 'This fortunate and happy sovereign had two sons, the elder named Sundar Pandi, who was legitimate, his mother being joined to the Dewar by lawful marriage, and the younger named Tira Pandi, was illegitimate, his mother being one of the mistresses, who continually attended the king in his banquet of pleasure.' 'As Tira Pandi was remarkable for his shrewdness and intrepidity, the ruler nominated him as his successor. His brother Sundar Pandi being enraged at this supersession killed his father in a moment of rashness and undutifulness, towards the close of the year A.H. 709 (A.D. 1310), and placed the crown on his head in the city of Mardi (Madura). He induced the troops who were there to support his interests, and conveyed some of the royal treasures, which were deposited there to the city of Mankul.'[1] Then there was a war between the brothers and a battle is said to have taken place, 'on the margin of a lake which, in their language, they call Talachi.' Both the brothers fled away from the field, each ignorant of the fate of the other; 'but Tira Pandi being unfortunate, (tira bakht), and having been wounded, fell into the hands of the enemy, and seven elephant loads of the gold also fell to the army of Sundar Pandi.' Vīra Pāṇḍya, however, according to this authority obtained the assistance of 'Manar Barmul, the son of the daughter of Kales Dewar, who espoused the cause of the Tira Pandi, being at the time at Karamhati, near Kalul.'[2] With this assistance Tira Pandi advanced to oppose him, at the head of his army 'in the middle of the year A.H. 710 (A.D. 1310).' '*Sundar Pandi*, trembling and alarmed, ***fled from his native country, and took refuge under the protection of Alau-d-din of Delhi***, and Tira Pandi became firmly established in his hereditary kingdom.' According to Wassaf's account therefore, Sundara Pāṇḍya found refuge in the court of Alau-d-din, and that gave the occasion for interference, if such an occasion were necessary for Malik Kafur who was already on this invasion. It is this state of affairs that Amir Khusru described when he

[1] This is not Namkal as surmised by Elliott, but in all probability one of the Mangalams, Mēla Mangalam or Kīḻa Mangalam, in the western hills, not far from Madura and quite close to Periyakuḷam. It is to this vicinity that the earlier Vīra Pāṇḍya fled for refuge driven by his more powerful rival Kulaśēkhara Pāṇḍya in the war of succession in the twelfth century; or Mangalam in the Sattur Taluka a place of consequence in the same war. See Lecture I above.

[2] Kalul is apparently Karur and Karamhatti may be error for Paramatti.

states that 'the two Rais of Ma'bar, the eldest named Bir Pāṇḍya, the youngest Sundara Pāṇḍya, who had up to that time continued on friendly terms, had advanced against each other with hostile intentions and that Bellal Deo, the Rai of Dhur Samundar, on learning this fact, had marched for the purpose of sacking their two empty cities, and plundering the merchants; but that, on hearing of the advance of the Muhammadan army, he had returned to his own country.'[1] On Wednesday, 18th of Shawwal, Malik Kafur set forward on his expedition to Ma'bar and arrived at the mountains which separate Ma'bar from the Hoysala country after five days. There were two passes through these mountains, which Amir Khusru calls 'Sarmali and Tabar.' After traversing the passes they arrived at night on the banks of the river 'Kanobari' and bivouacked for the night on the sands. They then set forward for 'Bir Dhul' and committed massacre and devastation all round it. The Rai Bir wished to seek security by fleeing 'to his islands in the ocean.' He was advised to seek protection on the land itself. He took a certain amount of treasure and property with him and fled for protection to 'Kandur.' Not finding it secure enough from the enemies he fled further into the jungles. Malik Kafur pursued him, and found at Kandur some Musalmans, who were subjects of the Hindu ruler. They offered to join the Muhammadans, and in spite of their being half-Hindus Malik Kafur spared their lives, 'as they could repeat the Kalima (the declaration of faith of the Muhammadans).' Malik Kafur then set forward after returning to 'Bir Dhul' in search of the Raja to Kandur, to which place apparently he had returned. He was there informed that the Raja had fled to a place which Amir Khusru calls '*Jalkota*' an old city of the ancestors of Bir. Pursuing him closely there, Malik Kafur

[1] Elliott, iii, p. 88.

Chidambaram. The tank within the temple
(by permission of Messrs. Wiele & Klein, Madras)

found that he had again escaped to the jungles, and the Malik had therefore to return to Kandur, where he searched for more elephants and perhaps even treasure. 'Here he heard that in *Brahmastpuri* there was a golden idol, round which many elephants were stabled.' Malik Kafur started on a night expedition against this place and in the morning seized no less than 250 elephants. He then determined on razing the beautiful temple to the ground—'you might say that it was the Paradise of Shaddad, which, after being lost, those "hellites" had found, and that it was the golden Lanka of Ram'—'in short, it was the holy place of the Hindus, which the Malik dug up from its foundations with the greatest care,' and the heads of the Brahmans and idolaters danced from their necks and fell to the ground at their feet, and blood flowed in torrents. 'The stone idols called *Ling Mahadeo*, which had been a long time established at that place, up to this time, the kick of the horse of Islam had not attempted to break.' The Musalmans destroyed all the *Lings*, 'and *Deo Narain* fell down, and the other gods who had fixed their seats there raised their feet, and jumped so high, that at one leap they reached the fort of Lanka, and in that affright the *Lings* themselves would have fled had they had any legs to stand on.' Much gold and many valuable jewels fell into the hands of the Musalmans, who returned to the royal canopy, after executing their holy project, on the 13th of Zi-l-ka'da A.H. 710 (A.D. April 1311). They destroyed all the temples at Birdhul, and placed the plunder in the public treasury.

Capture of Southern Mathra (Madura).—After five days, the royal canopy moved from Birdhul on Thursday, the 17th of Zi-l-ka'da, and arrived at '*Kham*', and five days afterwards they arrived at the city Mathra (Madura), the dwelling-place of the brother of the Rai, Sundar Pāṇḍya. They found the city empty for the Rai had fled with the Ranis, but had left two or three elephants in the temple of

Jagnar '(Jaganath, rather Śokkanātha ?)'. The elephants were captured and the temple burnt.

Amir Khusru in this work of his, Tarikh-i-'Alai, brings the campaign to a close with this. The number of elephants that Malik Kafur captured extended over a length of three parasangs according to him and counted 512 in number. He had besides taken five thousand horses and five hundred maunds of jewels of every description, diamonds, pearls, emeralds and rubies.

But in another work of his called 'Ashika,' he gives more details of this particular campaign. He says there that the army proceeded to Ma'bar 'that it might take the shores of the sea as far as Lanka and spread the odour of the amber scented faith.' The ruler of the place was according to him 'a Brahman named Pāṇḍya Guru.' He had many cities in his possession and his capital is said to have been 'Fatan,' where according to him there was an idol laden with jewels.

This 'Pāṇḍya Guru' might be one of the number of Pāṇḍyan Princes whose inscriptions have come down to us, other than the brothers Sundara Pāṇḍya and Vīra Pāṇḍya.[1] The fratricidal war was obviously for the 'kingship' which carried the overlordship of the other chieftaincies with it. (Cf. Marco Polo : passage cited above, Lecture II).

The ruler had many troops and ships, and Musalmans and Hindus were in his service. He was possessed of a thousand elephants of Ma'bar and innumerable horses. When the Muhammadan army arrived, the Raja fled from Fatan, where the Musalmans in the service of the Hindu Raja sought the protection of the Muhammadans. Five hundred elephants are said to have been taken, and after destroying the idol, Malik Kafur returned to Delhi. Appa-

[1] It is just possible that this Pāṇḍya guru was a priest or mahant with authority over Rāmēśvaram and other temples in the vicinity. There is no definite authority to lead to this conclusion however.

rently this is a continuation of the campaign from the Chola into the Pāṇḍya country, and ***Fatan*** must be the Paṭṭaṇam, the one of the two or three Paṭṭaṇams in the vicinity of Rāmēśvaram, if not Rāmēśvaram itself, and the temple therein referred to, is almost certainly the great temple in Rāmēśvaram. From all that is before us, it would be safer to regard this as a continuation of the campaign, which, according to the previous account, terminated in Madura, and to extend it to Rāmēśvaram. But the clear mention of Fatan leaves no alternative but to accept the progress of the Muhammadan raid up to Rāmēśvaram. The ports near this contained, at that time, a comparatively large Muhammadan population which finds mention in this work of Amir Khusru.

The Route of the Invasion.—In regard to the invasion of Dvārasamudra and Ma'bar the route taken is the road leading from Delhi straight across the middle of Rajputana to Gurgam ; Tankal on the Jamna, where the muster roll was taken, is not shown on the maps accessible to me. There is a place Kanhur, which may be identified with Kanhun in Rajputana, a little aside of the road from Ujjain to Delhi, and this was twenty-one days' march from Tankal. Another seventeen days brought the army to Gurgam, very probably the Kharagam of the maps, a little way to the south-west of Indore, and a little to the east of the main road to Dhar and Ujjain. Therefrom the army went to Deogir, probably by the main road from Dhar to Deogir. Thenceforward the road taken seems to be the road from Deogir to Bir, a few marches to the south-east of it. Therefrom winding south-westwards, an old road leads to Barsi Railway station, and thence across the Bhima, so that the three rivers Godaveri, Sini and Bhima are passed. The army then should have come upon the place called Bandri in the country of Paras Dalvi. Bandri is apparently Pandharpur just on the right side of the Bhima, and the five days' march from Kharababad of Paras Deo, which seems to be indicated, would answer well. The only difficulty in this route is what actually is intended by the name, Kharababad. It was possibly another name of Bir or some other town in that vicinity.[1] At Bandri, Malik Kafur was said to have halted to make enquiries about the countries farther south.

Panḍharpur seems to have been then a frontier station between the Mahratta country and the Karnāṭa of the Hoysalas. It was already pointed out that an inscription of Vīra Somēśvara has recently been discovered there, which perhaps marks it as the northern-most limit of the Hoysala dominions. The road thence to Dvārasamudra seems to have followed either of the two well-known roads, but probably the eastern road from Panḍharpur to Bijapur, from Bijapur to Harihar; from Harihar to Hiriyūr and thence across from the main road to Bāṇavar and Haḷebīḍ a possible and fairly convenient route of march even now. That fixes the route of march of Malik Kafur to Dvārasamudra. The route thence is not equally simple. According to Amir Khusru they marched five days to get to the mountains; that means, the distance from Haḷebīḍ to Hosur, was a five days' march. The road taken must surely have been not the road from Haḷebīḍ by way of Mysore down the Satiyamangalam ghat into the Coimbatore district. It appears to be the eastern road that was taken; therefore the army must have come back to Bāṇavar; from there they must have struck the main road somewhere about Chikkanāyakanhalli, and thence by way of Tumkur and Bangalore to Hosur. Of the two passes mentioned,

1 Bir would be conveniently situated as the head-quarters of a frontier province, from which to watch the movements of hostile powers such as the Kākatīyas on the one side and the Hoysalas on the other. Adoni and places along the line from Bir to Adoni figure often in these campaigns. South of Pandharpur was the territory of the Hoysalas. Bir would be placed beyond reach of the enemies and within striking distance of either frontier.

there is nothing satisfactorily answering to the Sarmali of Amir Khusru. From the way that he mentions the two, we have to look for both of them close to each other among the passes that lead from the Mysore plateau into the country below the ghats. One of the passes leads through the Mēlagiri hills, and that does not bring the Mēlagiris near in sound to Sarmali. The whole country on this side was known in those days as Puramalai Nāḍu, the country outside the hills. It is not certain whether something like that is not the cause of the confusion. But the other pass that he actually does mention as 'Tabar' is the pass on the main road, now commonly known as the Toppur Pass, well-known also in the campaigns of early British India. Getting across the mountains by the Toppur pass, the army reached the river 'Kanobari,' apparently Kaveri, and then bivouacked for the night on the sands. It is not clearly inferable from his account whether the army actually crossed the Kaveri and took the road on the right bank, or whether it pursued its way by the road on the eastern bank of the river. As apparently the Kaveri did not contain much water, they might have crossed the Kaveri and taken the western road till they came to Muśiri, where the main road gets across the Kaveri to the other side and joins the Namkal road. The objective of the march all along is said to have been the 'country of Bir' or what seems a city or town under the name 'Birdhul.' Since there is no mention in the narrative of the second crossing of the Kaveri, it is just possible the route taken was the other; from Toppur to Omalur and thence to Salem by Tiruchengode; from there to Namakal and down on the high road to Kaṇṇanūr and Śrīrangam by the left bank of the Kaveri itself. Whichever of the routes was taken it is clear that the road taken was the well-beaten road from above the ghats to Trichinopoly, the route taken by Hoysala Narasimha when he intervened effectively against the Pāṇḍya invasion of the Chola country, as I have already pointed out in the previous lectures. The campaign in this region hovered round the Chola capital, Gangaikoṇḍaśoḻapuram and the Hoysala capital of Kaṇṇanūr (Sanskrit, Khanḍanapura, and Kandur of the Muhammadan historians); Chidambaram, Śrīrangam and various other temples suffered.

The actual route taken from here to Madura is not quite so clear in the narrative. The only lead that the account gives us is that the army first moved on and encamped in a place called Kham, and from there it set forward and reached Madura in five marches. Taking it that the starting point of Malik Kafur was his camp at Kaṇṇanūr, there are three roads by which the advance could have been made. The one along the road following more or less the South India Railway line now to Dindigul and the Palnis, and thence along the road to Periakuḷam almost due west of Madura as far as a village called Butlagunḍu, and turning eastwards to Madura. Another a little to the east of it, proceeding straight down to Viralimalai, going further down through what is now the *Zamindari* of Marungāpuri through Koilpaṭṭi and Tovarankurichi, striking the great trunk road from Vaṭṭāṇam to Dindigul, at Nattam. The road thence leads between Śirumalai (the possible Sarmali of Amir Khusru) and Aḻagarmalai straight down to Madura. The third road of the present day, perhaps the most important at the present time, is the road leading from Trichinopoly by way of Kīranūr to the town of Pudukoṭṭa straight, and thence to Tirumeyyam; from there to Tiruppattūr and from Tiruppattūr to Madura.

The Śilappadhikāram describes the roadways feasible for travellers from Uraiyūr, the suburb of Trichinopoly, to Madura in early times; and then apparently there was only a single road going down to Koḍumbāḷūr not far from Viralimalai. This branched off from there into three, somewhat in the shape of a trident one leading westwards to a little way to the west of Madura from where one had to make a turn eastwards and reach Madura. The middle road took itself straight down, and was apparently the shortest; but it went through a desert tract and was infested by robbers. It was therefore not worth taking for a party in which there was a young and apparently well-bred lady. The third road slightly longer went through a much more hospitable country and took one on, through stages, to Tirumāliruṁśolai (Aḻagarmalai), said to be a place worth visiting for its own sake, and thence to Madura. This eastern-most road of the Śilappadhikāram is however not identical with the high road between Trichinopoly and Madura known to historians.

In the course of the Ceylon war of Parākrama Bāhu, Lankāpura the general marched in pursuit of Kulaśēkhara from Madura along the road from Madura to Tiruppattūr and followed up the march along the same high road from Tiruppattūr to Pon-Amarāvati. Here is a clear lead where to look for the high road from Madura to Trichinopoly. We have already spoken of the invasion of the Chola country by Māravarman Sundara Pāṇḍya I. His inscriptions, and perhaps even restorations of various temples along the high road are traceable from Tiruppattūr by way of Kaṇḍavarāyanpaṭṭi to Vēlankuḍi and thence to Pon-Amarāvati. At Tiruppattūr I was informed that an old road branching off from a point a few furlongs from Tiruppattūr along the Tiruppattūr-Tirumeyyam road took one to Kaṇḍavarāyanpaṭṭi, from which an old broad avenue road takes one to Tirukkaḷākkuḍi (written Tirukkoḷakkuḍi in inscriptions) and thence to Pūlānkurichi (Pūvālankurichi) on the Pon-Amarāvati way. The road continued southwards from Tiruppattūr to Tirukkoshṭiyūr, and from there through Madagupaṭṭi to Śivaganga. From Śivaganga there is the road proceeding to Mēlūr, and from there to Aḻagarmalai, from which Madura could be reached. For our present purpose the high road from Madura came down to Tiruppattūr and the same high road apparently carried one to Pon-Amarāvati;[1] that is the point that has to be made.

The bit of the old road between Tiruppattūr and Pon-Amarāvati which is said to be about six or seven miles long shows even old bridges. This confirms the statement of the Mahāvaṁśa that the high road went from Tiruppattūr to Pon-Amarāvati. The road must have continued from Pon-Amarāvati to Trichinopoly either through Pudukoṭṭa or just outside of it. The present day high road from Trichinopoly goes from Trichinopoly to Pudukoṭṭa, from Pudukoṭṭa to Tirumeyyam, and from Tirumeyyam to Tiruppattūr, leaving Pon-Amarāvati at the centre of the arc from Pudukoṭṭa to Tiruppattūr. As far as I have been able to make out there is no road connecting Pon-Amarāvati with Tirumeyyam, and therefore it is inevitable that a road from Pon-Amarāvati must have led towards Trichinopoly. The present day road to Pon-Amarāvati from Pudukoṭṭa, branches off a little way from Pudukoṭṭa along the Pudukoṭṭa-Kuḍumiyāmalai road. That road continues almost unbroken northwards to Annavāśal, from which another place Nārttāmalai (Nagarattārmalai) is reachable at a short distance cross country. I am told that an old road, the road is in use even now, leads from Koḍumbāḷūr to Kuḍumiyāmalai, and thence to Pudukoṭṭa, the Pon-Amarāvati road branching off from this. Inscriptions of Māravarman Sundara Pāṇḍya I are found in the temples ruined

[1] Strangely enough the revised *Madura Gazetteer* edited by Mr. Francis states on p. 33 that Pon-Amarāvati has not yet been identified. There never has been any doubt about the identity of Pon-Amarāvati, and the epigraphist's report treating of the War of the Ceylonese (1899) identifies the place with Pon-Amarāvati in Pudukoṭṭa. At any rate, there can be absolutely no doubt now in the face of the clear statement of the Mahāvaṁśa that the utmost boundary of the Pāṇḍya country was a line drawn through Pon-Amarāvati, Kīḷānilai, and Maṇamēlkuḍi, a little way south of the mouth of the southern Veḷḷār. Mr. Hemingway's Trichinopoly marks it on the map.

Madura. General View of the temple and town
(by permission of Messrs. Wiele & Klein, Madras)

and standing along this road. They are found in Pon-Amarāvati, in Iḷayāttākuḍi and in one part of Narttāmalai called Kaḍambarmalai. It seems likely therefore that the high road continued from Pon-Amarāvati towards Kuḍumiyāmalai across to Annavāśal and thence to Kaḍambarmalai, wherefrom it would follow the present road almost, to Trichinopoly, or might go round by way of Viralimalai and Koḍumbāḷūr to Trichinopoly. The road Malik Kafur followed seems to be the former. The Kham of Amir Khusru seems to be a corruption of, or a contraction from, Kaḍambavanam which must have been another name of what is called Kaḍambarmalai now, as the god of the temple in the locality is named Kaḍambavaneśvara. From Kaḍambavanam, Kham is a possible contraction in the mouth of a Muhammadan. This Kaḍambamalai must have been a fortified place. There are remains of what was intended to be a strong fortification on the hill and about; the temple is a structure altogether in the character of those of Māravarman Sundara Pāṇḍya I, the special feature of which is a high plinth, popularly called Sundara Pāṇḍyan Koraḍu. I have not been able to trace any inscription of a Pāṇḍya later than this Māravarman Sundara Pāṇḍya I in this place which is full of inscriptions. Kaḍambavanam is one of the names of Madura, and it is likely that the place was built by Māravarman Sundara I as a new frontier town.

Māravarman's aggressive activity along this line was apparently put a stop to by the occupation of Kaṇṇanūr by the Hoysalas, and in his later campaigns at any rate, Māravarman probably took a more eastern road by way of Vallam, Tanjore and further east. There are visible signs of wanton destruction in the locality, which may be due to the Muhammadan invaders; and the last of all Kaḍambarmalai would be about seventy-five miles, and therefore five marches, from Madura. It therefore seems likely that

Kaḍambavanam was the camping ground Kham of the Muhammadans after they left Trichinopoly. This identification receives further confirmation from an inscription of A.H. 761 (about A.D. 1359–60) in the Tirukkaḷākkuḍi temple which relates to a dispute between certain villagers in Pon-Amarāvati Nāḍu. A number of Muhammadan generals who went down to destroy Śūraikkuḍi are said to have been in camp at Māttūrkuḷam where they summoned the inhabitants of the two villages of Viraiyāchilai and Kōṭṭiyūr, to settle their disputes. This apparently means that Māttūrkuḷam was in the high road from Pon-Amarāvati to Trichinopoly. Mātturkuḷam is just in the line from Kuḍumiyāmalai almost on the Trichinopoly-Pudukoṭṭa road now. The road therefore seems then to have run from Trichinopoly to Māttūrkuḷam, from there to Kuḍumiyāmalai across by way of Śittannavāśal, a few miles from Kuḍumiyāmalai, and straight along to Pon-Amarāvati, thence to Kaṇḍavarāyanpaṭṭi, Tiruppattūr, and thence along the present high road to Madura. And this seems clearly the road taken by Malik Kafur in his invasion of Madura.

Brahmastpuri is Chidambaram.—There are three places that figure in this campaign frequently, 'Bir Dhul,' 'Kandur,' and 'Jalkotta.' Any identification of all these, from the nature of their names as given by Amir Khusru, must turn upon the identification of the great temple Brahmastpuri, which Malik Kafur plundered. According to the description given there, it was a temple roofed over with gold, set with gems. It contained both the Linga, emblematic of Śiva (Ling Mahadeo), and Vishṇu (Deo Narain). These indications give sufficient lead to identify the place with Chidambaram. Chidambaram is popularly known as Kanakasabhā or Ponnambalam (golden hall) from Pallava times. That was because the whole of the inner shrine of the temple was roofed over with gold, and that was renewed two or three times under the great Cholas.

The later members of this dynasty from Kulottunga I onwards, if not from Rājēndra I, were specially devoted to this temple, and seem to have always completed the ceremony of coronation in the capital Gangaikoṇḍaśōḷapuram by a visit to this temple. [1]

Hence at the time it must have been one of the richest temples in this part of the country. The name Brahmastpuri is apparently the slightly modified Brahmapuri, which is the sacerdotal (āgamic) name given to Chidambaram as a whole in Śaiva literature. There is one temple dedicated to Śiva, which goes by the specific name Brahmapuri, and the name of the deity itself is Brahmapurīśvara, and is known ordinarily as Tirukkaḷāñchēri, the northern part of Chidambaram, and this particular temple received a gift of 1,100 gold pieces annually for certain festivals, etc., from Kulottunga III. [2] Hence there is little doubt that the Brahmastpuri of Amir Khusru is Chidambaram.

Śrīrangam, a possible alternative.—The possible alternatives to this would be, having regard to the description of gold roofing, Śrīrangam. If exclusive attention should be paid to the name alone, Shiyāḻi would be an alternative; and the incidental statement in the description of Amir Khusru, who puns on the legless character of the Lingas, that they all at one kick from the horse of Islam jumped to the island of Lanka, may lead one to identify Brahmastpuri with Rāmēśvaram. This last or Shiyāḻi, so far as our present knowledge of these places goes, does not answer the other details. Śrīrangam may be just possible; but the difficulty against Śrīrangam is that the temple does not contain both the images of Śiva and Vishṇu like the other two above. If Chidambaram is Brahmastpuri, what is *Bir Dhul,* what is *Kandur* and what is *Jalkotta.* It must be

[1] *Vide* Kulottunga Śoḻan ulā. Madura Sangam manuscripts: lines 63-6.

[2] Epi. Rep. for 1914, sec. 17.

borne in mind here that at the time Sundra Pāṇḍya put the father to death, Kulaśēkhara, the father 'Kales Dewar,' was apparently in Madura. Sundara put him to death, took possession of the treasury and installed himself in Madura before Vīra Pāṇḍya could intervene. Hence it is clear that Vīra Pāṇḍya was not in government at Madura, and in all probability his government was elsewhere. We pointed out elsewhere that Māravarman Kulaśēkhara resided in his palace outside Jayankoṇḍaśoḻapuram, six miles from Gangaikoṇḍaśoḻapuram as his capital. That apparently was the capital of the Chola country under Pāṇḍyan rule. Either the whole of the town, or the new suburb in which Kulaśēkhara erected his palace, might have gone by the name Vīra Śoḻan for various reasons. Bir Dhul cannot be anything else than Vīra Śoḻan, in the mouth of the northern foreigner unless he meant 'the Chola country under Bir', as a whole. Amir Khusru speaks of the country as 'the country of Bir' which is synonymous with Vīra, may be Vīra Śoḻa or Vīra Pāṇḍya. Apparently Amir Khusru means Vīra Pāṇḍya. If Bir becomes Vīra, Dhul by itself cannot stand for any particular place, and seems to be the Tamil Śola either the country or the king, thus rendered in the phonology of the northern foreigner. Gangaikoṇḍaśoḻapuram, or its new neighbour might have borne this name as these often did change their names with successive rulers. If Jayangoṇḍaśoḻapuram, the possible capital of Vīra Pāṇḍya is the Bir Dhul, Kandur is almost certainly Kaṇṇanūr (the Khaṇḍanapuram of Sanskrit writers). If Jayangoṇḍaśoḻapuram were attacked, the ruler thus attacked would move for shelter to Kaṇṇanūr, the capital of the Hoysalas till recently, a place strongly fortified in their time, and occupying a strategic position along the main artery of communication between Trichinopoly and Tiruvaṇṇāmalai which at the time was one of the capitals of the Hoysalas. Wassaf states clearly that when Malik Kafur invaded Haḻēbīd, the Hoysala asked for help, and of the brothers it was Vīra Pāṇḍya that sent it. If that is so, when the Pāṇḍya's capital Bir Dhul had been attacked, he would naturally look for assistance to the Hoysala, and such assistance as the Hoysala could render must come from Tiruvaṇṇāmalai, the eastern capital, or from Mysore, wherefrom an army did come into the Chola country ordinarily by way of Tiruvaṇṇāmalai. Hence Kandult is unmistakably Kaṇṇanūr, north of Śrīrangam. The campaign oscillated between Jayangoṇḍaśoḻapuram (Bir-Dhul) and Kaṇṇanūr (Kandur); and that would certainly be justified by the respective position of these places. There is the additional recommendation that the Pāṇḍya retreated from Kandur for shelter to the forests; the locality of Kaṇṇanūr would suit it very well indeed as he could retire into the hilly tracts of the Kollimalais on the borders of Salem and South Arcot.

There is one other place that is to be settled, and that is Jalkoṭṭa. It is not possible to offer as satisfactory an identification of this place as there is nothing further to lead us to an identification except the name. If Jalkoṭṭa means anything at all, it must be water-fortress; and I take it, it apparently refers to an island protected by deep waters round it. The only place in the vicinity that I could think of is the famous Devakoṭṭa of the early British Campaigns at the mouth of the Coleroon. There are the remains of huge brick walls, of bricks of the same kind and size as those found in Gangaikoṇḍaśoḻapuram. One of the walls in the island at the mouth showed three parts—two brick walls of 2 to 2½ feet thick with an intervening mud wall about 6 feet. Another bit could be seen about five to six miles up the river and the present bed of the Coleroon seems to occupy the place of the rest of it. The course of the river has changed a great deal in the last few centuries. I am led to this suggestion by the strength of the fort on the island of which we have a very good description from the Jesuit priest Pimenta at the commencement of the seventeenth century, in addition to what we get from a number of works in Sanskrit and Telugu bearing on Tanjore history.[1] It was a place of considerable strength and great importance in the wars of the Portuguese and the Tanjore kings. It probably had this importance three centuries earlier, and was a place of refuge to monarchs of the Chola and the Pāṇḍya dynasties that held sway in this tract of country. That we have to look for these places in the Chola country and not in the Pāṇḍya is quite certain, as Amir Khusru takes us in a separate campaign to 'Southern Mathra' (Madura), and as a supplement, to a campaign against Faṭan, the capital, apparently of another Pāṇḍya, (may be Vīra himself), which, as was already indicated, must be looked for about Rāmēśvaram.

The sack of Śrīrangam by Malik Kafur.—In discussing the campaigns of Malik Kafur 'against the country of the yellow-faced Bir', we discussed the possibility of Brahmastpuri being Śrīrangam, and we have, for reasons given there, shown that Brahmastpuri must be Chidambaram and not Śrīrangam. If it is so, was the temple at Śrīrangam at all attacked by Malik Kafur? In the account of the campaigns of Amir Khusru there is no reference to the sack of this temple by name, but there is a clear statement that Malik Kafur sacked all the temples in the country round Kandur. We have for satisfactory reasons identified Kandur with the Khanḍanapuram of Sanskrit, and Kaṇṇanūr of Tamil literature, which became famous as the capital of the Hoysala Somēśvara under the name Tiruvikramapura. If the Pāṇḍya was defeated at Kaṇṇanūr, the temple of Śrīrangam could not have escaped ordinarily the ravages of the Muhammadans, having regard to the fact that the temple had been the recipient of the magnificent and vast

[1] Purchas, His piligrimes x, chapter vi. *Sources of Vijayanagar History*, Madras University. Extracts 90 and 91 in particular.

benefactions of Sundara Pāṇḍya, not to mention a host of others before him.

There is direct evidence to confirm this presumption in a work called Kōyiloḻuhu. This is a work which deals with all the benefactions made to the temple at Śrīrangam by people from its foundation to almost the eighteenth century. There are various editions of this work, differing in details, which cannot all of them be regarded accurate without confirmation. The more important of these, however, seem based upon the inscriptions in the temple, some of which may not be available at present. This work has a few paragraphs devoted to the sack of Śrīrangam and the carrying away of the idol of Ranganātha, apparently under Malik Kafur. The account begins that the king of Delhi having conquered Pratāpa Rudra, invaded both the Toṇḍamaṇḍalam and Śoḻamaṇḍalam. The invading armies spread along the whole country and made a general sack of temples carrying away the idols as well. In the course of this campaign, they entered Śrīrangam as well, by the north gate, which was in the charge of the Árya Bhaṭṭas, the Northern Brahmans. The guards, by name Panjukoṇḍān, were over-powered, the temple was entered into and all the property was carried away including the idol of the god. There was a woman who had made it her daily habit never to take her food without worshipping the god in the temple. She was a native of Karambanūr, otherwise called Uttamarkoil, on the other bank of the Coleroon. As the army was retreating after the sack, she gave up her household and followed the army in the guise of a mendicant having learnt that they were carrying away the idol of Rāmapriya as well from Tirunārāyaṇapuram (Melukoṭṭai). She reached ultimately the palace at Delhi where these idols were all locked up in a safe chamber. One of the younger princesses of the Sultan's family having been struck with the beauty of the Ranganātha idol, asked permission and obtained the idol to play with. She kept herself in the constant company of the idol. Knowing so much, perhaps feeling that the idol was in safe custody, the woman managed to steal away from the palace and journeyed back to Śrīrangam to give information of it to the people there.

The more important among the citizens having deliberated as to what they should do, walled up the north gate of the temple and left the temple vacant burying the goddess idol that escaped capture under a bilva tree (Aegla Marmelos). Sixty of these men placed themselves under the guidance of the woman mendicant and set forward on their journey to Delhi. She put on the former guise and got entry into the palace as before. In the meanwhile those that followed her managed to get audience of the Sultan, and by exhibiting both the music and the dance for which they were famous, as having had to perform daily before the god, they pleased the Sultan so greatly and declined all rewards offered by the Sultan, preferring instead the one idol of Ranganātha, among the many, as the reward. The Sultan ordered that these men might be allowed to take the idol of their choice. Not finding this particular idol in the store-room and knowing as they did that it was with the princess, they reported the matter to the Sultan, who in joke told them that if it was their god they might call him and take him away. They agreed and sang their prayers, which the idol answered by following them. Showing this to the Sultan they obtained his permission and started off with their idol over-night. When morning broke, the princess was disconsolate at the loss of her idol and declined to live if she could not have it. Search for the party proving useless, he placed her under an escort and sent her off for the idol. The Brahmans of Śrīrangam having had a start, marched along ahead and reached Tirupati safe before they could be overtaken by the princess and her escort. At Tirupati they heard of the arrival of the party of the princess and feeling themselves unsafe, the party broke up and dispersed themselves to avoid observation leaving the idol in charge of three men among them, the father and son, and the son's maternal uncle. The big party having thus disappeared, the escort marched on till they reached Śrīrangam. Finding that the northern gate of the temple was walled up and the temple empty, the princess died of a broken heart.

In the meanwhile, the three men in charge of the idol heard of the advance of the Muhammadans closer to the hill; fearing for their safety and that of the idol, the chief man tied himself down to the idol and asked the two others gently to let it down the slope of the hill, himself being always on the underside so that the idol may not suffer damage. Having got down safely, the three men lived on there in an isolated glen in the forest at the foot of the hill unfrequented by ordinary people. In the meanwhile, people at Śrīrangam thinking it impossible to recover the idol, made and consecrated others, instead of those of both the god and the goddess. In the meanwhile the three men continued to live on doing their daily service to the god in the usual fashion. For a period of fifty-nine and a half years from the date of the sack, of which two years were spent in the palace of the Sultan, the idol of Śrīrangam found its shrine in that sequestered glen. In the course of this long stay, the father and the uncle had died and the son had grown up to be an old man of eighty, looking more like a forest man than a civilized one. Feeling that his end was drawing near this one man showed himself to the hill folk about and let them understand how and why he happened to be there. Information of this reached the town by means of these people, and it happened to be the time of Gopana, who was in charge of Nārāyaṇapuram (Nārāyaṇavaram) near Chandragiri under the newly formed kingdom of Vijayanagar. He carried the idol to his later head-quarters at Ginji where he placed it in the temple called Singavaram even now, in a safe place difficult of approach even from Ginji itself. When Prince Kampana had over-powered the Muhammadan garrisons in the various localities in South India and brought the whole of it under the control of Vijayanagar, Gopana, his chief adviser got the idol re-installed in the temple at Śrīrangam in the Śaka year, 1293, A.D. 1370-71, in the year Paritāpi, month Vaikāśi, date 17.

The last date 1370-71 is admittedly taken from the inscription which gives a chronogram, which is interpreted here as 1293. Counting back fifty-nine and a half years from this will take us to 1310-11. This is most naturally referred to the invasion of Malik Kafur and cannot refer to one of the later invasions. But there is one apparent objection to accept this account. There is another sack of Śrīrangam referred to in the same work and of a later date certainly when the idol of Ranganātha had to be taken towards the south and ultimately brought back by way of Malayāḷam to Calicut, and across to Tirupati. We shall have to refer to this in another connection.

The memory of this particular migration of the idol is preserved in the temple where in the north-eastern corner of the outer Maṇḍapa, in the first line round the sanctum, there is a chamber containing a wall painting of this Suratāṇi (Sultana), popularly called Tulukkachchi Nāchiyār. At break of day worship is offered to her and to the god, with bread and butter, which is a special feature of this particular temple in regard to this particular deity.

Epigraphical Evidence.—There are a few references in inscriptions in this part of the country which throw considerable light upon the Muhammadan invasions having gone as far as the Pāṇḍya country. The earliest so far available is No. 434 of 1903 of the Madras Epigraphist's collection, which refers itself to the fourteenth year of Venṛu Maṇkoṇḍa Śambuvarāyan, whose date of accession is A.D. 1322 according to the late professor Kielhorn. This would mean that the reference is of date A.D. 1335-36, and it speaks of the Muhammadan invasions in 'previous days' and the destruction of the country by them. This record is in Tiruvāmāttūr a place in the South Arcot district. The next reference is in records of Tiruppattūr (in the Ramnad district just outside the southern border of Pudukoṭṭa) referring themselves to the years forty-four and forty-six of Vīra Pāṇḍya, in which it is stated that Tiruppattūr temple was in the occupation of the Muhammadans during their campaign in the south, and the temple was reconsecrated in the said years by a certain Viśaiyālaya Dēvan. The name Viśaiyālaya figures in inscriptions of Māravarman Kulaśēkhara, and refers possibly to the same officer as the one referred to in the records of this Vīra Pāṇḍya.[1] If that were so, the date of these records would be A.D. 1339-40 and A.D 1341-42. The Vīra Pāṇḍya referred to above must be Jaṭāvarman Vīra Pāṇḍya against whom Malik Kafur undertook the invasion of the south and whose date of accession is A.D. 1295-96. The next later record is one of the seventh year of Rājanārayaṇa Śambuvarāyan, whose sixth year, according to Kielhorn, is A.D. 1345, and therefore the actual date of reference is A.D. 1346. But the most important document in this connection is c. 64 of 1916 at Tirukaḷākkuḍi which refers explicitly to the invasion and occupation by the Muhammadans, the appropriation of temple lands, the neglect of temple worship, etc., till Kampana Uḍaiyār came and put an end to the Muhammadan domination and appointed officers (Nāyakanmārs) for supervision of temple worship and

[1] A family of these chiefs is known associated with Śūraikkuḍi or *Vannian* Śūraikkuḍi, to distinguish it from another place of the name, on the road to Tiruppattūr from Kānādukāttan. About a dozen chiefs of this family have records and are known by the general style 'Araiyan Viśaiyālaya Dēvan'.

management. This record refers itself to the thirty-first year of a Māravarman Vīra Pāṇḍya and gives astronomical details which, according to Rao Bahadur Mr. Krishna Sastrigal, work out correctly to A.D. 1358.[1] The next one is No. 18 of 1899 at Tirupputkuḻi of A.D. 1365, which states in clear terms that Kampana conquered Rāja Gambhīra Rājya, and was pleased to rule the earth permanently. This date A.D. 1358 is taken as a starting point by Mr. Sastrigal, and calculating back from it he fixes the date of Māravarman Vīra Pāṇḍya's accession as A.D. 1326-27 on the assumption of a forty-eight years' occupation by the Muhammadans beginning with Malik Kafur. This point will come in for discussion in connection with the dynasty of the Sultans of Madura. It is enough to state here that the assumption of the official date for the Sultans of Madura who ruled for forty-eight years in all is wrong, and hence this date for Māravarman Vīra Paṇḍya is untenable if it depended upon that assumption alone. For the present purpose this series of epigraphical references makes it clear beyond doubt that the early Muhammadan invasions reached certainly into the Pāṇḍya country, and raises a very strong presumption that it did go farther south both to Madura and to Rāmēśvaram as Amir Khusru claims, having regard to the character of the invasion as a mere raid undertaken for the sole purpose of plunder.

Alau-d-din's Empire.—Malik Kafur returned to Delhi about the end of the year A.D. 1311 [2] or early in A.D. 1312, with all the great booty that he had taken in his invasion of Ma'bar, and presented himself before Alau-d-din. From that time till the death of Alau-d-din in the year A.D. 1315 there

[1] Epi. Rep. for 1916, Sec. 33.

[2] This date of Amir Khusru seems quite correct. The Koiloḻuhu referring to the sack of the Śrīrangam temple states specifically that the Ranganātha idol was fifty-nine and a half years out of the temple down to its restoration in A.D. 1370-71, according to the inscription in the temple. *Epigraphia Indica*, vol. vi, No. 33.

was no further invasion of the South by the Muhammadans. Alau-d-din's administration was one of a thorough-going character, as was already stated. He had put down internal rebellion with a high hand, and introduced order and efficiency in his administration, both civil and military, and by that means he had successfully kept the Mughals out of the Indian frontiers. He had besides so far been successful in his invasions of the Dekhan and the South, that, although these distant kingdoms were not actually annexed to his government, they were reduced to such subordination that they could be regarded as a part of his own empire. It looked as though the empire was quite at peace and there was not the slightest likelihood of any disturbance.

Domestic troubles of Alau-d-din's reign.—Anxieties and cares, however, assailed the king almost from the moment of the return of Malik Kafur from his southern expedition. The causes of these are easy to trace, and these were the causes that subverted his own government, luckily for him after his death, and that of his great successor Muhammad-bin Tughlak. These can be grouped under three heads: (1) It was pointed out already that Jalal-ud-din settled several of the Mughal centurions (Amirs of hundred and more, called 'Amir Judeida' by other historians) who had become Muhammadans, in various places providing them estates or other means of livelihood.. At the commencement of the reign of Alau-d-din, he took advantage of his revenue organization to cut the income of these Mughals close, along with those of others, even depriving some of them of their means of livelihood. This naturally created discontent, and the discontent gathered head on the occasion of a possible Mughal invasion. Some of them, the more impetous among them, conspired to assassinate the king. This conspiracy was taken full advantage of, and Alau-d-din ordered a general massacre of these new Mussalmans to take place .simultaneously wherever they were.

Such of them as did not escape by chance or design were put to death, their houses plundered, their women and children turned into the streets, and whatever of property they had was swept into the public treasury. By this drastic measure he made internal rebellions by these chieftains impossible although such of them as escaped to more distant provinces were quite ready to create trouble as we shall see. (2) The violence and jealousy of his temper, which shows itself in these acts, began to extend itself further in the last years of his reign. He grew jealous of those old nobles and officers, who were mainly responsible for the administration of the kingdom. Fearing risings on their part, he removed several of them and put in their stead young slaves and eunuchs, who became his favourites, notably Malik Kafur. His treatment of his sons carried in it another fruitful cause of discontent. While yet they were too young for exercise of authority, he advanced them to responsible dignities, which naturally turned their heads and brought about first misunderstandings, and then graver consequences. (3) His infatuation for Malik Kafur the greatest of his favourites, led him to prefer the slave above all others, whatever their rank or position. The officer that resented this preference the most was Alp Khan, the father-in-law of Kizer Khan and a brother of his mother. Through the influence of Malik Kafur Alp Khan, the Governor of Gujarat, was assassinated, and even Kizer Khan and his mother were ill-treated and turned out of their palaces. These disturbances near the throne naturally loosened the hold upon the distant provinces, and, as was usually the case, revolts broke out in Gujarat. The officer sent to put down the rebellion was killed and the rebels had the upper hand of it. Other rebellions followed when Alau-d-din got seriously ill. It was generally believed that the illness was aggravated and helped out to a fatal termination by Malik Kafur himself.

Malik Kafur supreme, and his assassination.—The death of Alau-d-din left Malik Kafur in the plenitude of his power. He made use of it to aggrandize himself at the expense of everybody else. He threw all the grown-up sons of the late king into prison, and with the assent of the nobles placed an infant son upon the throne, himself undertaking the conduct of Government. Kizer Khan and his brother Shadi Khan, who were older and in prison in Gwalior were blinded, and the queen-dowager, the mother of Kizer Khan, was sent out into miserable retirement. He threw Mubarak into close confinement with the intention ultimately to have him blinded. These high-handed acts of his made him very unpopular in a short time, and the crowning act of his, to gather together all the more important nobles in the capital and assassinate them, was anticipated by his own assassination by a body of *paiks*—'slaves of the late king, whose duty it was to be in charge of the Hazar Sutun,' the Durbar hall of the palace. Thirty-five days after the death of Alau-d-din these men assassinated Malik Kafur, brought forth Mubarak Khan from his prison, and placed him in the position of authority as Naib (director) to the infant king. Mubarak had to begin his reign as director for the infant, and after a short while when he felt his position safe, he set aside the infant brother and ascended the throne himself. Almost the first act of his was to get rid of his dangerous allies, 'the guards of the Hazar Sutun.' He distributed them in distant places and got them put to death to put them beyond possibility of becoming dangerous. The accession of the Sultan Kutub-ud-din Mubarak Shah took place about the middle of A.D. 1316.

Kutub-ud-din Mubarak Shah.—Mubarak began his reign by a declaration of amnesty for all political prisoners and exiles of the late reign. He ordered six months' pay to be given to the army, and increase of allowance and grants to nobles. He also adopted other measures to give relief to the people from the heavy tribute and oppressive demands of the late reign, 'and penalties, extortion, beating, chains, and blows were set aside in revenue matters.' He allowed the rigorous measures of the late reign to fall into desuetude, and signs of prosperity began to appear among the people. After so much promise of a good administration the Sultan gave himself up to his pleasures, involving as a consequence the neglect of administration.

The rise of Khusru Khan.—Along with this he began to exhibit the other failing, favouritism to an unworthy slave. A young Parwari by name Hasan was brought up by one of the officers of the Court. The Sultan took a liking for this young man and in the very first year of his reign raised him to distinction with the title Khusru Khan. So attached was he to this young slave that he raised him at one jump to the position of Malik Naib Kafur, and combined with that high office that of the Wazir. The abolition of all the regulations of Alau-d-din except those against drinking exhibited itself in the rise of prices and perhaps the return of prosperity to the people; and if Barni could be believed, bribery, extortion and malversation followed in train. The regulations against drink were also neglected, and the example of the habits of dissipation of the monarch was but too readily followed, and even improved upon, by his subjects. Fortunately for him the Mughals did not appear in his reign on the borders. His few years of rule were years of prosperity in respect of agriculture, and there was no great disturbance in any quarter. In the first year of his reign he sent out an army under 'Einu-l-Mulk Multani to put down the rebellion in Gujarat and the province was soon got into order. He appointed his own father-in-law, Malik Dinar, Zafar Khan, governor of Gujarat. Several other old and experienced governors of Alau-d-din were retained at their posts, and they contributed to the continuance of orderly administration, in spite of the relaxation in regard to the regulations of Alau-d-din.

Loss of hold upon the tributary kingdoms.—So far as the Dekhan and South India were concerned, the few years of disturbance following the return of Malik Kafur to Delhi, and the domestic trouble which occupied his attention completely were quite enough to destroy the hold of the central government upon the subordinate Hindu kingdoms. It was stated already that soon after the return of Malik Kafur to Delhi, the number of elephants and the amount of tribute due from Warangal were sent by Rudra Deo. The following three or four years were quite enough to make him negligent in this matter. During that short period a change had taken place in the government of Deogir. Ram Deo had already died in the reign of Alau-d-din and had been succeeded by Shankar Deo his eldest son; and a second change had taken place by the time Mubarak had ascended the throne, and the chief power was in the hands of a son-in-law of the late Ram Deo of Deogir. His name was Harapāla Deo, and, like an ambitious young man that he was, he thought that it was an advantageous time to throw off the yoke recently imposed upon them by the Muhammadans. In regard to the distant south, Ma'bar, Malik Kafur's conquest did not extend to anything beyond a magnificent raid as far as Rāmēśvaram, and the destruction of a number of places of importance. There seems, however, little doubt that he left a garrison behind in Madura, the head-quarters of the Pāṇḍya Kulaśēkhara, who had fled for protection to Delhi. Whether the garrison was left to safeguard the interests of Kulaśēkhara is not clearly stated, but seems quite likely. There are good reasons for believing that a Musalman garrison continued in Madura. If it did, its authority must have been confined very narrowly, not extending in all probability to very much beyond the territory immediately round Madura. In the year following the return of Malik Kafur to Delhi, we find an enterprising Travancore ruler in occupation of practically the whole of the Chola country. This was Ravi Varman Kulaśēkhara, who was born in the year A.D. 1266-7. He fought early against a Vīra Pāṇḍya, in all likelihood the Bir Pandi or the Tira Pandi of the Muhammadan historians, and marched into the territory of the Pāṇḍyas and the Cholas soon after Malik Kafur left for Delhi. He was as far north as Tiruvaḍi in the South Arcot district in A.D. 1313. In A.D. 1313-14 he was in Kānchi, having celebrated his coronation on the banks of river Vēgavati in his fourth year, a stream that runs through the town of Kānchi.[1] If this means anything, he felt justified in anointing himself ruler over the Tamil country in succession to the Imperial Cholas, and their Pāṇḍya successors. Records in Śrīrangam of the same year, or the following, show him as having overcome in battle a rival of his by name Vīra Pāṇḍya, whom he drove for shelter to Konkan.[2] Another record of his in Poonamalli gives him credit for a victory over a Sundara Pāṇḍya. This record shows the two fishes of the Pāṇḍyas surmounted by an elephant-goad, a certain indication of Kēraḷa ascendency over the Pāṇḍya. The presence of this ruler in the Tamil country and what he did there during the period indicate that the garrison left in Madura could have been only a guard of protection to the Pāṇḍya Kulaśēkhara and could have been no more.[3] So then when Mubarak ascended the throne and was ready to turn his attention to the South in the second year of his administration he had to do the conquest of South India over again.

[1] *Epigraphia Indica*, vol. viii, No. 8.

[2] Epi. Coll. for 1911. No. 34; for a record of his fifth year, see Epi. Rep. for 1909, Sec 74.

[3] For Ravivarman Kulaśēkhara see my article 'A medieval Kēraḷa Ruler' in the *Ernakulam College Magazine* for July 1919.

Hoyśālēsvara temple ; Halebid. General View, back
(by permission of the Mysore Archæological Department)

Dvārasamudra re-built before A.D. 1316.—The kingdom of the Hoysalas of Dvārasamudra remained quite intact all this while, and was not much affected even by the progress of the Kēraḷa ruler Ravivarman Kulaśēkhara. During the period of activity of the latter in the Tamil country, the Hoysala apparently withdrew into his ancestral dominions and appears to have been attending to the work of restoring order in his kingdom, which had suffered by the invasion of the Muhammadans considerably, though not to the extent that the Tamil kingdoms did. Reference was already made to the return of the Hoysala prince from Delhi in A.D. 1313,[1] and to the fact that the entry of the prince again into the capital of his father was celebrated by a grant to a temple which might be just one of the items of celebration, and need hardly be regarded as the whole of it. Another record of Vīra Baḷḷāḷa III dated the equivalent of A.D. 1316, states in clear terms that the Baḷḷāḷa was ruling in great happiness *after having re-built his capital at Dhorasamudra.*[2] This rebuilding of the capital is a certain indication of the reviving security of the Hoysala, and we might see a reflex of the disturbances at head-quarters in the hopefulness with which the southern governments went about setting their own kingdoms in order with a view to further eventualities. We do not hear of any activity on the part of the Hoysala in the Tamil country till about the year A.D. 1328. Absence of information is not always synonymous with absence of occurrences worth recording in history; but at the same time it looks as if the Hoysala intervention, which might well have begun soon after A.D. 1316, became really effective only about the year A.D. 1328, the date of the recorded residence of the Hoysala at Tiruvaṇṇāmalai.[3] That incident will

[1] Sh. 68 *Epigraphia Car.*, vol. viii.
[2] Md. 100 *Epigraphia Car.*, vol.iii.
[3] Db. 14 *Epigraphia Car.* ix.

come in its proper place later. The sudden retirement of Ravivarman Kulaśēkhara might have been due in part at any rate to the attempt of the Hoysala, to recover his lost dominions in the Tamil country[1] though the chief cause must have been the southward march of Pratāpa Rudra's general Muppiḍināyaka whose records we find both in Kānchi and *Jambukēśvaram* (on the island of Śrīrangam, near Trichinopoly). The need therefore for a fresh attempt at the conquest of the southern kingdoms as soon as Mubarak felt settled upon the throne is very clear.

Reconquest of the Dakhan.—Mubarak marched to Deogir defeated Harapāla in battle, took him prisoner and flayed him alive. When the rains began, the Mahrattas had been brought into subjection; the Sultan remained in Deogir itself during the rains appointing Malik Yek Lakhi, an old servant of Alau-d-din, 'who for many years was Naib of the Barids (spies),' as governor of the Mahārāshṭra. It was now that Mubarak appointed 'feudatories, rulers and revenue collectors over the territories of the Mahrattas.' This means that the Mahratta country was brought directly under Muhammadan rule, and the country was distributed among a certain number of Muhammadan governors. In the words of Col. Haig, 'Kutub-ud-din Mubarak Shah remained during the rainy season at Deogir engaged in bringing the Mahratta country for the first time under Muhammadan rule, and in building the great mosque which still stands at Deogir. This structure is a monument of the establishment of Islam in the south. The numerous pillars which support its roof are purely Hindu in design, and were evidently taken from some temple which stood on or near the spot where the mosque now stands. The effect of the Hindu carvings in the temple of monotheism is most incongruous, perhaps designedly so, for Kutub-ud-

[1] Epi. Rep. for 1916, Sec. 531 and *Ibid* for 1909, Sec. 73.

din Mubarak, who was three parts debauchee and one part theologian, evidently intended them to bear witness to future ages of the downfall of Hinduism and the establishment of Islam. The emperor, during his stay in Deogir, *established military posts throughout the Gulbarga, Sagar, and Dhorasamudra country*[1] and parcelled out the Mahārāshṭra among Muhammadan jagirdars."[2]

Khusru Khan's invasion of Warangal.—It was in all probability for establishing the military posts above referred to that an expedition against Warangal was entrusted to Khusru Khan, of which Barni makes no mention. Amir Khusru, however, who completed his work Nuh Siphir (nine spheres) in A.D. 1318, has a detailed account of Khusru Khan's invasion and siege of Warangal. In Deogir itself Khusru Khan was detached first against Raghu, the minister of Ram Deo, and then, against Harpal (Harapāla) Deo himself. It must have been after this that he marched southwards towards Warangal. Warangal seems to have been closely besieged as on the former occasions, and was compelled to submit. The negotiations also took a turn similar to that of Malik Kafur's Campaign, the Khan stating that 'the Khalifa who sent me to this country ordered me to demand three conditions from the Hindus; first. that they should make profession of the faith in order that its tidings may be proclaimed throughout the world; second, that, in the event of refusal, a capitation tax should be levied; and the third is, if the compliance with this demand is refused to place their heads under the sword. It is my recommendation that the Rai come forth and place his head upon the ground, in front of the royal pavilion.' These terms meant conversion to Islam, or the surrender

[1] The statement is a little too hyperbolical, as appears from the Hoysala Inscriptions, and the first campaign of Alau-d-din Bahman Shah according to the Burhan-i-Ma'asir.

[2] Historic Landmarks of the Dakhan 625.

of all property and agreement to pay Jazia, or death in the alternative, terms quite similar to those offered by Malik Kafur before. The Raja agreed to surrender all his wealth and to pay tribute, and after he satisfied the Khan that he had secreted no treasure, the Khan accepted the terms. The written agreement also arrived in due course. 'The Khan then received from the Rai five districts (mauza) of his country (A'kta), an annual tribute of more than a hundred strong elephants, as large as demons, twelve thousand horses, and gold and jewels and gems beyond compute. The Rai assented to the whole, with heart and soul, and wrote an agreement to this effect and confirmed it.'[1] As a token of subordination to the Empire at Delhi Khusru Khan renewed the canopy and standard given to the Rai, and returned to Deogir in a hurry, as he was summoned in haste. Before Khusru Khan reached Deogir however, Mubarak Shah left for Delhi on the 5th of August A.D. 1318.

Mubarak's return to Delhi.—Before leaving on this expedition to Warangal Khusru Khan was raised by the Sultan to a distinction even higher than that attained by Malik Kafur and was granted a canopy with the special commission to invade Ma'bar. He probably started on that expedition after the Sultan left for Delhi. On the Sultan's return march to Delhi, at Ghati-Sakun, an attempt on the life of the Sultan was about to be made by Malik Asadu-d-din, a cousin of Alau-d-din. One of the conspirators revealed the plot to the Sultan, and all the conspirators were immediately captured and put to death; and the whole family of the principal conspirator, in Delhi, who had no knowledge of the conspiracy were also similarly treated. Then the Sultan grew exceedingly suspicious and, according to Barni, got all the sons of Alau-d-din in prison

1 Elliott iii. 558-60.

at Gwalior put to death. He then grew very high-handed in all that he did, and resigned himself practically into the hands of Khusru Khan whom Barni describes as a low designing schemer. Some of his schemes to put to death the principal nobles, to get them out of the way of his schemes, were brought to the ears of the Sultan, who subjected to disgraceful punishment those that made bold to warn him of his own danger. He put to death his own father-in-law Zafar Khan, Governor of Gujarat and appointed in his stead an uncle of Khusru Khan. A rebellion broke out against the new governor; and persons of a respectable character were appointed to governorships afterwards. There was a revolt in Deogir by the governor Malik Yek Lakhi, who was cruelly punished and publicly disgraced. Luckily, however, others appointed in his place happened to be tried men and of good character. They carried on the administration satisfactorily at Deogir. It was during this period of his reign that he ordered the construction of a Jami Masjid at Delhi and when that was completed, he gave orders that the city and fort of Delhi begun by Alau-d-din and left unfinished, should be completed.

Khusru Khan's invasion of Ma'bar and return to Delhi.—Khusru Khan's invasion of Ma'bar, as Barni describes it, was uneventful. He marched towards the country, the kings fled before him and about a hundred elephants left in two cities fell into the hands of Khusru Khan. The rains set in, and Khusru had to remain there during the rains. To the horror of Barni, Khusru Khan seized the person of Taki Khan, a Sunni and, appropriating his money, put him to death.[1] While here, he was plotting against the more influential nobles and maturing his own plans to carry through his final schemes of usurping the throne himself.

[1] Elliott, iii. 219.

The Sultan was so infatuated with him that he was able to prevail against the most influential among the nobles of the court. When ultimately he returned to Delhi he found himself in great power, and Mubarak trusted himself altogether in his hands. Introducing with the permission of the Sultan a body of three hundred men from his own country of Gujarat, he got possession of the palace in the night and succeeded in assassinating Mubarak Shah, and proclaimed himself emperor in his stead. The doings of this favourite are looked upon, at least by the Muhammadan historians, as a deliberate Hinduising movement with a view to putting an end to the power of the hereditary nobles among the Muhammadans and raising to their positions renegades and slaves with a view ultimately to bring about the restoration of Hindu monarchy, a movement we meet with again in the reign of Muhammad-bin-Tughlakh, perhaps in a much more pronounced form. This naturally created a party of the more orthodox Musalmans, who found a capable leader in Ghazi Malik, governor of Deobalpur. At the time when Khusru Khan overthrew Mubarak, the eldest son of this Ghazi Malik, Muhammad Fakhrud-din Juna, who became afterwards Sultan Muhammad Tughlakh, was in Delhi. Khusru made him his 'master of the horse,' and treated him with respect and gave him robes of honour. This did not reconcile him to the rule of the base Khusru as the 'storms of violence and cruelty reached to the skies. Copies of the holy scripture were used as seats, and idols were set up in the pulpit of mosques.' . . . 'It was Khusru's design to increase the power and importance of the Parwaris and Hindus, and to make their party grow; he therefore opened the treasury and scattered money about . . . . calling himself Sultan Nasiru-d-din. The base born slave had his title repeated in the Kutba (public prayer) and impressed upon coins.' There was such an ascendancy of the Hindus in the capital that both the Ghazi Malik and his friends found their position dangerous.

The Tughlakh Revolution.—Two months after the accession of the new Sultan, Malik Fakhru-d-din made his plans, mounted his horse one afternoon and fleeing with a few slaves from Delhi 'confided himself to God.' He was able to elude his pursuers, and reached Sarsuti in safety. He was met there by an escort of 200 horse sent by his father and reached his family safe. That was the signal for a rising of the Musalmans against Khusru. Khusru's army was defeated by Ghazi Malik and Bahram Abiya of Uch. A week after this victory, Malik Ghazi marched upon Delhi itself. Khusru came out of Delhi to meet him, having emptied the treasury in rewarding his followers, and destroyed everything worth preserving. The battle fought in the environs of Delhi went against Khusru, who fled from the field. Ghazi Malik stood victor, and Khusru and his followers were hunted out of their hiding places and were beheaded. Spending the night at Indarpet, Ghazi Malik on the following morning took possession of Delhi. Seating himself in the Hazar Sutun, Ghazi Malik gave public thanks for his victory and wished the nobles to assemble in order to decide who was to succeed next. None of Alau-d-din's descendants being left, everybody unanimously acclaimed Ghazi Malik, Sultan, who accepted the position with reluctance and ascended the throne as Sultan Ghiyasu-d-din Tughlakh Shah in the palace of Siri in A.D. 1320.

LECTURE V

THE TUGHLAK INVASIONS

Ghiyasu-d-din Tughlak.—The accession of Ghiyasu-d-din Tughlak marks the beginning of a period that promised an ordered administration for Hindustan, and a re-assertion of the hold of the Muhammadans upon the Dakhan and South Indian kingdoms. Almost the first act of the reign of this king was the discovery of the relatives of Alau-d-din and the making of adequate provision for them. He bestowed as usual honours and titles upon his friends and relations, among the latter, the five sons of his. He gave his eldest son the title of Ulugh Khan and a royal canopy, at the same time declaring him heir-apparent. He made his friend Bahram Abiya of Uch, Kishlu Khan, and honoured him with the name of brother, adding to his province of Uch both Multan and Sind. He made his sister's son Bahau-d-din, Muster-master (Ariz-i-Mamalik) with the territory of Samana. He ordered other measures which undoubtedly were of benefit to the people, and showed unmistakably the statesman in the ruler. The revenue assessment was fixed at a tenth or eleventh of the produce either by estimate or by actual measure. His officers were ordered to see that cultivation increased year by year, and taxation was regulated so as to leave a margin of prosperity to the rayats. Even the Hindus were allowed to benefit by his rule, though they were taxed so that they might not be 'blinded with wealth'. His civil measures were so excellent that Amir Khusru embodied his judgment in verse as follows :—

> He never did anything that was not replete with wisdom and sense.
> He might be said to wear a hundred doctors' hoods under his crown.

Warangal : Fort, temple, gateways
(by permission of H.E.H. the Nizam's Archæological Department)

These arrangements apparently brought under his control without question all Hindustan excepting distant Bengal, the Government of which continued to be under men who claimed kinship with the family of Ghiyasu-d-din Balban. The province of Deogir in the Dakhan placed under a Muhammadan governor by Sultan Mubarak continued loyal.

Invasion of Warangal under Ulugh Khan.—The first disturbance seems to have arisen in Warangal where Rudra Deo seemed inclined to shake himself free from the subordination to the Muhammadans. An invasion therefore had to be fitted out under his son Ulugh Khan. The great expedition started forward under the chief command of the heir-apparent, but assisted by a staff of able officers. If the description of the operations round Warangal and the resulting failure could be accepted as fact, the so-called previous conquests of the place could not have been as thorough as our Muhammadan authorities claim them to have been. The fortifications were of the same strength and were composed of the same double line of walls, mud and stone. The siege operations had to be conducted as elaborately now as ever before. After the usual operations the besieged were reduced to extremities and sued for peace, when the intrigues and dissensions which broke out in the camp made the continuance of the siege impossible. Some among the officers that constituted his staff took advantage of the absence of letters from head-quarters, and circulated a rumour that a revolution had taken place at head-quarters, as a result of which, they said Ghiyasu-d-din was killed or set aside, and another ruler was occupying the throne. The army broke up, and Ulugh Khan had no alternative but to retreat upon Deogir. But among the conspirators themselves there were dissensions, and they dispersed with the consequence that most of them were defeated in detail, and either killed by the Hindus or taken prisoner and sent over to Ulugh Khan. This latter remained for four months at Deogir, during which time he received communications and reinforcements from his father. The culprits taken alive were sent to Delhi and received exemplary punishments. This is the account of Barni who undoubtedly is apologist for Muhammad Tughlak. According to Ibn Batuta however, the disturbance was due to an actual effort on the part of Ulugh Khan to set up independently of his father, who himself is said to have been aware of it. But all the same the father sent the reinforcements to enable the invasion to be successful. Ulugh Khan returned to the siege, and, taking the fort of Bidr (Bider, the Badrakot of Ibn Batuta), proceeded thence to the siege of Warangal. The outer fort was taken, and the whole of the royal family and treasure fell into the hands of the besiegers. Ulugh Khan sent a despatch of victory, together with the Raja of Warangal, his family and treasure. He changed the name of Warangal to Sultanpur, and conquering the country of Tilang (Telingana) marched forward towards Jajnagar, the capital of Orissa. He captured forty elephants there and returned to head-quarters by way of Telingana.

An abortive Mughal Invasion.—About this time the Mughals made an effort to get across the frontiers into India, but Ghiyasu-d-din's generals succeeded in defeating them and keeping them out, sending two of their generals prisoners to Delhi. Ghiyasu-d-din made Tughlakabad his capital where he remained till certain nobleman came from Lakhnauti complaining of oppression by the Sultan of Bengal. The Sultan resolved to march upon Lakhnauti, and sent to Ulugh Khan at Warangal summoning him to the capital. When he returned the Sultan made him his vice-gerent and started on his expedition to Lakhnauti.

Ghiyasu-d-din's Invasion of Bengal.—Bengal at that time formed two governments with capitals at Lakhnauti and Sunargaon. Lakhnauti was under the rule of Sultan

Shamsu-d-din, son of Sultan Nasiru-d-din, son of Sultan Ghiyasu-d-din Balban. Shamsu-d-din died soon after, and was succeeded by his son Shahabu-d-din. His younger brother Ghiyasu-d-din seized the kingdom and killed most of his brothers. Two of them, however, Shahabu-d-din and Nasiru-d-din, fled to the Tughlak and urged him to march against the fratricide. It was in these circumstances, according to Ibn Batuta, that the invasion against Lakhnauti was undertaken. Lakhnauti readily surrendered, but Ghiyasu-d-din Bahadur made some resistance at Sunargaon. He was at last defeated and taken prisoner, and sent over to Delhi. The conquered territory, however, was made over to Nasiru-d-din the fugitive brother, and the Sultan set forward on his victorious return to Delhi. The Sultan was received on his return in a wooden structure, called 'Kushk', specially erected for the occasion at Afghanpur, about a march from the city. After dinner when the nobles came out to wash their hands the building collapsed, and among the victims were the Sultan and his favourite son Mahmud. Barni ascribes this to an accident and Ferishta apparently agress with him. Ibn Batuta, however, makes a detailed narration of the circumstances that brought this fateful catastrophe about. He apparently had no doubt that it was brought about by Ulugh Khan's design, and quotes the authority of Shaik Ruknu-d-din who was then 'near the Sultan, and that the Sultan's favourite son, Mahmud was with them.' The circumstance that Ahmad, the son of Ayyaz who, as Malik Zada, constructed the structure for Ulugh Khan, became afterwards, under Sultan Muhammad, Khwaja-i-Jahan is perhaps decisive in favour of the collapse having been brought about by design.[1] Whether it was brought about by accident or design Ghiyasu-d-din Tughlak died as a result of the occurrence, and Ulugh Khan ascended

[1] Elliott, iii. 610-11.

the throne as Sultan Abu-l-Mujahid Muhammad Shah, ordinarily known Muhammad-bin-Tughlak.

Sultan Muhammad.—Sultan Muhammad ascended the throne at the camp of Afghanpur and removed to Delhi on the fortieth day after. With his accession the spread of Muhammadan power in the Dakhan reached its greatest extent, though its unenduring character was even then apparent. Sultan Muhammad was an accomplished scholar, philosopher, and mathematician, and wrote Persian poetry. He excelled in letter-writing and his epistles became a pattern for subsequent ages. He was religious-minded and simple in his habits, and had all the virtues of a devout Musalman. His character was disfigured however, by a strain of cruelty and impetuosity of temper which caused inordinate blood-shed. He was a man of ideas, several of them in advance of his age. Once he made up his mind he wanted that his ideas should be carried out at all costs. Any failure of his schemes resulted in the most cruel punishments of those entrusted with their execution.

The extent of his Empire, the highest reached under the Muhammadans.—At the outset of his reign he had formed certain plans in his own mind and turned his energies to the successful carrying out of these. The first almost to call for his attention was the revenue administration of the empire. In the year or two following, Sultan Muhammad exerted himself to bring under control, the more distant provinces which were halting in their allegiance. It was about this time A.D. 1327–28 that he undertook an invasion of Warangal[1] and Dvārasamudra, and brought them back into allegiance, so that at the end of the first period, about A.D. 1330, his empire attained to the greatest extent Muhammadan empire ever did in India extending as it did from Sonargam to Gujarat, and from

[1] Elliott, iii. Tarikh-i-Firoz Shahi of Shamasu-i Siraj 'Afif, p. 367.

Lahore to Ma'bar. At this time his empire was composed of twenty-three provinces enumerated as follows by one of the historians of his reign :—Shahubu-d-din Abul Abbas Ahmad : (1) Delhi, (2) Dawakir (Deogir), (3) Multan, (4) Kahran (Kuhram), (5) Samana, (6) Siwistan, (7) Uch, (8) Hasi (Hansi), (9) Sarsuti (Sirsah), (10) Ma'bar, (11) Tilank (Telingana), (12) Guzarat, (13) Badaun, (14) Oudh, (15) Kanauj, (16) Lakhnauti, (17) Bihar, (18) Karra, (19) Malwa, (20) Lahore, (21) Kalanor (possibly Kalanjar rather than Gwalior), (22) Jajnagar, (23) Tilang-Darusamand (the country between Telingana and Dvārasamudra).[1]

Financial needs and revenue measures.—The government of this vast empire called for qualities which were not among those possessed by Sultan Muhammad. Such good influences as could be brought to bear upon him, could not prevail against his own schemes for the extension and maintenance of his empire. At the very outset of his reign he adopted a wrong policy in regard to the Mughals. When they first invaded under Tumarshirīn, instead of leading an army against them as Alau-d-din did before, he bought them off by a heavy payment which only tempted them to appear again.[2] He was naturally liberal and rewarded those that sought his patronage lavishly. This liberality together with the price which he had to pay for purchasing peace from the Mughals emptied his treasury. To make up for this depletion he adopted methods for enhancing the land revenue which had grave consequences. If Barni is to be believed, the Hindus abandoned cultivation and fled to the jungles, a procedure which they adopted only in great extremities. It was in this extremity that he had recourse to the mad project of going on a hunting excursion against these ryots, and carrying it out literally.

[1] Elliott, iii. 574–5.

[2] Brigg's Ferishta, i. 413, Cambray's edition, Calcutta.

His ambitious projects.—Two magnificent projects, one against Khorassan and Persia, and the other against China had formed in his mind, which, as usual with him, he determined to carry out. He raised an army of three hundred and seventy thousand soldiers who, after waiting for a year, found their pay falling into arrears and became clamorous. They had to be disbanded and the project was abandoned for the time. But a year's maintenance of such a vast army must none the less have exhausted the treasury. He then had recourse to the other expedient of issuing token coins. Instead of copying the Chinese practice of issuing paper notes he adopted copper tokens to pass as silver *tanka.* This naturally led to false coinage. All genuine coin passed out of circulation and the currency got completely discredited. Quite naturally this was the occasion for revolts and the more distant provinces began first.

The revolt of Bengal.—The first to revolt must have been Bengal to which Ghyasu-d-din Bahadur Bura was restored by Muhammad. He seems to have rebelled, was taken prisoner, flayed alive and his stuffed skin sent round to the various provinces, as a warning against similar acts. His successor Fakhru-d-din followed his example in Bengal, but remained unconquered.

Rebellion in Ma'bar.—What happened in Bengal happened also in distant Ma'bar. An army sent to punish the rebels remained there and did not return, and Jalalu-d-din Ahsan Khaṇ set up independently there.[1] We have coins of Muhammad bin Tughlak of dates A.D. 1330 and 1333; but those of date A.D. 1335 and after, are issued in the name of the rebel, so that this rebellion in South India must have taken place in or a little before A.D. 1335. According

[1] Hultzsch in *J R A S*, 1909, pp. 667–83. We have an inscription of his ninth year in Rāngiam (Rājaśingamangalam) in Pon-Amarāvati nāḍu in the Pudukoṭṭa colln.

to Ibn Batuta, Muhammad himself marched to put down this rebel. At Badrakot (Bider) pestilence broke out in camp, he himself having had an attack of the disease. A rumour got abroad he was dead and even Deogir broke out in rebellion. When he reached Daulatabad, the rebel fled to Konkan. These rebellions followed, according to Ibn Batuta that of the king's cousin Bahau-d-din Gushtasp the muster-master under Ghyasu-d-din,[1] now Governor of Sagar near Gulbarga as otherwise the friendly hospitality of the Raja of Kampili at such a great cost would be difficult to understand. Ferishta actually notes that the place was in the 'Carnatic' and that Bahau-d-din was defeated before Deogir.[2] Muhammad bin Tughlak set forward to suppress the rebellion, defeated the rebel at Deogir and sent forward an army to lay siege to Kampili, where Bahau-d-din had fled for shelter. The fugitive was given asylum, and the Rajah resolved to stand the siege and take the consequences rather than surrender the fugitive. When the siege was prosecuted with vigour and had reached the last stage, the Raja sent forward Bahau-d-din to his neighbour Baḷḷāḷa Rāja of Dvārasamudra, and killing his women and younger children, rushed upon the besiegers and died fighting. Eleven of the sons of the late Raja were among the prisoners taken who were compelled to become Muhammadans. Some among them rose to important positions in the service of Muhammad.[3] Before the army set forward on the march to Dvārasamudra, the Hoysala king found it prudent to surrender the fugitive Bahau-d-din who was brought before the Sultan, and by his orders was flayed alive. His skin was stuffed and sent to the various provinces, in the same manner as was done in the case of the rebellious Governor of Bengal. The Sultan perpetrated the atrocity of even cooking the

[1] Elliott, iii. 618-19. [2] I. 418. [3] Ibn Batuta : Elliott, iii 615.

flesh of the cousin and serving it to the wife and children of the victim. These incidents are ascribed to the date equal to A.D. 1342 by Ferishta. He is wrong by over seven years, as the coins of Madura Sultans prove beyond a doubt. Ibn Batuta appears to place the rebellion of Bahau-d-din quite early in the reign, if he meant any sequence in his narrative.[1] It was during his stay in Deogir while on this campaign that the thought struck the Sultan that Deogir would be much more centrally situated for the capital of his vast empire than Delhi, according to Ferishta [2] who seems to make Muhammad's invasion of A.D. 1327–28 the same as the one against *Bahau-d-din.*

Change of capital from Delhi to Deogir.—When the idea entered his head he resolved at once to transfer his capital to Deogir. He appears, however, to have made a point of consulting his ministers who thought Ujjain would serve the purpose equally well. But Muhammad, as usual, had made up his mind before, and in the year A.D. 1328 ordered the change of capital from Delhi to Deogir.[3] This order did not mean merely the transference of the Imperial Head-quarters from Delhi to Deogir, but the transfer of the whole body of inhabitants in the city which entailed untold misery upon the people. The order was carried out, how-ever to the degree of thoroughness that involved the firing off of a maimed man from a catapult, and the dragging of a blind man by the leg, as these were the only two inhabitants of Delhi who remained behind without obeying the order. The Sultan was about to remove himself to Deogir when he had to march northwards to meet the rebellion of Kishlu Khan and pass on from there to Delhi because of a serious distress and a possible disturbance. It was then that the

[1] Hultzsch's article in the *J R A S*, referred to above.
[2] I. 419 Edn. quoted above.
[3] There is a gold coin of date A.H. 727 (A.D. 1326) struck at Deogir, No. 174 of Thomas, p. 209.

Daulatabad Fort. General View
(by permission of H.E.H. the Nizam's Government Archæological Department)

expedition of the one hundred thousand sent against China having laboured up the Himalayas, reached the other side only to meet a powerful army of the Chinese ; and, turned back by the opposing Chinese, it had to return when the monsoon rains broke in. Very few of this magnificent army of invasion returned to tell the tale, and these few that took the pains to do so were decapitated for having brought the bad news. That was the signal for a rebellion in the home provinces, and so much distress prevailed that the king had to remove himself from Delhi. He formed the camp in the Doab where he was furnished with supplies by Einu-l-Mulk, the governor of Oudh. It was apparently during his stay in Delhi after putting down Kishlu Khan's rebellion that he made the last effort to recover his authority in the distant south, but the invasion stopped short at Deogir. Muhammad sent forward a party which reached Madura but made common cause with the rebels. It was while returning from this abortive invasion that he ordered the return of the inhabitants of Deogir back to Delhi.

Interference in Provincial Administration.—When the Sultan was at Deogir on the occasion of the rebellion of Ma'bar, he had placed the Government of Deogir under Katlagh Khan. At the same time he appointed Malik Kabil, Governor of Tilang, made Nusrat Khan, Governor of Bidar, and created another Sub-Governor for Berar. Katlagh Khan carried on the administration so well that he infused some confidence in the people, and was able to amass a considerable amount of wealth in the treasury. He found it, however, impossible to transmit the accumulated wealth to Delhi as the roads were unsafe owing to the prevalence of famine in Malva. But the distress that prevailed at the head-quarters was taken advantage of by mischief-makers to prejudice the king against Katlagh Khan. The Sultan now perpetrated the double blunder of recalling Katlagh Khan from Deogir, and proposing to appoint instead

Einu-l-Mulk of Oudh. This naturally dissatisfied both, and had dangerous consequences upon the empire. Einu-l-Mulk and his brothers revolted, fell upon the camp of the king himself and captured many of his elephants. The rebellion was at last got under, and several of the rebels punished. Einu-l-Mulk was however pardoned, and he retained his position in the King's favour. Katlagh Khan's position at Deogir was taken by a brother of his own who was governor of Broach, by name Maulana Nizamu-d-din. This latter had none of the qualifications required in a governor of Deogir, and let the vast province get out of hand. Einu-l-Mulk not being appointed, the king had now recourse to a new device which like so many others of Sultan Muhammad defeated its own ends.

Parties among the Muhammadans in the Empire.—Ever since the days of Jalalu-d-din there were three sections of Muhammadans who perhaps had not yet hardened into three distinct parties. In the reign of Sultan Muhammad they were getting to be distinct and held themselves aloof from each other, perhaps with some hostility of interests against one another. There were the hereditary Muhammadan noble families who, having been companions in arms with the members of the ruling dynasty, looked upon themselves generally as pillars of the empire. These were naturally men of influence, each one with his own particular following. Then there was the body of men, usually slaves, taken prisoners in war, or purchased, as Malik Kafur 'hazardinari' (he who cost 1,000 dinars). These were dependent entirely upon royal favour and could be dealt with more summarily by the sovereign for the time being. They were found to be efficient instruments of the monarchs against the influential nobles of the empire. Lastly, since the days of Jalalu-d-din Khilji a certain number of 'Amirs of Hundred' from the Mughal armies, had settled in the country. These were commanders of a hundred or more in the Mughal Army, who resolved to settle in the country becoming Mussalmans after the Mughal defeat. They were given various settlements, and provision was made for their maintenance by Jalalu-d-din. His successor dispossessed such of them as were within his reach, and perpetrated a massacre of a considerable number of them. Ever since this event these men perhaps considered themselves free from any allegiance to the monarch, and conducted themselves like the famous ' Knights of the Empire ' of Europe. They were the cause of great trouble at this time though they conducted themselves well enough when they were treated with consideration.

Rebellion of Kishlu Khan of Multan.—Muhammad Tughlak now fetched up a grievance against the hereditary nobles because an intimate friend of his father, who fought with him against Khusru, Bahram Abiya, Governor of Multan and Sindh, revolted against him. This governor was given the title of Kishlu Khan and the dignity of being addressed brother, by the late Sultan, and had his government extended by the addition of both Multan and Sindh to his original Uch. He caused no trouble till the stuffed bodies of both Ghiyasu-d-din Bahadur Bura of Bengal and Bahau-d-din of Sagar were sent in exhibition to his province. When they entered his capital he actually ordered the remains to be buried, and since then was preparing himself for the worst. An agent sent by the Sultan behaved impertinently, and provoked the noble into cutting off his head. That was the signal for his rebellion. Muhammad marched forward to put down the rebellion and returned victorious to Delhi. This must have happened before A.D. 1334 when Ibn Batuta passing through Sindh saw the head of Behram exhibited in front of his own hall of audience in Multan.[1] But soon after, a rebellion broke

[1] Elliott, iii. 616.

out in the same province from one Sahu Afghan whom the emperor succeeded in turning back into Afghanistan itself. He thereafter preferred to appoint slaves and servants of his to various important governments, rather than hereditary noblemen. When Katlagh Khan was recalled from Deogir he split the governorship of the Dakhan into two, Deogir and Malva, and sent one Aziz Himar to the government of Malva. This appointment was practically the beginning of the end of Muhammad's rule and came sometime about A.D. 1343.

Affairs in the Dakhan.—In regard to the Dakhan, however, we have to go back a little earlier. The emperor was still engaged in putting down the rebellion of Sahu Afghan in Multan and later in Sannam and Samana, when rebellion broke out among the Hindus of Warangal. Katlagh Khan was at Deogir and Malik Makbul was the naib Vizier in Warangal. Here is what took place in the words of Barni :—'While this was going on a revolt broke out among the Hindus of Warangal. Kanya Naik had gathered strength in this country. Malik Makbul, the Naib Vizier, fled to Delhi, the Hindus took possession of Arangal, which was thus entirely lost. About the same time, *one of the relations of Kanya Naik whom the Sultan had sent to Kambala, apostatized from Islam and* stirred up a revolt. The land of Kambala also was thus lost, and fell into the hands of the Hindus, Deogir and Guzarat alone remained secure.'[1] It was after this that the Sultan moved into the Doab and erected his head-quarters at Sarg-Dwari. Soon after Nasrat Khan revolted at Bidar, and Ali Shah, nephew of Zafar Khan, at Gulbarga. The Sultan ordered Katlagh Khan to proceed against the latter who had not only taken possession of Gulbarga but even made himself master of Bidar. Katlagh Khan put down the rebellion successfully and

[1] Elliott, iii. 245.

returned to Deogir. The recall of Katlagh Khan and the appointment of the weak Nizamu-d-din at Deogir together with the appointment of Azir Himar to the governorship of Malva with instructions to get rid of the foreign Amirs there, certainly set in train a movement which brought about the final destruction of the vast empire of Sultan Muhammad.

Mission from the Khalifa of Egypt.—In A.D. 1343, however, the Sultan received a mission from the Kalifa of Egypt which satisfied him that his title to rule the Indian Empire received the confirmation of the head of Islam. The interval between this transaction and the final recall of Katlagh Khan in or soon after A.D. 1345, the Sultan made use of for reorganizing the revenue system and reforming it with a certain amount of success. Therefore about the year A.D. 1345, the empire was apparently at peace, only Bengal and Ma'bar being successfully held by the rebels.

The foreign Amirs, 'Amir Judeida'.—We have already pointed out that of the three parties of Muhammadans in the country, the foreign Amirs, Amir Judeida as they are called, proved the most troublesome when they felt they were not properly treated. The reorganization of the Government of the Dakhan consequent on the recall of Katlagh Khan was taken advantage of by the Sultan to get rid of these foreign Amirs who had made themselves most obnoxious in Gujarat and Malva. One of the confidential instructions given to his favourite Aziz Himar was to get rid of these foreign Amirs. Aziz Himar managed to call together a large number of them at his headquarters under some pretext, and charging them with being responsible for the disturbances in the empire got them all beheaded. The favourite was of course rewarded by the Sultan, but the news of this perfidious massacre set the smouldering discontent of these Amirs aflame. The foreign Amirs in

Gujarat defeated Mukbil, the Naib Vizier, and carried off all the horses and treasure, destroying at the same time all the goods that merchants carried under the Naib's convoy. Securing so much useful material of war, the rebels proceeded to Cambay as a place of refuge. But the Sultan promptly marched to put down the insurrection in spite of the faithful Katlagh Khan volunteering to lead the punitive expedition. He appointed another governor for Gujarat, and entrusted the government of Delhi to his nephew Feroz and two others, Malik Kabir and Ahmad Ayyaz. Before, however, the Sultan could march towards Gujarat, Aziz Hamir, Governor of Malva, marched against the insurgents, was defeated and put to death. This new success of the insurgents put more heart into those of the foreign Amirs who still hung back from open rebellion. When at last the Sultan arrived at Nahrwala, the capital of Gujarat, he left a detachment under the new governor there, and proceeded against the rebels towards Abugir. There he defeated and dispersed them. The remnants of the Amirs of Gujarat fled with their wives and property towards Deogir. The Sultan sent Malik Makbul, with some of the foreign Amirs of Broach and with the fresh troops from Delhi, in pursuit of the fugitives. They were overtaken on the banks of the Narbada, were defeated and in great part destroyed, and their wives and children fell into the hands of the Naib. Such of them as managed to escape fled for protection to the Hindu chief Man Deo, the Raja of Baglana, who made them prisoners and plundered them in his turn. The evil influence of the Amirs of Gujarat was put an end to, as Barni says. Here again the Sultan perpetrated another act of faithlessness against these Amirs by ordering Malik Kabul to seize and put to death all the foreign Amirs of Broach who were in his camp. The few that escaped this massacre fled to Deogir or dispersed themselves among the chiefs of Gujarat.

The Dakhan Amirs driven into Revolt.—The Sultan remained sometime in Gujarat conducting a rigorous enquiry into the arrears of revenue, and making arrangements to collect them. As was usual with him he punished those that had shown opposition to his or his governor's actions with his accustomed cruelty, thereby creating a considerable volume of general discontent. He ordered a similar inquiry in respect of the province of Deogir, and entrusted this important commission to two men whom Ziau-d-din Barni refers to with the utmost contempt. The deputation of these two creatures of the Sultan, of whom one had already appeared and the other one was on his way sent a thrill into the hearts of the Musulmans of Deogir. At the same time the Sultan sent two well-known noblemen to Deogir with a military commission to Maulana Nizamu-d-din, who was the governor at the time. The governor was asked to despatch fifteen hundred chosen horse under the two noblemen sent. He was also to send along with them the chief foreign Amirs. Those 'at Rachoor (Raichur), Moodkul (Mudkal), Koolburga (Gulbarga), Bidur (Bidar), Bejapoor (Bijapur), Gunjouti (Gangavati), Raibagh, Gilhurry, Hookerry, and Berar,'[1] responded to the governor's summons and came with their followers. When these appeared at Deogir they were sent along with the fifteen hundred horse, under the conduct of the two nobles who carried the king's commission. They marched towards Broach, and at the end of the first day's journey, the foreign Amirs suspected that they were being led to their execution. They therefore broke out into open resistance, killed the two nobles under whose conduct they were proceeding and returned to Deogir. They entered the royal palace there, seized Nizamu-d-din the governor, and put him in confinement. They cut to pieces the agent of the

[1] Brigg's Ferishta, i. 437. Cambray's Edition.

king who had already arrived there, and took possession of the treasures kept in the citadel of Dharagir. Distributing the treasures among themselves, they made one of themselves, Ismail Makh Afghan, called Ismail Fath in Ferishta, their leader, placed him on the throne, and distributed the Mahratta country among themselves. These transactions naturally brought them a fresh accession of strength, as all the foreign Amirs of Gujarat, who had survived the massacres and the war, proceeded to Deogir and joined their confreres. The Sultan on hearing of the revolt marched at the head of a large force, and, arriving at Deogir, attacked and defeated them. The newly elected king with his family and treasure immured himself in the fort of Dharagir, and the other Amirs dispersed to their own Jagirs. After plundering Deogir the Sultan sent Imadu-l-Mulk after the insurgents who fled to their Jagirs towards Gulbarga.

Rebellion of Taghi in Gujarat.—While the Sultan was engaged at Deogir settling the affairs of the place and providing for the settlement of the Mahratta country, information reached him that a slave by name Taghi had raised a revolt in Gujarat. This slave of one of the generals of Muhammad had gathered together some of the 'foreign Amirs' in Gujarat who still retained any power, marched to Nahrwala and made the governor and his officers prisoners. With a following of Hindus and Muhammadans he plundered Cambay and marched upon Broach itself. On hearing of what had taken place the Sultan marched immediately to Broach in spite of the want of supplies for the army. He arrived at Broach and encamped on the banks of the Narbada. On hearing of the arrival of the Sultan the rebel abandoned the town and fled with three hundred horse. The Sultan sent forward a detachment of cavalry which overtook the rebel, defeated him and dispersed his followers. After spending two or three days in Broach, the Sultan marched forward towards Cambay, and thence proceeded to Ahmadabad, hearing that the rebel was there. When the Sultan arrived at Ahmadabad the rebel fled to Nahrwala wherefrom he made bold to march against the Sultan in Ahmadabad. The rebel army was easily defeated by the Sultan and cut to pieces. Several of the 'foreign Amirs' in the army of Taghi became prisoners, and the whole of his baggage was captured. The remnant of the army was put to the sword. Taghi, however, managed to escape, and fleeing across Gujarat ultimately found refuge in Sindh. The Sultan spent some time in Gujarat receiving the submission of the various chiefs and rulers.

Muhammad in Gujarat, successful rebellion in Deogir.—Close upon the heels of Taghi the Sultan set forward and arrived at Nahrwala two or three days after. There he spent sometime in settling the affairs of Gujarat. 'The Mukadams, the Ranas, and the Mahants of Gujarat came in and paid their homage and received robes and rewards. In a short time the inhabitants who had been scattered abroad returned to their homes and were delivered from the ravages of the rebel.' While he was thus engaged at Nahrwala information came from Deogir that Hasan Kangu and other rebels, who had fled from Deogir towards Gulbarga, returned at the head of a large army, attacked Imadu-l-Mulk and slew him in battle, scattering his army. The remnant of the imperial army left Deogir and retreated towards Dhar. Hasan Kangu then proceeded victoriously to Deogir and was proclaimed king, his predecessor in that dignity resigning his title and retiring into private life. Intelligence of the whole transaction was conveyed to Muhammad. He could see very well that he had lost the affections of the people, and this made a very deep impression upon him. He still continued in Nahrwala and had summoned from head-quarters Ahmad Ayyaz and other nobles with an army with a view to sending them against Deogir. In the meanwhile information arrived that Hasan

Kangu, the successful rebel at Deogir, had drawn together a very large army round him at Deogir. Prudently resolving to leave him alone for a time, the Sultan resolved to put down the traitor Taghi first, before he took any steps against Deogir, and moved forward with the reinforcements towards Karnal (Girnar). It was in these circumstances that the Sultan felt so depressed as to consult Barni in regard to what kings did in similar circumstances. Barni offered the advice, which was quite sound in the circumstances, that he should abdicate in favour of his heir-apparent, or should retire from active exercise of authority, leaving it to his ministers to carry on the business. The Sultan, however, in sheer desperation came to the opposite resolution, quite in keeping with his character, of continuing to scourge the people till he had chastened them by constant suffering. According to Barni the Sultan spent three years in Gujarat. The first he spent in settling the affairs of the country round Mandal and Teri. The second he passed near the fort of Karnal (Girnar) where the rebel Taghi was at the time. The Hindu chief of Karnal was about to surrender Taghi who having got wind of his host's intention, fled to the Sumera Rajputs of Thatta. After the rainy season of that year was over the Sultan took Karnal and brought all the coast under subjection to him. He passed from there to Kondal (Gondal) where he fell ill of fever and had to remain there for some time to recover. While there, he heard of the death of Malik Kabir who was his regent in Delhi. Sending forward Ahmad Ayyaz and Malik Makbul to take charge of the capital, he gathered as large a force as he possibly could at Kondal, and marched towards Thatta crossing the river by means of boats requisitioned from Deobalpur, Multan, Uch and Siwistan. When near Thatta he was joined by a contingent of Mughals under Altun Bahadur sent by the Amir of Farghana. While about three or four days march from Thatta he contracted a fever by eating some fish. The fever increased in violence during the last two or three days of his illness and before he could give final orders for the siege of Thatta, he died on the 21st of Muharram A.H. 752, A.D. March 1351.

Muhammad's Empire at his death.—At his death the empire which, about twenty years previously in the reign of Sultan Muhammad himself, extended from Madura in the south to Kashmir, and from the western passes to the mouths of the Ganges, had shrunk to comparatively narrow dimensions. Muhammad's authority certainly did extend over the country north of the Vindhyas, the western boundary remained intact. The smaller half in the east, the Bengals had effectively cut themselves off and had not been brought under his authority again. For more than fifteen years the province of Ma'bar had remained quite independent of him. His authority over the territories of the Hoysalas was but nominal. The Sultan's overlordship was perhaps a little more recognized by the Raja of Warangal at least in name; the province of the Dakhan or Deogir had stood defiant and practically independent during the last three or four years of his life. Muhammad Tughlak therefore had, among the Muhammadan monarchs, the credit of having ruled over the greatest extent of India, his empire exceeding in extent even that of Aurangzeb. He had also the misfortune to see before he died that that vast empire had shrunk to something smaller than that to which the slave kings laid claim. For this calamity he himself was in the main responsible. He made an attempt to expand his empire, in days when communications were at the very best imperfect, to a distance of six months' journey from headquarters in spite of the declared policy of Alau-d-din to the contrary. He succeeded in this effort; but he tried to maintain this vast empire by a policy of mistrust and repression which carried its own condemnation; and with such a policy failure was inevitable.

A NOTE ON THE CHRONOLOGY OF MUHAMMAD TUGHLAK'S REIGN

The central fact of Muhammad Tughlak's reign is the revolt of Ma'bar and its setting up independently of him with a sultanate at Madura under the general sent by Muhammad-bin-Tughlak himself. This was Jalalu-d-din Asan Shah, who was the father-in-law of the traveller Ibn Batuta, and whose coins are extant in some number. Dr. E. Hultzsch who examined these coins and published the results of his study in the *Journal of the Royal Asiatic Society* for 1909 ascribes this event to A.D. 1335. The latest coin of Muhammad-bin-Tughlak he finds in the south is of date A.D. 1334. The earliest of Jalalu-d-din is dated A.D. 1335 and carries on it the superscription of which the details are given by Ibn Batuta himself. Dr. Vincent Smith in his recent publication *The Oxford History of India* has the following on page 242. 'The turning point was reached in A.D. 1338-9 equal to A.H. 739 when both Bengal and Ma'bar or Coromandel revolted and escaped from the Delhi tyranny.' The grounds upon which he gives the actual date A.D. 1338-9 are not clear. There is no reference in the chapter to Dr. Hultzsch's article and perhaps he bases this actual date on older information. On the following page 243, he has the following sentence apparently taken from Ferishta, in substance at any rate, 'about the same time approximately 1340, Saiyid Hasan, the Governor of Ma'bar or Coromandel revolted and slew the Sultan's officers.' This date is far too late on the evidence of South Indian coins. Similarly in regard to the change of capital to Deogiri this book has adopted the date A.D. 1326-27 (A.H. 727), admittedly on the basis of the account as given in Ibn Batuta, it may be that Ibn Batuta's narrative in this part is arranged chronologically. Ziau-d-din Barni who certainly did know what he was writing about says actually that the change of capital had taken place when the Sultan went against Kishlu Khan. His rebellion apparently was what directly encouraged the movement in Ma'bar, particularly as the exhibition of Bahau-d-din's corpse brought about the rebellion of this powerful governor of Sind. This diverted the attention of the Sultan to such a degree, 'that he did not proceed to Deogir whither the citizens and their families had removed. Whilst he remained at Delhi, the nobles and the soldiers continued with him, but their wives and children were at Deogir.' The change of capital therefore must have taken place soon after, and in consequence of, the rebellion of Bahau-d-din and in the interval between that and the rebellion of Kishlu Khan in Sind, whose head was seen by Ibn Baṭuta in Multan on his journey up to Delhi in A.D. 1333-34. We may perhaps date the change of capital in A.D. 1327-8 of which year A.H. 727 we have one gold coin of Muhammad bearing upon it the name Deogir.

This arrangement receives unlooked for confirmation from an inscription at Panaiyūr in the Tirumeyyam Talūk of the Pudukoṭṭa State which refers itself to the ninth year of 'Muhammadi Surattān' (Muhammad Sultan). This would be the year A.D. 1334 when his authority was acknowledged as a matter of course in the southern part of the Pudukoṭṭa State. The Sultanate of Madura then must be held to have begun in A.D. 1335 and that is the beginning of the end of Muhammad's empire. There are a number of inscriptions which refer themselves to the Hijira year in the district of Ramnad, of which one is published along with this. They refer themselves in general terms to the rule of Rājādhirāja Sakala Nṛpakulakkōn; the dates given are 732, 761 and 771 in these records which have been referred to the Kollamāṇḍu (Malabar era) in the Epigraphist's report. But the record from Kaṇḍadēvi published in this work makes it clear that it is the Muhammadan era that is referred to, as the Muhammadan month and its equivalent Tamil month are given in the inscription itself. The record of 732 refers itself to the time of 'Ādi Surattān' (First Sultan). These finds put it beyond doubt that the era under reference is the Hijira era, and that the authority of Muhammad Tughlak was acknowledged in the far south up to the year A.D. 1334, and the authority of the Muhammadans, apparently the Sultans of Madura, up to A.D. 1371.

Both Ziau-d-din Barni and Ibn Batuta agree that on hearing of the rebellion of Ma'bar, the Sultan marched at the head of his army to put down the rebellion. They again agree that he took ill at Bidar and had to abandon the enterprise, contenting himself with sending an army. When he was in Deogir on his return journey he ordered the inhabitants of Delhi then in Deogir to return, himself advancing slowly owing to illness. This must have been in the year or two following the revolt of Ma'bar in A.D. 1335. After some time came the rebellion of Sahu Afghan in Multan. In the course of Muhammad's suppression of this rebellion came the organized revolt of the Southern Hindus, Warangal, Kampli with perhaps Dvārasamudra behind them. The foundations of Vijayanagar were laid in the fortification of Virūpākshapaṭṭaṇa and the installation of the Hoysala Prince there in the position of heir-apparent respectively in A.D. 1339 and A.D. 1340.

LECTURE VI

MUHAMMADAN KINGDOMS IN THE DAKHAN AND SOUTH INDIA

Foundation of the Sultanate at Madura.—At the time of death of the Sultan, Muhammad Tughlak, India south of the Vindhyas was divided into four well-marked divisions as before. The first might well be called the Dakhan with its capital at Deogir till recently under the Muhammadan governors of the empire, but asserting during the last four years of the Sultan's life, a defiant independence. Along side of it and occupying the other half of the Dakhan plateau and the corresponding coast districts, was the tributary Hindu kingdom of Telingana with its capital still at Warangal. South of the Krishna extended the territory of another tributary Hindu ruler, but more nominally subordinate than Warangal. This was the Hoysala kingdom which stretched from sea to sea and from the river Krishna almost to the Kaveri. South of this was the Pāṇḍya country in the days of its widest expansion; but at the time, divided among a number of petty Pāṇḍyan rulers, members in all probability of the main ruling family of the Pāṇḍyas. In the heart of this country was established a definite Musalman state which up to the year A.D. 1335 was subordinate to Muhammad Tughlak. In that year the Muhammadan governor of Madura threw off the yoke and declared himself independent. This Muhammadan ruler of Madura laid claim to authority over all Ma'bar, that is the whole of the Coromandel coast extending from Quilon to Nellore—in other words all the Tamil country. The actual extent of his territory, however, seems to have been limited to the territory of the Pāṇḍyas and the southern part of that of the Cholas, the Kaveri, possibly the southern Peṇṇār, marking the limit between them and the Hoysalas. These four states remained independent at the time that Muhammad Tughlak died.

The year A.D. 1335 which marks the declaration of independence by Sultan Jalalu-d-din Ahsan Shah at Madura marks an epoch in the history of South India, just as it marks, the turning point in the successful career of Sultan Muhammad Tughlak. The declaration of independence by this remote province was the signal at the time for the middle states of the Hindus, either openly to throw off the yoke, or to set in train the movement which culminated in the abolition of Muhammadan rule in the south of India. Adequate knowledge of the history therefore of the Madura Sultanate, and of the newly founded Muhammadan kingdom of Deogir during the first decades of its existence, is a necessary preliminary to the correct understanding of the Hindu movements which culminated in the foundation of the empire of Vijayanagar.

The Muhammadan Kingdom of Madura.—Malik Kafur's invasion of the south reaching as far as Madura and Rāmēśvaram, was described at length in a previous lecture. Amir Khusru's circumstantial account of this southern invasion was given in full. It was also pointed out that although a few places he mentions are not yet capable of satisfactory identification, enough of his account could be made out to justify the statement that the objective of Malik Kafur after he left the territory of the Hoysalas was the country of Vīra Pāṇḍya.[1] There is very little doubt left that he marched in support of Vīra Pāṇḍya's rival Sundara Pāṇḍya whose territory proper was Madura and

[1] The Malik pursued the 'yellow faced Bir' to Birdhul 'an old city of the ancestors of Bir.' Elliott iii. 90. Paras Dalvi desired that 'Bir Dhul' and 'Bir Pāṇḍya' might be reduced. Ibid, p. 88. This could mean no more than the Chola and Pāṇḍya country of Bir, of Vīra Pāṇḍya.

the country round it. When he returned early in A.D. 1312 Malik Kafur in all probability left a garrison behind to safeguard the position of his protege Sundara Pāṇḍya. Almost the next year we find the Malabar King Ravi Varman Kulaśēkhara of Keraḷa in occupation of the country from the South Peṇṇār to as far north as Poonamalle, nay even to Nellore, indicating clearly that the so-called Muhammadan conquest meant at best no more than the occupation of Madura and a comparatively narrow district round it. Sultan Mubarak Khilji sent Khusru Khan against Ma'bar in A.D. 1318 either to regain the lost hold of the Muhammadans, or it may be to make a fresh conquest of it. Whatever was the actual purpose, Khusru remained a whole year in Ma'bar and hatched his plot there to subvert the ruling dynasty at Delhi. Barni complains of his ill-treatment of the Muhammadan merchants there, and states that he developed his hinduising plot while there. Barni certainly cannot be held to mean that he took any direct part in encouraging the Hindus to throw off the Muhammadan yoke in the South. For South Indian History this may be held to mean no more than that he brought back to loyalty a certain amount of territory which remained under their control in the distant South, if even that. The revolution that followed immediately loosened the hold of the Muhammadans in the South, or at least cut off communication between the head-quarters and the distant Muhammadan garrison in Madura. Although Muhammad Tughlak was compelled to retire from Warangal in A.D. 1328, one of his invasions to Ma'bar appears to have successfully reasserted the authority of Delhi in Madura.

Muhammad's Conquest of the South.—An account of the sack of Śrīrangam by the Muhammadans preserved in the works on the Vaishṇava Guruparamparā (succession of pontiffs in Śrīrangam) is reminiscent of the invasion ordered by Muhammad from Warangal in A.D. 1327-8. The account is given in some detail in connection with the lives of Piḷḷai Lokāchārya and Vēdānta Dēśika in the Sanskrit work Prapannāmṛtam, a work composed in the first decades of the seventeenth century. Some details of this story are found preserved in a Telugu work called *Āchārya Sūkti Muktāvaḷi*. One part of this story relating to the temple ritual is preserved in Koyiloḻuhu, which gives a date. A comparison of all these leaves no doubt that they refer to the same incident as the same characters figure in it, and the other details of the main story are practically the same. The date given in the Koyiloḻuhu is 1149 Śaka coupled with the name of the year Akshaya. The given year seems to be an error for 1249. The year Akshaya does not correspond to Śaka 1149 but does to Śaka 1249 except for a slight discrepancy. If this correction in the century is accepted the date would correspond to A.D. 1327-8, when an invasion was sent into the south by Muhammad-bin-Tughlak to re-assert the authority of the Muhammadans in the south. The story briefly is this :

While the annual festival in which the god is taken over-night to the banks of the Coleroon river, a little to the south-east of Śrīrangam—a festival lasting a few hours—was being celebrated, tidings came that an army of the Muhammadans had come in and occupied parts of the Tonḍamanḍalam (the two Arcots and Chingleput) and a small body of troops was marching rapidly towards Śamaya-varam about five miles from the north bank of the Coleroon. The principal Brahman citizens of the town, who had assembled at the celebration of the festival and who were in charge of the temple, not having got through the festival cast lots in the presence of the idol whether to stay or to go. They got an answer directing them to stay. They stayed over therefore to complete the festival, and in the meanwhile information was brought to them that the flying column of the Muhammadans was dashing past Śamaya-varam. They therefore made haste to wind up proceedings, and, sending away the god and the goddess, in a small palanquin under the escort of Lokāchārya (Piḷḷai Lokāchārya) and a few stout-hearted followers and carriers, the assembled multitude got themselves ready for the attack. They had not to wait long before they were actually attacked, and destroyed in large numbers. From out of this massacre Vēdāntachārya escaped, with the two little sons of Śrutaprakāśikāchārya, and the single manuscript of his famous commentary on the Śrī Bhāshya, and betook himself through unfrequented roadways to Satyamangalam on the borders of Mysore. Lokāchārya and his companions took their way to the south for safety. Fearing that they would be overtaken if they went along the road, they seemed to have kept more or less close to the road, but avoided the road-way and proceeded slowly through jungles and unfrequented tracts across the state of Pudukoṭṭa. They seemed to have marched in safety till they got to the southern frontier. Near Tiruppattūr they branched off, avoiding the main road from Tiruppattūr to Madura, probably because they had heard of the near approach of the enemy. Lokāchārya fled for shelter to Tirukkoshṭiyūr about six miles from Tiruppattūr on the modern road from Tiruppattūr to Śivaganga. It was probably on that occasion that the Muhammadan forces encamped in the temple precincts at Tiruppattūr, and it was too dangerous a proximity for Lokāchārya and his companions to continue in Tirukkoshṭiyūr. They therefore made a further detour to the east and getting through a more or less dense forest region, they came to a place called Jyotishkuḍi (Jyotishmatīpura), where they lived a few months. During their residence there, information reached them that the bulk of the citizens of Śrīrangam were massacred, the temple itself sacked and desecrated, and all those citizens that Lokāchārya knew and cared for had suffered death. On hearing this distressing account of what happened to his friends and companions he got ill and died. His companions stayed there till they completed the funeral ceremonies of their venerable leader, and marched across from there for greater safety to Sundarāchalam (Aḻagar-malai), where they stayed for about a year. Finding their position untenable even there, they marched down farther south by way of Eṭṭiyāpuram zamindari till they reached Āḻvār-Tirunagari and then across into the Travancore country. Going along from temple to temple of the Vaishṇava holy places on the west coast they reached at last Calicut. Starting from there again after some time they got into the Mysore country and stayed a short time in Terukkaṇāmbi. Setting forward therefrom again they reached as far as Punganur, apparently towards Tirupati. Finding the march dangerous, they retreated towards Tirunārāyaṇapuram (Mēlkoṭṭai), where they remained for some considerable length of time. When they felt the road ways safe, they carried the image across to Tirupati. The story closes that from Tirupati, the image was taken over to Ginji by Gopana and ultimately got back to Śrīrangam.

This last incident seems merely the copy of what actually did take place in respect of their Ranganātha idol when Śrīrangam was sacked by Malik Kafur. The riddle is solved by what the accounts state as having taken place when the images were ultimately brought to Śrīrangam. When specifically stating that there were two images, the story relates that when the old image which the youngest of the three attendants preserved at the foot of the Tirupati hill, was brought at the instance of Gopana into Śrīrangam, they were all puzzled as to which was the genuine original image of the God. Not finding one old enough to bear testimony on direct knowledge, they ultimately lighted upon a blind washerman who was much past ninety years and who actually said that he had been for over half a century washing the clothes of the god and would by the smell of the water with which the god was bathed tell accurately which was the old image. The test was applied and he pointed to what was the original idol of the God. It is not an impossible inference to make from this story that the original image and the one that was substituted for it after that was carried away were both of them brought back by Gopana and the difficulty was to decide which of the two was the original image and therefore to be installed in the temple. So the discrepancy between the two stories as to the migration of the idol of Ranganātha is only apparent so far as the story goes, and is easily reconcilable ; but how far the stories themselves are reliable is matter upon which light would be desirable.

In our discussion of the route taken by Malik Kafur, we have already indicated that the ordinary route taken by the invasion was in all probability the road from Trichinopoly to Māttūrkoḷam, and then perhaps to Kaḍambaravanam (Nārttāmalai), and from there to Pon-Amarāvati straight, cutting the Kuḍumiyāmalai road where at present the Pon-Amarāvati road leads off from it, or somewhere near. That apparently was the high road during the period of the Muhammadan invasions of South India. These fugitives from Śrīrangam, the account clearly states, kept alongside of the road but avoided it so that they may not be overtaken. They preferred to get along through forest tracts by secret path-ways not losing altogether the thread of the road. This direction would imply that their objective was the region round Tiruppattūr. The pursuing party would certainly have taken the road and clattered down along it to reach Tiruppattūr on the high road to Madura. These fugitives would naturally go to places where there were Vishṇu temples which would afford accommodation and protection at once to themselves and the god (idol) in their charge. There is no vestige of it as far as my local enquiries went in Tirumeyyam which might have been along their route. They probably travelled further east than that, and finding perhaps the Muhammadans already in occupation of Tiruppattūr, or what is more likely, anticipating them, marched off to the great Vishṇu shrine at Tirukkoshṭiyūr. There again the people of the locality have no memory of any asylum these fugitives found; but I discovered that in a chamber where there are images consecrated to the Āḻvārs in the temple there is an image of Piḷḷai Lokāchārya. It may possibly be that this Āchārya is done the honour because of his association with the temple on this occasion. It was then they discovered that even that was too close to the pursuing party to be safe, and they made a detour this time into the depths of the forest country by retiring into Jyotishkuḍi. There are two places which may be equated with this Jyotishkuḍi. The now important Śaiva centre of Kāḷaiyār Kovil is known by the name Jyotirvanam (the forest of Jyoti trees, Cardiospermum halicacabum), because that part of the forest was famous for Jyoti trees. This is the famous fortress of Kānappēr which figures as an important centre round which the Ceylon general had to fight on three occasions to take possession of it, and which he made his head-quarters for his campaigns further north; and as Kānappēr this figures as an old fortress in very early classical Tamil literature. What is more, local tradition tells us that just at the corner of the great tank attached to the Śaiva temple, remote from this temple, there was a shrine of Vishṇu, which had suffered so much damage that sometime in the course of the last century or two they removed the Vishṇu image and placed it in the back enclosure of this Śiva temple. It is very likely that the forests surrounding this temple-town would have provided the asylum that these fugitives sought, and this is what seems to be referred to in the account as Jyotishkuḍi. There is, however, another place about fifteen miles from this, straight down along the road to Paramaguḍi, but easier reached along a road about twenty-one miles from Śivaganga. That is the famous place of Iḷayānguḍi, which contains both a Śiva and a Vishṇu temple. The Śiva temple contains inscriptions of the Chola Rājēndra of the eleventh century, which call the temple Rājēndra Cholīśvara, while the local inhabitants give the name Jyotīśvara, apparently from the miracle performed by Śiva in behalf of Iḷayānguḍi Māṛanār. Śiva appeared as a devout Śaiva, hungry and wet on a rainy night before the Nāyanār (devotee of Śiva). When he and his wife got some food ready under almost impossible conditions and invited the guest to partake of it, Śiva showed himself in a blaze of light.[1]

Local enquiries there showed that the Vishṇu temple of Krishna-Vēṇugopāla was older than this. One of the early Śaiva devotees takes his name from this place Iḷaiyānguḍi and is called Iḷaiyānguḍimāranāyanār as was stated already. The whole place is now more a Muhammadan town, and the place has practically ceased to be the Brahman centre that it once must have been. Two miles from this is a Muhammadan village now called Śoduguḍi which, in the registers of the Zamindari, appears as a Dharmāsanam village, that is a gift to the Brahmans ; now it is entirely a Muhammadan village. This Śoduguḍi contains an obscure Vaishṇava temple, and it was suggested as a possible alternative to Kāḷaiyār Kovil as the equivalent of Jyotishkuḍi. For one thing Śoduguḍi is perhaps a little too for out and has not the attractions of Kāḷaiyār Kovil, which should have readily recommended themselves to the fugitives. Śoduguḍi by itself has none of the earlier associations of Kāḷaiyār Kovil and must have involved another very hard journey through forests. The actual Sanskrit name is

1 pp. 77–79 : Sēkkiḷār's *Periya Purāṇam* or *Ārumuga Nāvalar's Prose Version*, pp. 68–70.

given as Jyotishmatīpuram, the city of the Jyotishmatī trees. Jyotishmatī is the name of the tree Cardiospermum halicacabum. It seems more likely therefore that Kāḷaiyār Kovil is the Jyotishkuḍi, where they found shelter and where Piḷḷai Lokāchārya breathed his last, while Iḷaiyānguḍi, not Śoduguḍi is quite possible. The only other possibility is a little Brahman village about twelve miles from Aḻagarmalai, but there is nothing whatever to recommend it as the place. Aḻagar Tirumalai or Tirumālirunjolai is reachable by a shorter road from Kāḷaiyār Kovil, and by a somewhat longer road from Iḷaiyānguḍi, and that would be the place to which they would naturally retire for greater protection from either place. The well referred to in the account above from which water was drawn for divine service by the fugitives, is pointed out in this last place, but there is no recollection, in the locality of this particular incident, or of the image of Ranganātha having been there at all. When the Muhammadans got a firm footing in Madura, Tirumālirunjolai would certainly have become untenable and these fugitives with their idols must have retired farther into Tinnevelly, and thence into the Travancore country for safety. A study of the Muhammadan coins found in Madura confirms the second Muhammadan conquest of Madura implied in this account of the sack of Śrīrangam.

We have coins of Muhammadan Tughlak among those found in Madura bearing the dates 1330, 1333 and 1334, a clear indication of the recognition of the authority of the Delhi Sultan in the distant south.[1] The coins of Jalalu-d-din Ahsan Shah so far available to us bear the equivalent of A.D. 1335, as the earliest date. This could be held to

[1] There is a Tamil inscription in the as yet unpublished collection at Pudukoṭṭa referring itself to the ninth year of *Muhammadi Suratana* (Sultan Muhammad). The record is in the Gñānapurīśvara temple at Panaiyūr in the Tirumeyyan Taluk of Pudukoṭṭa, and refers to the *settlement of a dispute without the interposition of Government or Royal officers.*

mark the date of his successful rebellion.[1] According to Ibn Batuta, Muhammad appointed Shariff Jalalu-d-din Ahsan Shah to be governor of 'the country of Ma'bar, which is at a distance of six months journey from Delhi. This Jalalu-d-din rebelled, usurped the ruling power, killed the lieutenants and agents of the sovereign, and struck in his own name gold and silver money.'[2] The details that he gives of the legends upon the coins make it quite certain that this is the Jalalu-d-din Ahsan Shah of the Madura coins, which give the date, A.D. 1335, of the earliest known coins in his own name, as was pointed out above. This has to be noted carefully as it invalidates altogether the chronology of Ferishta. According to him this date would be about seven years later, namely A.D. 1341.[3] It is this Ahsan Shah that both Barni and Ferishta refer to as Syed, Hasan, and Hussun, respectively. Jalalu-d-din Ahsan Shah apparently overthrew the army sent by the Sultan Muhammad and declared himself independent in the next few years when he felt certain that Muhammad was not likely to march upon him himself owing perhaps to the rebellion in the home provinces, such as Multan and Sindh. Ibn Batuta knew Jalalu-d-din as he had married one of the Sheriff's daughters, and was the friend of the Sheriff's son Ibrahim, the purse bearer of the Emperor Muhammad. When Muhammad heard of the rebellion, Ibrahim was sawn in two by Muhammad's order for the rebellion of the father. This Ahsan Shah was murdered by one of his nobles in A.D. 1340 and he was succeeded by Alau-d-din Udauji one of the officers of Jalalu-d-din. This Udauji ruled for about a year. At the end of it, after a successful battle with the

1 There is another inscription in the Pudukoṭṭa collection at Rāngiam referring itself to Ādi Sultan's year 732, apparently the Hijra year, with details of date, the equivalent of Monday, March 9, A.D. 1332. Ādi Sultan is in all likelihood Muhammad ; but it is barely possible it refers to Jalalu-d-din who must have become governor of Ma'bar in this year.

2 Elliott, iii. 618.

3 Brigg's Ferishta, vol. i, p. 23, Calcutta Edition of Cambray.

Hindus (infidels), when he removed his helmet to drink water, he was shot dead on the spot by an arrow from an unknown hand. A son-in-law of his who assumed the title Qutbu-d-din succeeded. He was killed in forty days, and was succeeded by Ghiyathu-d-din Dhāmaghani originally a trooper in the service of the Delhi Ṣultan. He had subsequently married one of the daughters of Ahsan Shah, and became a brother-in-law of Ibn Batuta. While Ibn Batuta was in South India on his way to China on the mission on which he was despatched by Muhammad in A.D. 1342, he met with an accident on the seas, and was hospitably received by this brother-in-law of his who, at the time, was engaged in a campaign against the infidels near Harekatu of Ibn Batuta (identified with Arcot in the translation). Ghiyathu-d-din sent a party to receive Ibn Batuta and take him to his camp. Ibn Batuta gives some interesting details of Ghiyathu-d-din's doings which throw a lurid light upon the character of Muhammadan rule in the South. While Ibn Batuta accompanied him, when he moved from the camp towards the capital, he happened to fall in with a number of 'idolaters' with their women and children in clearing a road through the forest. He made them carry a number of stakes sharpened at both ends, and when morning broke he divided these prisoners into four groups, and led one party to each gate of the four entrances to the camp. The stakes that they carried were then driven into the ground at one end and the unfortunate wretches were impaled alive thereon. Their wives and children had their throats cut and were left fastened to the posts. Ibn Batuta exclaims in horror 'it was for this reason that God hastened the death of Ghiyathu-d-din.' It is hardly necessary to add to this blood-curdling story others from Ibn Batuta.

His wars against the Hoysalas.—The Muhammadans could not have been left in peace, and there appears to have been ceaseless petty warfare particularly on the frontier.

Bēlūr : Royal Residence, N. W. View
(by permission of the Mysore Archæological Department)

Ibn Baṭuta mentions a great victory that his host gained over 'Bilal Deo' (Vīra Baḷḷāḷa III). This last great Baḷḷāḷa had at least three capitals Dvārasamudra in Mysore, Kundāṇi in Salem, and Tiruvaṇṇāmalai in North Arcot. During the last fifteen years of his reign he was constantly in the last place, apparently because of the predatory activities of these southern Muhammadans, and the need for protection along this frontier. Tiruvaṇṇāmalai is on the main line of communication between Madura and the North. According to Ibn Batuta, Baḷḷāḷa aimed at the conquest of the whole of the Coromandel Coast, and was able to put into the field a hundred thousand men not counting about twenty thousand Muhammadans whose services he enlisted. As against this, according to him, the Muhammadans had about six thousand troops of which the half were worthless. 'The conflict began at the town of Kabban,[1] and the Hindus routed their enemies who retreated to Mutrah (Madura) their capital.' The Baḷḷāḷa encamped close to the former, which is described as one of the chief strongholds of the Muhammadans, and invested the place closely. Finding it impossible to defend themselves any longer the garrison asked for terms, and the Hoysala king offered to let them return to Madura under a safe conduct if they surrendered the town. He gave them also a fortnight's respite to send to the headquarters and obtain permission. On receipt of this offer which was read out in the mosque in the presence of all who had assembled for prayer the Muhammadans in Madura thought that the surrender of this fortress on any terms would be followed by their own destruction, and resolved to make an effort at raising the siege. They therefore secretly marched against the Hindu camp and threw the besieging army into confusion and ultimate flight. The old sovereign, who was about eighty years at the time according to Ibn

[1] Kaṇṇanūr-Koppam, near Śrīrangam.

Batuta, endeavoured to mount a horse and escape, but he was taken prisoner by Nasiru-d-din, the nephew of the Sultan of Madura. Not recognizing the old man, Nasiru-d-din was about to kill him, when a slave in attendance exclaimed 'it is the king'. 'Whereupon he (the Baḷḷāḷa) was taken prisoner and treated with apparent consideration; and, whilst under promise of eventual release, all his riches were extorted from him. He was then murdered and his skin stuffed with straw was hung from the walls of Mutrah (Madura)', where Ibn Batuta says he saw it suspended.[1] This was the lamentable fate of the last great king of that dynasty. This event must have taken place just in the last known year of Ghiyathu-d-din because soon after his return to Madura he lost his only son, his wife and his mother, by an attack of cholera, and himself died a fortnight later 'from the effects of an aphrodisiac prepared by a Yogin (a mendicant given to the practice of exhibiting supernormal power).' All these events had taken place before Ibn Batuta left Madura in the reign of his successor Nasiru-d-din.[2]

The Sultans of Madura subsequent to Ibn Batuta's departure.—This series of transactions took place between the years A.D. 1342 when Ibn Batuta was despatched from Delhi on his mission to China, and A.D. 1344 when finally he embarked for China from the port of Fatan (Paṭṭaṇam). The last known inscriptional date for Baḷḷāḷa III is 1342. He died about the end of that year,[3] Ghiyathu-d-din following in the course of a few weeks. Ghiyathu-d-din was succeeded by his nephew Nasiru-d-din who is said to have been a domestic servant at Delhi wherefrom he fled to his uncle Ghiyathu-d-din, soon after he became king. He

[1] *Madras Journal of Literature and Science for* 1888-89, p. 53.
[2] For the whole of this see Ibn Batuta, French translation by C. Defremery and B. R. Sanguinetti, iv, pp. 185-200. An English translation is appended.
[3] September 8, 1342, is the date of his death, according to Kd. 75. Ep. Car. vi.

obtained the consent of the nobles and the army for his accession by a lavish distribution of gold. Ibn Batuta himself received three hundred pieces of gold and a robe of honour. One of Nasiru-d-din's first acts was the killing of a son of his own paternal aunt because he happened to be the husband of Ghiyathu-d-din's daughter. Having murdered the husband he married the widowed princess. It was in this reign that Ibn Batuta was provided with a number of ships to proceed on his journey. He embarked at Fatan (Paṭṭaṇam) again, paid a short visit to the Maldives and Honawar, and set forward from there on a voyage taking Bengal, Sumatra and Java on the way to China ultimately. The only extant coin of Nasiru-d-din is dated A.H. 745 which would correspond to A.D. 1344. Then follows a break in the coins till we come upon one of Adil Shah with date A.H. 757 corresponding to A.D. 1356–57. He was followed in A.H. 761 (A.D. 1359) by Fakru-d-din Mubarak Shah for whom we have a number of coins bearing dates from A.H. 761 to 770 (A.D. 1368). Then came the last of the Sultans, Allau-d-din Sikandar Shah whose coins bear dates A.H. 774-779 (A.D. 1372-77). This find of coins of the Sultans of Madura [1] so far available gives us the history of Madura under the Muhammadans, meagre as it is. But it is well supplemented by Ibn Batuta for the greater part of the period. The dates of these coins range from A.D. 1335 to A.D. 1377-78 with what seems a comparatively large gap from A.D. 1344-1357, almost corresponding to the period of active rule of the Bahmani Sultan Alau-d-din I. What this gap might mean will appear later. The power of the Muhammadans in Madura appears to have come definitely to an end about A.D. 1377-78, the last year of the Vijayanagar ruler Bukka.

Muhammadan dynasties of Madura.—The dynasty of

[1] For this refer to Dr. E. Hultzsch's article in the *JRAS*, 1909. This supersedes previous contribution by Rodgers and others.

the Sultans of Madura which flourished in the period of A.D. 1335 to A.D. 1378, a period of about forty-five years, has been confounded with the incorrect succession list given by Nelson in the manual of the Madura country, and adopted therefrom by Mr. Sewell in his Antiquities of the Madras Presidency, volume ii. Quite recent reports of the Epigraphist to the Madras Government adopt the same scheme also.[1] An examination of the list given both in Nelson and Sewell shows that the dynasty began with Ādi Sultan Malik Nēmi on the authority of the Mackenzie manuscripts—one of those documents based on the local accounts obtained and recorded by Colonel Mackenzie's staff early in the nineteenth century. Of the six names that follow, it is possible to identify two or three with the Sultans of the coins of Madura whose history I have detailed above. The last three or four names seem not possible to recover or to equate satisfactorily. Adopting this list from Sewell, the Muhammadan dynasty is made to begin in A.D. 1310 and come to an end forty-eight years after, in A.D. 1358. This arrangement, it is hardly necessary to point out, is untenable since the discovery of the coins of Madura and their study. No Muhammadan dynasty of Madura could be held to begin earlier than A.D. 1335[2] and the dynasty lasted till A.D. 1378 according to these coins with a rather wide gap from A.D. 1345 to 1357. Further criticism of Nelson's list would be superfluous.

The Hoysalas during the period.—During the period of active rule of this dynasty, the Hoysala ruler was Vīra Ballāḷa III who ascended the throne in A.D. 1292 and continued to rule till A.D. 1342. During the last twenty years of his reign he had to be very active on the Tamil frontier. We have already pointed out that in the year A.D. 1316 he had restored his capital of Dvārasamudra so far that he is

1 Report for 1916, sec. 33, p. 126.
2 Refer to note above regarding the ninth year of Muhammad on p. 164.

Tiruvaṇṇāmalai, General View of town and temple
(by permission of the Madras Archæological Department)

said to have been ruling in great happiness [1] at his ancestral capital. This rebuilding of the capital by the Hoysala exhibits the Hindu rulers of the South taking advantage of the confusion that prevailed at head-quarters before Mubarak made his position secure on the throne at Delhi. We do not hear much of Vīra Baḷḷāḷa III from inscriptional sources till A.D. 1328-29, the year in which Muhammad-bin-Tughlak sent an invasion to the south after his own abortive expedition to Warangal. In spite of the re-building of his capital, the Hoysala does not figure either in the organization of the Mahratta country by Mubarak and the placing of Muhammadan garrisons in the various forts along the Hoysala frontier; or in the subsequent invasions of the Ma'bar (Tamil country) by Khusru Khan. He probably was able to reorganize his resources quietly and unobserved. It was possibly about this time that he went farther afield from Dvārasamudra and laid the foundations of the city generally called Hosapaṭṭaṇa or Virūpākshapaṭṭaṇa, which ultimately became Vijayanagar, to secure his northern frontier. In the year A.D. 1328–29,[2] we hear of Vīra Baḷḷāḷa for the first time at Uṇṇamulai Paṭṭaṇam (Tiruvaṇṇāmalai).[3] He was ruling in peace and happiness at the same place in A.D. 1342. In the meanwhile one record of his states that in A.D. 1339 (Śaka 1261) he was ruling in happiness in Śrī Vīra Vijaya Virūpākshapura [4] as his residential capital (Nelevīḍu). He is further described in this record as the sole monarch by his own valour.[5] In the following

1 Md. 100 Ep. Car. iii. 2 Db. 14 Ep. Car. ix.

3 It must be noted that the two names are not the same though they both refer to the same place. The first means 'lady of unsucked breast' a name of Pārvatī. The second means the hill unreachable. These are respectively the names of the Goddess and God, at Tiruvaṇṇāmalai.

4 Vīra Bāḷḷaḷa anointed his son with the style Vīra Vijaya Virūpaksha Baḷḷāḷa. The new capital bears this name also in this record. Compare with these the statement of Ferishta that the Baḷḷāḷa called the city after his son's name Beeja. *Briggs I.* 427.

5 Hoskote 43 Ep. Car. ix.

year a grant refers to the 'Paṭṭābhishēka (anointment) of the prince' while Vīra Baḷḷāḷa was ruling.[1] This is apparently a reference to the coronation of the prince which, according to a Chikkamagaḷūr inscription, is said to have taken place at Hosapaṭṭaṇa. There is an inscription in the temple at Hampi referring itself to the Hoysalas,[2] indicating thereby that Hampi was in the territory of the Hoysalas. There is further an inscription of A.D. 1354 (Śaka 1276) which states that Bukka was ruling from Hosapaṭṭaṇa. The next year he is said to be in Vidyānagara his capital. This series of facts would put it beyond doubt that Hosapaṭṭaṇa and Vidyānagara are the same Vīrupakshapaṭṭaṇa or Hampi, and that this had been recently fortified against eventualities sometime in or before A.D. 1339[3] by the Hoysala Vīra Baḷḷāḷa III himself. It is clearly stated in another record of Bukka that it is after the conquest of all the kingdoms that Bukka changed the name of his capital city to Vijayanagar.[4] It would be a safe inference therefore to make from this sequence of facts that Vīra Baḷḷāḷa III was apparently preparing himself for possible campaigns both on the northern frontier and on the southern, and had his son anointed against eventualities, though this could only have meant the anointment of the prince in the *Yauva Rajya* (heir-apparentcy) as Vīra Baḷḷāḷa is definitely stated to be ruling. The next year a record from Mālūr gives Vīra Ballāla his full titles, and among them is one which ascribes to him the setting up of a pillar of victory at the beginning of 'the bridge' at Rāmēśvaram (Sētu Mūla Jayastambha.[5] This would be of date A.D. 1342 (April-May). The next year (the Śaka year) he is said to be

[1] Bn. III. Ep. Car. ix. [2] *A.S.R.* 1907-08, p. 236, note 2.

[3] Mr. Rice notes the date as 1329 on page 107 of Mysore and Coorg from inscriptions. It is obviously an error as Śaka 1261 cannot be A.D. 1329.

[4] 'Vijitya viśvam Vijayābhidhānām viśvōttaram yō nagarīm viyadatta. Cn. 156 of A.D. 1378 Ep. Car. v.

[5] Mr. 82 Ep. Car, 10.

fighting at Trichinopoly against the Muhammadans. This statement is found clearly enough in a *vīragal* (hero-stone) at a village in the Kaḍūr district. It was a stone set up in honour of a *gauḍa* (a rural magnate) Kankayya who fell in battle with the Muhammadans 'and went to heaven along with the king.' The stone was in fact set up in Śaka 1290 in the year Plavanga, but the actual occurrence of the death, referred to in the record,[1] is stated to have taken place (twenty-five years earlier) in the year Chitrabhānu preceding, Āśvyūja Śu. 8 (a date corresponding to A.D. 8th September 1342). But the most important point in the reading of this inscription is the place. I have been able to examine the inscription through the kindness of Rao Bahadur R. Narasimhachariar, Director of Archæological Researches in Mysore, and the reading is *Chirichirapaḷi.* It is only the latter 'ra' that is worn in the first half, but there is little doubt that it is 'ra'. The whole word therefore is a Kannaḍa pronunciation of Trichinopoly, which must be the locality of the battle in which Vīra Baḷḷāḷa III fell.[2] We have a more or less circumstantial account of this transaction from Ibn Batuta, who was in the country at the time, and was in Madura soon after. The battle took place apparently as was stated already between Gyathu-d-din, the Sultan of Madura and a relative of Ibn Batuta, and Vīra Baḷḷāḷa III. But Ibn Batuta calls the place of battle Cobban, the nearest South Indian equivalent of which could be only Koppam. With this particular record of Vīra Baḷḷāḷa before us we must of necessity look out for a Koppam of some strategical importance to have become the scene of such constant wars between the

[1] Kd. 75. Ep. Car. vi.

[2] Mr. Rice has wrongly read the name as *Beribi* (Mysore and Coorg) from inscriptions, page 108. This error is found in the translation of Kd. 75. Ep. Car. vi. The transliteration gives it as Chirichi-paḷiyalu. The Kannaḍa version gives it Chirichi-paḷi. Hence the difficulty and the need for verification.

Muhammadans and the Hoysalas. Luckily for us we have a reference to a Koppam in an inscription of Jaṭāvarman Sundara Pāṇḍya I. In the preamble to this inscription[1] he refers to the place Kaṇṇanūr as Kaṇṇanūr-Koppam. And this is obviously the Koppam, or Cobban of Ibn Batuta. In connection with this identificaton it must be borne in mind that according to the account of this Muhammadan traveller who certainly did know what he was describing, this Cobban was a place of vital strategical importance; for, according to him, if Cobban fell the position of the Muhammadans in Madura, would have become impossible. To this description Kaṇṇanūr would answer very well. That Kaṇṇanūr passed into the possession of the Muhammadans either during the invasion of Malik Kafur himself, or in the interval between that and this last battle is clear as the place which was the capital of Vīra Rāmanātha, and perhaps even his son, to the time of accession of Vīra Baḷḷāḷa III, does not find mention in any of the records of this Vīra Baḷḷāḷa. The change of capital to Tiruvaṇṇāmalai in A.D. 1328 as we know it, it might have been much earlier, finds an explanation in this that Kaṇṇanūr must have been lost to the Hoysalas before that period and must have become the base of active operations against the Hoysala territory in the Tamil country. It is as a counterwork to the Muhammadan position in Kaṇṇanūr which is on the trunk road leading from the north to Madura that Tiruvaṇṇāmalai must have been pitched upon as the capital of the Hoysalas. Tiruvaṇṇāmalai connects with the Hoysala capitals Kundāṇi and Dvārasamudra, on the one hand, and with Kaṇṇanur on the other, and is certainly well situated for preventing reinforcements reaching the Muhammadans from the north. The distance between Trichinopoly and Kaṇṇanūr is only about eight or nine

[1] Śen Tamil, vol. 4, p. 515, reprinted with translation below.

miles at the best, and if anything like a large army of 1,00,000 operated on the side of the Hoysalas, as Ibn Batuta clearly states that that was the strength of the army, this distance between the two camps would be even necessary.[1] The town Trichinopoly is referred to by that name, although not yet found in inscriptional records, in the Tēvāram of Sambandar in the seventh century A.D. and is referred to as the head-quarters of a small division, Tiruchirāppaḷḷi Uśāvaḍi,[2] under Dēvarāya I in the fifteenth century. There is the probability that the place is referred to by this name in the fourteenth century in a Pudukoṭṭa Inscription of the eighth year of Tribhuvanachakravartin Parākrama Pāṇḍya which contains a signature Tiruchirāpaḷḷi Uḍaiyān. Hence it is clear that the Cobban of Ibn Batuta is no other than Kaṇṇanūr, and it is in that vicinity that the last battle of Vīra Baḷḷāḷa III was fought.

About eleven months after this event we have a record of a grant made on the occasion of the coronation of the Hoysala prince by Baḷḷappa Daṇṇāyaka. This Baḷḷappa figures several times in the records of Vīra Baḷḷāḷa III, and it is just possible that he was 'the son-in-law of the Baḷḷāḷa' of the Kolar records. In this grant which is dated Śaka 1265 Svabhānu, sometime in A.D. 1343 (July-August), Vīra Baḷḷāḷa is not mentioned as ruler, and we are therefore led to infer that this time it is the anointment of the prince as sovereign. The last record of this new ruler, who might for convenience be named Baḷḷāḷa IV, or Virūpāksha Baḷḷāḷa, is one dated the following Vyaya which refers itself to the time of Baḷḷāḷarāya. This would be the equivalent of A.D. 1346-47, and we hear no more of the Hoysalas after this date.

Ibn Batuta in South India.—It was during this period

[1] Consult Orme's early campaigns of the British in this locality, or better Mr. Hemingway's *Trichinopoly Gazetteer*.

[2] Ep. Rep. for 1914, sec. 27.

that the Algerian traveller Ibn Batuta who entered India in A.D. 1333 and resided in the court of Sultan Muhammad for about ten years, stayed sometime in South India in the course of his embassy to China in behalf of the emperor. Sultan Muhammad received an embassy from China requesting permission to repair or rebuild a temple in a place called Sambhal, probably the one in Eastern Rajaputana. The Sultan declined permission on the ground that under the Muhammadan law it was not permissible to allow of the erection of heretical temples unless those that wish to build them paid the Jiziya (poll-tax on infidels). If the Celestial Emperor would agree to put himself on those terms Muhammad would have no objection to grant the permission. Ibn Batuta with the necessary paraphernalia of the mission started from Delhi and proceeded across India to the coast of Konkan, wherefrom he proceeded along the coast by way of Goa, but took ship for Calicut at a port called Kandahar. He halted at Honawar (Hinur) where he remained a guest of Sultan Jamalu-d-din Muhammad. After a three days' sail from there he reached the island Sindabur; therefrom he set forward on the two months' march along the coast to Kuḷam (Quilon). He had to pass through the territory of 'the twelve Sultans of Malabar,' passing through the towns of Abusah and Fakanur. He came to Mangalore after a three days' sail from the latter place. The next important port that he touched at was Hili (near Cannanore) which at that time was one of the three ports of call for the Chinese merchants on the Malabar coast, namely, Hili, Calicut and Kuḷam. Starting again from there, he passed Jarfattan and two other coast towns, Dahfattan and Budfattan, till he reached Fandaraina. Starting thence he reached Calicut where the embassy was to take ship on its voyage to China. There happened to be at the time in this port thirteen Chinese vessels composed of the three kinds; large ships or *Junks*, the middle-sized ones called *Zan*, and the small ones known as *Kakams*. Each junk was manned by 600 sailors and carried 400 warriors. They contained decks, cabins, saloons and holds for merchandize. Each oar of these ships was worked by fifteen men, and every junk was accompanied by three of the smaller craft. Three of these ships were set apart for the imperial mission, and before all of the men could embark all the junks had to leave the port owing to stress of weather, and several of them suffered shipwreck. Ibn Batuta who remained on the shore was left there and the Kakam containing all his belongings set sail as soon as it saw the fate that had overtaken the fleet as a whole. Ibn Batuta hearing that the Kakam would put in at Kuḷam started towards the place by the river-way and reached Kuḷam in safety in ten days. He found it a handsome town frequented by Chinese merchants, the port being most conveniently situated for them. The town was under its Hindu ruler. He therefore met the Chinese envoys who had travelled down from Delhi and who had also suffered shipwreck in the voyage. Giving up the idea of returning to Delhi which he entertained for a little while, he accepted the advice of an imperial agent at Calicut and proceeded to Honawar, where he was the respected guest of the Sultan. He took part in an expedition against the island of Sindabur which was ultimately conquered by the Sultan of Honawar. While there he learnt from two of his slaves that managed to return to India, that all his property including his slaves were taken possession of by others and had been dispersed over Java, China and Bengal. Notwithstanding this depressing news he returned to Sindabur as he promised, and, as disturbances broke out there again, he left the place and reaching Calicut resolved to pay a visit to the Maldive islands. There he stayed for sometime and contracted relations that made his departure difficult. Finally he managed to obtain permission to depart. He then paid a visit to Ceylon, where landing at Puttalam he found the Indian chieftain Āriya Chakrâvarti in possession of the locality who received him kindly and conversed with him in Persian. Through his good offices and with the escort provided by him he paid a visit to Adam's Peak, and returned to Puttalam. He started from there for Ma'bar and in the course of his voyage, he suffered shipwreck. When he had almost given himself up for lost, some native inhabitants of the coast near about rescued him from this perilous position. On reaching ashore he sent word to the Sultan of Ma'bar, Ghiyathu-d-din who had married a sister of one of the wives that Ibn Batuta had married in Delhi. But Ghiyathu-d-din was at the time engaged in the siege of a place called Harikatu, wherefrom he sent an escort to fetch Ibn Batuta. Ibn Batuta arrived in camp on the second day. What Ibn Batuta saw there, and what he really has to say about the doings of Ghiyathu-d-din, we have already related in part before. He was a cruel monarch engaged constantly in war against the Hindus under the Hoysala monarch Vīra Baḷḷāḷa III. In addition to the single instance of cruelty given there, Ibn Batuta details other instances. Ibn Batuta persuaded the Sultan to fit out an expedition for the conquest of the Maldive islands and was himself entrusted with the commission. This had to stand over for sometime as the chief admiral, Khojah Sarlak as he is called, insisted that it would take at least three months to fit out the expedition, during which time Ibn Batuta had no alternative but to wait. In the meanwhile was fought the decisive battle of Cobban, as Ibn Batuta calls it, and the death of the family of Ghiyathu-d-din and himself followed soon after. Under his successor Nasiru-d-din, Ibn Batuta stayed for a short while in Madura. It was then that he insisted upon returning in spite of the fact that the fleet of Khojah Sarlak was not yet ready. Nasiru-d-din issued orders to place such ships as were available in the port of Fatan at his disposal. Ibn Batuta reached Fatan and took ship there to the Maldives back again on his way to Calicut and Honawar; from Calicut he took ship again, and this time he had a prosperous voyage till he reached Bengal. What is of importance to South Indian History is that he left Delhi early in A.D. 1342 and left Fatan sometime in A.D. 1343–44; and what he relates of South India has reference to this particular period. We have already seen, on the authority of the inscription on the *Vīragal* in the Kadur district, that Vīra Baḷḷāḷa III died on the 8th of September 1342. Ghiyathu-d-din's death must have followed in the next few months, that is about the end of the year or early in the next. We have coins of Ghiyathu-d-din of date A.H. 745. The equivalent of this, in Christian era, would be A.D. 1343–44. It must have been early in the year 1344 that he left Madura for Fatan, and he took his departure from Calicut later in the year for China.

Break in the Coinage of the Sultans of Madura, A.D. 1343–44 to 1355–56.—To return to the Sultans of Madura we have coins of Nasiru-d-din, the successor of Ghiyathu-d-din, only of date A.H. 745. That would mean A.D. 1344. From that date to A.H. 757 (A.D. 1356) there is a break in the coinage for a period of about twelve years. It would be rather difficult to believe that this is due to a mere accident. We have already stated that between the Sultans of Madura and the Hoysalas there were constant wars along the Kaveri-Coleroon frontier—the same frontier in which the Pāṇḍyas and the Hoysalas had constantly to fight in the period immediately preceding. The death of Vīra Baḷḷāḷa could not have put an end to this war. His successor Baḷḷāḷa IV must have continued the wars of his father for the next two or three years during which time he must have been ruling. The last inscriptional date we get for him is a date in A.D. 1346, as was already pointed out. It is just possible that he also fell in fighting against the Sultans of Madura about that particular period, say about A.D. 1345, that Muhammad bin Tughlak had involved himself in the greatest difficulties in his empire, and there was a famine if the chronology of the Muhammadan historians could be accepted without question. The Sultan, Muhammad, perpetrated the double blunder of recalling the capable Katlagh Khan from Deogir and appointing the incompetent and unpopular slave Aziz Himar, Governor of Malva, whose perfidy to 'the foreign amirs', at the instance of the Sultan himself, created the rebellion in Gujarat which terminated only after the death of the Sultan. Nasarat Khan broke out in rebellion in Bidar and Einu-l-Mulk of Oudh followed near the imperial head-quarters at Sarg-Dwari. It is to this date that the Muhammadan historians refer the rising in Telingana under Krishnappa Nayaka,[1] one of the sons of Pratāparudra II of Warangal. This series of rebellions all over the empire would not have been lost upon the more distant south. There is an inscription of date A.D. 1328 when a Māchaya Daṇṇāyaka was ruling at Penugoṇḍa as a subordinate of Vīra Baḷḷāḷa III. Somewhat later Ibn Batuta himself says that his friend at Honawar, Jamalu-d-din Muhammad was the greatest Sultan in the West Coast. He was himself subordinate to 'an infidel king whose name is Horaib.' This Horaib could be no other than Hariappa Uḍaiyar or Harihara, the eldest of the five brothers to whom is given the credit of having founded the empire of Vijayanagar. This must have been before A.D. 1344. The latest known date for this

[1] This was apparently the eldest son and successor of Pratāparudra who died according to Shamsi Siraj Afif on his way to Delhi whereto Muhammad sent him probably in A.D. 1328. (Elliott iii. 367). This is confirmed by a Telugu historical manuscript Pratāpacharitam, according to which his death took place at Mantenna on the Godavari. This Mantenna is otherwise called Mantrakūṭa and figures in the inscriptions of the Kākatīya Rudra I (*vide* Anamakoṇḍa Ins. *Indian Antiquary*, xi. 20.)

Vijayanagar : East General View from the Hēmakūṭam Hill
(by permission of the Madras Archæological Department)

Harihara is A.D. 1346.[1] A record of date equal to A. D. 1352 (Śaka 1274)[2] refers to 'Vīra Bukka Rāyalu, ruling at Dhorasamudra and Penugoṇḍa.' The same grant refers to Bukka as an 'elevator of the Hoysala empire.' It would be difficult to regard this position of Bukka as having been achieved in a very short time, and by a person unconnected with the Hoysala administration. There is one other fact which exhibits a similar tendency and which must be noted here. In the early wars of Alau-d-din Bahmani when he marched south from Daulatabad after the death of Muhammad bin Tughlak there figures on the southern frontier, and therefore the more uncertain frontier of his, a Hindu chieftain by name Harib in the region of the Konkan coast up to Jamkhaṇḍi. A little further to the east of it between Bijapur and Gulbarga figures another Hindu chief by name Kapras ; and further east another Hindu chieftain still of the name Kampraz. This has reference to the year A.D. 1352. These three Hindu chieftains are obviously no other than Hariappa (Harib), Bukkappa Razu (Kapraz) and Kampa Razu (Kampana, Kamparazu), the three elder of the five brothers to whom inscriptions of the time ascribe the foundation of the empire of Vijayanagar ; the two other brothers Muddappa and Mārappa are found just behind this front line. One of them was the Viceroy obviously under Hariappa of the Malē and Tuḷu Rājya with his capital at Āraga in the Shimoga district of Mysore, and the other was in charge of Muḷbāgal Mahārājya in the south-eastern corner of Mysore, and fronting the Tamil country. This series of facts that emerge from a scrutiny of the inscriptional records of the period leads necessarily to the inference that the wars were still going on, and the kingdom of the Hoysala had to fight on the two sides, of which the northern side presented this impenetrable wall of garrisons under the five brothers,

[1] A. S. R. 1907-08, p. 236 and Refces. in Note 7.
[2] Ep. Rep. for 1918, Sec. 47 .

fighting to stem the new flood of Bahmani invasions and keep it within its bounds.

The explanation of the break in the coinage of the Sultans of Madura.—What actually did take place in the same period on the southern frontier is not equally clear; but a record at Tirukaḷākkuḍi referring itself to the thirty-first year of a Māravarman Vīra Pāṇḍya, which gives details of date to equate it satisfactorily, refers to the conquest of the Muhammadans in the south by Kumāra Kampana, the son of the third of the five brothers, Bukka. This record states 'the times were Tulukkan (Muhammadan) times; the *dēvadāna* (gifts to gods) lands of the gods were taxed with *kuḍimai* (dues of cultivation); the temple worship, however, had to be conducted without any reduction; the *ulavu* or cultivation of the temple lands was done by turns by the tenants of the village; at this juncture Kampana Uḍaiyār came on his southern campaigns, destroying Tulukkans, established a stable administration throughout the country and appointed many chiefs (Nāyakkanmār) for inspection and supervision in order that the worship in all temples might be revived regularly as of old'.[1] The date of this record from the astronomical details given has been equated with A.D. 1358 (Friday, September 7). If by 1358 all this had been done by Kumāra Kampana—and there is no particular reason to doubt the record—then the invasion by Kampana of the south must have taken place somewhat earlier. Does this not offer the explanation of the break in the coinage of the Sultans of Madura? If it does, it means the Vijayanagar invasions had taken place during this period, and either the Madura Sultan Nasiru-d-din himself (or his successor) had suffered a crushing defeat at the hands of the Hindus and the rule of the Muhammadans had been put an end to, at least temporarily. Its revival

[1] Ep. Rep. 1916, Sec. 33.

about this time, A.D. 1355-56, in Madura must be a comparatively faint effort, and when even the nominal rule in Madura was put an end to sometime in A.D. 1375-6, the time had arrived for the Vijayanagar ruler Harihara II to announce himself formally to the world as the 'Emperor of the South'.

There are two records found in the temple at Tiruppattūr, now in the Ramnad district, which belong to the forty-fourth and forty-sixth years of a Jaṭāvarman Tribhuvana Chakravartin Vīrā Pāṇḍya Dēva, which refer to these Muhammadan invasions also, and throw a certain amount of light upon the history of the period. The Jaṭāvarman Vīra Pāṇḍya of these records is undoubtedly the Vīra Pāṇḍya against whom Malik Kafur undertook his invasions of the south. The Śiva temple at Tiruppattūr is said in one of these records to have been in the 'occupation of the encamped Muhammadans whose time it was', and in consequence to have been ruined. In this condition a certain Viśaiyālaya Dēvar of Śūraikkuḍi, otherwise Araiyan Periyanāyanār reconsecrated the temple. Out of gratitude for this pious act of his, by which the people believed they were saved from some impending calamity, they assigned to him a specified quantity of corn from the harvest reaped by every individual each year, and conferred on him also certain privileges in the temple.[1] All this took place in the forty-fourth year of the Pāṇḍya referred to above. According to the calculations of the late Professor Kielhorn, confirmed by those of Mr. Swamikaṇṇu Piḷḷai, this Vīra Pāṇḍya ascended the throne in A.D. 1296-97 and the reconsecration of the Tiruppattūr temple must have taken place therefore in the year A.D. 1340, when apparently Vīra Pāṇḍya was still alive, and his authority was recognized in this part of the country. The other record referring to this event is of a

[1] This family of Śuraik-kuḍi chiefs played an important part in this period and the immediately following, as there are a number of records of these in the Pudukoṭṭa collection.

date two years later, that is A.D. 1342. It will be well to remember that the years A.D. 1340-42 were the years in which the Hoysala Vīra Baḷḷāḷa III made a serious effort at hemming in the Muhammadans into Madura with a view ultimately to turn them out of the place. It is an inscription of A.D. 1340, as was pointed out already, that lays claim to his having erected a pillar of victory at 'the root' (Sētumūla) of Adam's Bridge. It must also be noted that it is about the end of the year A.D. 1342 that he died as the result of a battle at Kaṇṇanūr. The Tiruppattūr records indicate that he was in the main so successful in the effort that even restoration work could be undertaken. The statement of Ibn Batuta that this Hindu ruler wanted to take the whole of Ma'bar is thus justified.

It was apparently after the death of this Vīra Baḷḷāḷa and possibly after that of his son, that the chieftain brothers who took upon themselves the responsibility of clearing South India of the Muhammadans should have continued the policy of the last Hoysalas. It is worth remarking that the wars of Kumāra Kampana, the son of Bukka, detailed in the Kamparāya Charitam of Gangādēvi may have to be brought in into this interval A.D. 1343 to A.D. 1355-56. The two enemies against whom Kamparāya won victories were the Śambuvarāyans of the North Arcot and Chingleput districts, and the Sultan of Madura. Without going into the full details, this poem and several other works, Telugu and Sanskrit, state that Kampa and his colleagues in the campaign overthrew one Śambuvarāyan, and restored the kingdom to another taking the title Śambuvarāya (or Sans. Champurāya) Sthāpanāchārya (he that established Śambuvarāya in his position). It must also be remembered that the kingdom of these chieftains is called Rāja Gambhīrā Rājyam.[1] This Rājagambhīra Rājyam was hitherto taken

[1] Tirupputkuḻi Inscription of A.D. 1365 No. 18 of 1899.

to mean either the Pāṇḍya country because a certain Pāṇḍya assumed the title, or the Chola country because a Chola king, at a slightly earlier period, had assumed this title. But it now turns out to be neither. The name of the kingdom seems to be derived from the hill fortress which was its citadel, and which apparently refers to Paḍaivīḍu in the Arni Jaghir. This is not all. One of the predecessors of this Śambuvarāyan[1] called himself Rājagambhīra Śambuvarāyan in an inscription of A.D. 1258 in Paḍaivīḍu itself. The epic of Gangādēvi refers to the siege of the hill Rājagambhīram in the course of the war,[2] thus making it clear that the Rājagambhīra Rājyam was no other than the kingdom of the Śambuvarāyans. It looks very probable that it was Sakalaloka Chakravartin Venṟu Maṇgoṇḍa Śambuvarāyan, whose date of accession is Śaka 1245 (A.D. 1322–23) that was overthrown by Kampana sometime about A.D. 1347, which is the first date of his successor Sakalaloka Chakravartin Rāja Nārāyaṇa Śambuvarāyan. This achievement of Kumāra Kampana must have followed close upon the disappearance of the last Hoysala Baḷḷāḷa IV, either by natural death or otherwise, as his last date is A.D. 1346. It is in this campaign that he is taken further as far as Madura, where he overthrew in actual battle, and killed, the Sultan of Madura. Among the attributes given to this Sultan by the poetess is one, which seems to mean much more than meets the eye. He is described to be 'one who reduced to a low condition the Chola and Pāṇḍya by his valour, who proved the hatchet to the creeper, the prosperity of the Baḷḷāḷa.'[3] This gives a clear indication that

[1] South Indian Inscriptions, i. 78 of Śaka 1180.

[2] Atha tasya purīmēva nītvā śibiratām nṛpaḥ । achalam Rājagambhīramrundat dviṣadāśṛtam॥ Kamparāyacharitam iv. 32.

[3] Parākramā (dhah) kṛta Chola Pāṇḍyam, Vallāḷa sampallatikā Kuṭhāram !
Raṇōnmukham Kampanṛpōpiyanandit Vīraḥ Suratrāṇamudagraśauryaḥ !
NOTE.—Instead of dhah (nnyak) is the manuscripts reading. Kamparāya charitam Trivendram Edition, p. 82,

the activities of this Sultan of Madura was destructive to the prosperity of the Hoysalas. This reference may be held directly to indicate that the particular Sultan who was responsible for the death of the Hoysala, was Sultan Nasiru-d-din who succeeded his uncle Ghiyathu-d-din in A.D. 1343. There is only one date on his coins, as was pointed out already, and that is A.H. 745.; and an interregnum of twelve years followed immediately after this date. It is this state of things that we seem to find an echo of in the Tarik-i Firoz Shahi of Shams-i Siraj 'Afif. 'While the Sultan was at Delhi, attending to the affairs of his kingdom, ambassadors arrived from Ma'bar to state a grievance to him. Kurbat Hasan Kangu was king in Ma'bar when Sultan Muhammad Shah died, and when Sultan Firuz succeeded, his edicts were sent into Ma'bar, but the people of that country rebelled, and, going to Daulatabad, they made Kurbat Kangu King of Ma'bar. When this Kurbat held his court, he appeared decked out hand and foot with female ornaments, and made himself notorious for his puerile actions. The men of Ma'bar saw this, and being greatly incensed against him, they rebelled. The neighbouring chief, named Bakan, at the head of a body of men and elephants, marched into Ma'bar and made Kurbat Hasan Kangu prisoner. He made himself master of all Ma'bar, which belonged to the Muhammadans; their women suffered violence and captivity in the hands of the Hindus and Bakan established himself as ruler of Ma'bar.' As his army was all along engaged in war and wanted rest, the Sultan declined to interfere according to this author. When sometime after his army volunteered to go for the conquest of Ma'bar, the Sultan was persuaded to decline to interfere again on the advice of his general Khan-i-Jahan who objected to going to war against Musalmans. What is worth remarking in this extract is that notwithstanding the confusion in the name of Kurbat Hasan Kangu and

Daulatabad, the whole transaction seems to refer to what took place in the region of the Coromandel and not in the Dekhan. The puerile action the Sultan is charged with has not been ascribed to the founder of the Bahmani Kingdom in any other account; and the whole matter has reference to what took place immediately after the death of Sultan Muhammad in A.D. 1351. By this time the five brothers who were the successors of the Hoysalas in their campaigns against the Muhammadans of Madura, had achieved all that is ascribed to the chief Bakan, who could be no other than the Bukka of Hindu historical records. So in the early fifties of the thirteenth century the Muhammadan power in South India suffered an eclipse from which it emerged, for a period of about twenty years, only to suffer extinction. When again that power was put an end to, the restoration of the country to the Hindus is signalized by the restoration of Śrīrangam to its ancient glory and greatness in A.D. 1370-71. This brings us to the end of the Muhammadan rule in the south; and the assumption of imperial titles by the Vijayangar ruler Harihara II comes in at a period when there was not the faintest chance of any recovery by the Muhammadans of their position in South India. It is the position of the Muhammadans in the South that explains what appears the inexplicable delay in the assumption of imperial titles by the first two rulers of Vijayanagar even when their possession of the South did become an accomplished fact.

Harihara II, assumed for the first time, the full style of Vijayanagar Emperors, 'the illustrious king of kings and the supreme lord of kings; the lord of the eastern, southern, western and northern oceans; the unopposed; a Vainatēya (Garuḍa) to the snakes (which are) wicked kings and princes; an adamantine cage for refugees; the Dharma (Yudhiṣṭira) of the *Kali* age; the ear ornament to the goddess of the *Karṇāṭaka* (country); the supporter of the four castes and orders ; he whose proclamations are engraved on the slopes of the principal mountains ; he who is formidable on battle-fields ; the moon to the day-lotuses (which are) hostile kings ; a brother to the wives of others ; he whose only delight is the fame of virtue ; the destroyer of the pride of the *Tiger ;* the master in establishing the *Chera, Chola,* and *Pāṇḍya* (kings) ; the ***publisher of the commentaries on the Vedas ; the master in establishing the ordinances prescribed by the Vedas*** ; he who has provided the Adhvaryu (priests) with employment ; the auspicious ornament of kings ; he whose eloquence is well-known,' thereby symbolizing the assumption of supreme authority and signifying what that authority actually stood for. We may pardon the egotism, and appreciate the praiseworthy effort underlying it.

GEOGRAPHICAL NOTES

1. *Aṇivaḷakki or Aṇivalakoṭa.*—From the narrative of the Ceylon invasion this place was the alternative head-quarters of the army of Ceylon apparently not very far from Neṭṭūr. Neṭṭūr is five miles west of Iḷaiyāngudi and seven or eight miles north of Paramagudi. Aṇivaḷakki will have to be looked for in that locality. I have not been able to locate the place satisfactorily so far.

2. *Battelar.*—This is a place, where according to Marco Polo, the pearl fishers collected first before putting out to sea. From the description that he gives in Chapter XVI of Book III (Vol. ii, p. 331) it is clear that he is referring to a place of this name on the Indian coast and not to the place of the name in Ceylon. Ibn Batuta's Batthalah is the place of the name in Ceylon, and that is undoubtedly Puttalam. The Battelar of Marco Polo seems to be a confusion by analogy, and refers undoubtedly to the Vēdāḷai of the Hindus. Vēdāḷai is just at the head of the Gulf and on the south side of what is now the peninsula of Maṇḍapam. In the immediate neighbourhood, there is another harbour called Tōṇitturai, meaning a place of assemblage for boats. It seems therefore that Vēdāḷai is the Battelar of Marco Polo. This probability finds confirmation as the place was regarded of sufficient consequence to be taken possession of by the Ceylon general in his war against Kulaśēkhara for the reason apparently that it was the starting point for the navy of Kulaśēkhara.

3. *Bir Dhul.*—This designation in Amir Khusru has long been a puzzle. So far as Amir Khusru is concerned this seems to refer to the head-quarters of Bir (Vīra), and is used synonymously as referring to the country of Bir. The suggestion is offered that it stands for Vīra Śoḷan which at the time might have been an alternative designation of the head-quarters of the Chola country under the Pāṇḍya ruler, which must have been either Gangaikoṇḍaśoḷapuram or Jayangoṇḍaśoḷapuram for

reasons given in the text (p. 110). Abulfeda, however, refers to it as Biyār Dāwal. I am informed that the collocation of letters is capable of being read Biyāra Dāwal. In either case there is no doubt that the first part of the word stands for the same as Amir Khusru's Bir which is the Vīra Pāṇḍya of the records of the country. The latter half of the expression of Abulfeda seems more clearly to indicate Dāwal, perhaps a part of Dawalat, which might mean wealth or possessions of which the Dhul of Amir Khusru may be a modification. In either case it could mean only the country which went to make up the fortune of this particular Pāṇḍyan prince. Sir Henry Yule on the basis of the location of Bir Dhul would make the inference that the part of the Coromandal coast visited by Marco Polo in this region must be looked for in the Chola country rather than in the Pāṇḍya. He has the following about it:—'As regards the position of the port of Ma'bar visited, but not named, by Marco Polo, and at or near which Sundara Pāṇḍya seems to have resided, I am inclined to look for it rather in Tanjore than on the Gulf of Mannar south of the Rāmēśvaram shallows. The difficulties in this view are the indication of its being "sixty miles west of Ceylon," and the special mention of the pearl fishery in connection with it. We cannot, however, lay much stress upon Polo's orientation.'

'When his general direction is from east to west, every new place reached is for him west of that last visited; whilst the Kaveri delta is as near the north point of Ceylon as Ramnad is to Aripo. The pearl difficulty may be solved by the probability that the dominion of Sonder Bandi extended to the coast of the Gulf of Mannar.' (Marco Polo by Yule and Cordier ii, p. 335.) I doubt very much that we are warranted in thus altering the account of Marco Polo. The place that he landed in would depend entirely upon the port he left in Ceylon and one would rather be inclined to take it that his indication sixty miles from Ceylon should rather be taken for our guide. While there is absolutely no doubt that Ibn Batuta embarked at Puttalam (Batthela) in Ceylon, the Ceylon general seems to have embarked from a place much farther north and after sailing a day and a night he disembarked at the eastern end of the island of Rāmēśvaram. That may be a distance of about sixty miles, a little more or less. As Marco Polo was coming from the east one would naturally expect that he touched at a northern port somewhere in Jaffna and he gives a westward direction and sixty miles of sailing distance. I believe he meant to be precise, and when he goes the length of describing that it is the pearl fishery country we find he was warranted in so saying. The pearl country was not confined to 'the Gulf of Mannar, south of the Rāmēśvaram shallows' as Sir Henry Yule seems to take it. There are two divisions which go by the name Miḻalai-Kūṟṟam and Muttūṟṟu-Kūṟṟam which find reference in classical Tamil literature. The latter certainly means the division where 'pearl springs,' meaning no more than that the pearl-oyster is produced and could be fished for there as in other place. We have a record in Hanumantaguḍi about a mile and a half east of Dēvakoṭṭa, which refers to a particular village as being in Muttūṟṟu-kūṟṟam, and, to give us further lead as it were, the village Anjukkoṭṭai is also said to be in that division. Dēvakoṭṭa and Anjukkoṭṭai are not very far from each other, the latter being a few miles from Kāḷaiyār Kovil. This division was known to have been productive of pearls in early days and a recent investigation in the port of Tonḍi due east from Kāḷaiyār Kovil did show the existence of pearl, though not of a promising kind. It might have been a more fertile field for pearls in earlier times. The other division referred to is just on the north of it along the coast and reaches into the Chola country flanking Pudukoṭṭa. It is one of the ports in this (Muttūṟṟuk-kūṟṟam) region that Polo certainly visited as, according to classical Tamil literature, Tonḍi was the great mart of the eastern Chinese trade. This is generally called in these authorities Śoḻan Tonḍi to distinguish it from Kuṭṭuvan (Chēra) Tonḍi. In this particular, Marco Polo is apparently right and modern commentators wrong. In regard to the fertility of the country, from such descriptions as we get of it, the region must have been a very fertile spot centuries ago and surely that was included in the territory both of Sundara Pānḍya, and after him, his successor Vīra Pāndya, the enemy of the Muhammadans.

4. *Brahmastpuri.*—The whole argument for identifying it with Chidambaram is given in the text (p. 108). The only

alternative in the name is Shiyāḷi, which is also a Brahmapuram, but the other details of the narrative will not fit in with it.

5. *Bhandri.*—This is almost certainly Panḍhārpur which in all probability was the southern limit of the dominions of Rama Deo according to Amir Khusru's itinerary for Malik Kafur. It was five days' march from Kharababad and would answer well if Kharababad were Bir. There is an inscription of Vīra Somēś-vara in Panḍhārpur which would bring it at least quite on the frontier of his territory, if not in it.

6. *Dēvipaṭṭaṇam.*—This is a port now in the Ramnad district about eleven miles almost due north of Ramnad. From what was said under Bir Dhul above this would come in the division Muttūṟṟu-Kūrram. It must have been a place of great importance once although the sea in the port is very shallow now. This is apparently what is referred to as 'Mali Fattan,' and that its name is so given in a medieval map ought to be regarded as settling the point finally.

7. *Fittan.*—This name which appears in the accounts of the Muhammadan historians has not so far been satisfactorily identified. The equivalent of this is Paṭṭaṇam, the Tamil word. Wassaf's Fittan, Mali Fittan and Kabil must be held to stand for Paṭṭaṇam, Mēlapaṭṭaṇam and Kāyalpaṭṭaṇam. Reading Wassaf with Ibn Batuta we have to take it that the Fittan or Fattan was the port of Madura from which people embarked on their voyages elsewhere, and in which normally they would disembark for getting into the country. If that is the normal port of entry in those days, there is no reason why we should regard Marco Polo to have actually landed elsewhere. One reason that has been urged by Sir Henry Yule in his edition of Marco Polo (Vol. ii, p. 335) is that Polo refers to the place of his landing as in the country of Soli, a province of Sundara Pānḍya. In the eighties and nineties of the thirteenth century when Marco Polo visited India, a considerable part, nay even the whole of the Chola country was under Pānḍyan authority. If he landed in the territory of Sundara Pānḍya, the third of the name in that particular period he might well have regarded himself as having landed in the Chola country because he was governor by pre-eminence of the Chola territory. It would be

hardly necessary, because of this particular difficulty, to look for Fittan anywhere in the Chola country, and to equate it with Kaveripatam which does not find any mention in any of the records of the period. No doubt Negapatam, particularly Nagūr (Nagore), was in this period a port of some consequence and enjoyed a considerable amount of trade with the outside world. The deciding factor ought to be that Sultan Ghiyathuddin of Madura asked Ibn Batuta to await his return to Fattan, ordered the equipment of a fleet to carry Ibn Batuta on his invasion of the Maldives from Fattan, and, when Ibn Batuta insisted upon going away in the reign of his successor, he was sent forward to Fattan to be provided with such ships as were available for his voyage to the West Coast. The whole indication of this is that Paṭṭaṇam or port was easily and ordinarily reached from Madura, and if, according to Yule, a mediæval map of about that period marked Dēviapaṭṭiṇam as Mali Fattan, it admits of no doubt that the Fattan must be where perhaps the present day Marakāyarpaṭṭaṇam is. That Dēviya Paṭṭaṇam was in that period a place of consequence can perhaps be inferred from the fact that the Ceylon general marched towards it soon after fortifying Kunḍugāl and took that port. Hence Paṭṭaṇam was in all probability the locality now known as Marakāyarpaṭṭaṇam with the possible alternative of Rāmēśvarapaṭṭaṇam, which then must have been in the peninsula not on an island as it is at present.

Wassaf mentions that Jamalu-d-din's ambassador to China died on the sea two days' sail from Fattan, and was buried in or near Fattan itself. There is the Mussalman tomb not far from Marakāyarpaṭṭaṇam which now-a-days goes by the name Śiniyappa Paḷḷivāśal. My local enquiry there elicited that it is so-called because of a Fakir in residence there. He saw some people who went on driving a number of animals laden with sacks of sugar. When the holy man enquired what it was they carried, the drivers gave it out, to hide the fact from him, that it was salt; and when they moved away from the Fakir some distance they opened one of the bags for some purpose and discovered it was salt actually. On further examination they discovered the whole of the sugar bags were converted to salt. This story notwithstanding, it is just possible that the Śiniyappa perhaps contains a reference to the local Muhammadan trader who went on an embassy to China and returned from there. If the ambassador was locally called Śiniyappa, the grave in the place would be the grave of this man.

8. *Gurgam.*—The place at which the Muhammadan army under Malik Kafur arrived after thirty-eight days' march crossing the mountains and the rivers of Vindhyan group, is identified with a place marked Kharegam, to the south-east of Indore across the mountains.

9. *Hercatou.*—This is the place to which Ibn Batuta was taken by Kamaru-d-din who was sent in charge of the escort to fetch him by his brother-in-law Ghiyazu-d-din, Sultan of Madura, who was then laying siege to a town in the immediate neighbourhood. Hercatou has been identified by the French translators with Arcot. This identification involves a number of assumptions which require to be examined carefully. Ibn Batuta left Puttalam in Ceylon and sailed for the country of Ma'bar; the port of landing certainly would be somewhere immediately north or immediately south of the present day island of Rāmēśvaram. He was caught in a storm and was rescued by some of the native inhabitants of the locality. Through their good offices he sent intimation of his arrival to his brother-in-law, the Sultan, to the place where he was engaged in the siege. The Sultan sent Kamaru-d-din who brought one palanquin and six horses. They started and reached the fort of Hercatou, where, according to him, they spent the night. Leaving the girls and some of the party behind, Ibn Batuta reached the Sultan the second day after setting out from the port where he landed. Now if Hercatou is Arcot the port where he landed must be about a day's march from that place according to him. If the identification with Arcot is correct, the port would have to be necessarily either Madras itself or some other place quite close, and then the place that the Sultan was besieging must be very near also. From Madras or somewhere near, Arcot would be more than a single day's march, but the place that the Sultan was besieging might certainly have been somewhere nearer; but then the question would be whether a place in the vicinity of Arcot would exactly answer to the further progress of

the party as described by Ibn Batuta. After leaving the camp Ibn Batuta went along with the Sultan to Fattan till the campaign should be over and then apparently they proceeded to Madura. If Fattan is to be looked for in the peninsula opposite Rāmēśvaram, Arcot for Hercatou would be too far and the country they had to pass through will not be the forest country that it is described to be. Besides we know from various inscriptions that the authority of Vīra Baḷḷāḷa had at the time extended to the southern frontier of Pudukoṭṭa where about the time restoration of temples, etc., had already begun under Vijayālaya Dēva of Śūraikkuḍi. If the Madura Sultan had gone as far north as Arcot he would run the imminent risk of his communication being cut off by the Hoysala in occupation of Tiruvaṇṇāmalai. As a matter of fact Ibn Batuta clearly says that Vīra Baḷḷāḷa made an effort to take possession of the whole of Ma'bar and it was at about this time that he is described as planting a pillar of victory at the 'root' of the Rāmēśvaram 'Bridge.' We therefore feel justified in looking for the place of landing somewhere south on the Ramnad coast or the extreme south of the Tanjore coast rather than anywhere near Madras. This locality would answer to the dense forests through which the army had to pass and the indication given of their going forward to Fattan and thence to Madura. There is a place called Ariyakuḍi within a day's march from the coast, if Ibn Batuta's ship had been lashed ashore somewhere about Vaṭṭāṇam or Mimaśal where there must have been ports in those days. Ariyakuḍi is a place of some importance now and contains a rich temple believed to be even old. It is not at present a fortified place, but there are places very near it which are fortified and which were in those days regarded as fortified stations on the frontier of the Chola country. From there if an army retired or had to march towards Fattan it would have had necessarily to pass through forest country and nothing else, and the further description of Ibn Batuta would be correct to a nicety. Ibn Batuta's Hercatou therefore must be looked for somewhere in that vicinity and it might possibly have been Ariyakuḍi which is near enough in sound.

Ibn Batuta himself however, seems to give us the lead to look for his port of landing at Fattan. Soon after landing he calls the territory in which he landed as belonging to the Sultan of Madura, which a port near Madras could not well be. He has the following sentence later on in the narrative: 'He (Nasiru-d-din) made Malik Bedred-din (Malik Badru-d-din) Vizier, the same man whom his uncle sent *to meet me when I was at Fattan.*' If this could be held to be the person that was called Kamaru-d-din who was sent with an escort to fetch Ibn Batuta, it admits hardly of any doubt that he actually landed at Fattan. In which case, we shall have to look for Hercatou much nearer Fattan than even Ariyakuḍi. But it is just possible that the reference here is to the period of Ibn Batuta's stay in Fattan where he waited for the arrival of Sultan Ghyazu-d-din.

10. *Jagnar.*—The translator of Amir Khusru in vol. iii. of Elliott's *History of India as told by Her Own Historians* renders this as Jagannāth. The actual equation ought to be Śokkanātha, one of the alternative Tamil names of Sundarēśa in the large temple at Madura. Sundarēśa and Śokkanātha are synonyms, the first part of the latter word being Tamil and the second of course Sanskrit. The Tamil Śokka is the same as Sanskrit Sundara.

11. *Jalkoṭṭa.*—In the form in which this word occurs a satisfactory identification seems hardly possible. The identification offered in the text (p. 111) is but a suggestion which seems probable from the circumstances of the narrative.

12. *Jayangoṇḍaśoḻapuram.*—This is about six miles from Gangaigoṇḍaśoḻapuram on the road to Uḍaiyārpāḷayam. The Pāṇḍya Māravarman Kulaśēkhara, A.D. 1168 to 1311, is said to have had his palace outside this town in a garden, and that is the only occasion in which, so far as we know at present, it was the capital city. Jayangoṇḍa Śoḻa was a title assumed by the great Chola Rājādhiraja, the immediate successor of Rājēndra I; probably he founded the city and by him it was intended to be a royal city as well. Bir Dhul of the Muhammadan historians is identifiable with this on the supposition that it might have had an alternative name Vīra Śoḻapuram as the capital of Vīra Pāṇḍya, the son of Kulaśēkhara and possibly his successor in these parts; or the last great Chola Kulottunga III who called

himself Tribhuvanavīra, might have given the name to the capital in his reign.

13. *Kānappēr.*—The modern name of this place is Kaḷaiyārkovil. It figures with the former name both in classical Tamil literature and in the campaigns of the Ceylonese general. Kānappēr was a remarkable fortress in the days of the early Tamil classics and had for its chief the invincible Vēngai Mārban (the man of the tiger-breast or preferably of the Margossa garland, possibly a totemic symbol). He was overthrown by the Pāṇḍyan Ugrapperuvaḷudi. It contains a Śiva temple of which the structure is rather modern and seems to have been more or less completely renewed in the days of the usurper chieftain Chinna Marudu of Ramnad. In the old days the place seems to have been surrounded by dense forests and might have belonged to the division which was called Kāna Nāḍu (forest-country) including within it a considerable part of what is now Ramnad district and the southern portion of Pudukoṭṭa. The Chetty townlet of Kānāḍukāttan seem to be a place where a frontier guard was located. This Kānappēr figured several times in the campaigns of the Ceylonese general in the war of the Pāṇḍya succession, and was reputed a fortress of very great strength though there is now no vestige of it. This bit of forest country seems to have been marked off into forests of various trees of which the country round Kānappēr, for a radius of seven or eight miles, was a forest of Jyōti or Jyōtishmatī trees (Cardiospermum halicacabum). The bit of country immediately south of it is described as a forest of Margossa. Reasons have been given in the text for regarding this place as the Jyōtishkuḍi to which the Vaishṇava fugitives of Śrīrangam retired when the second sack of the temple took place. It is reachable from Dēvakoṭṭa or Śivaganga, and even from Tiruppattūr. A road south connects it with the railway station Paramaguḍi.

14. *Kandūr.*—The place captured and destroyed by Malik Kafur, identified with Kaṇṇanūr, which see below.

15. *Kaṇṇanūr.*—Kaṇṇanūr, Sanskrit Khanḍanapura, is known in Hoysala inscriptions as Trivikramapura. It is about five miles north of the island of Śrīrangam and was the place chosen and fortified by the Hoysala Somēśvara when he had effected a

permanent lodgment in the Chola country to keep the aggressive Pāṇḍyas out. Both Somēśvara and his son Rāmanātha, had it as their capital. Though the Pāṇḍyas got so far the upper hand of it that they took the place several times, it continued in the possession of the Hoysalas till the Muhammadans took it ultimately; and ever since, it remained their chief encampment in that part of the country from which they sallied out in their various expeditions. Kaṇṇanūr is for reasons given in the text identified both with Kandūr of the early Muhammadan invasions which destroyed the place gradually, and with the Kobban of Ibn Batuta in the battle at which place Vīra Baḷḷāḷa III was put to death.

16. *Kanhun.*—There is a place Kanhur a little to the east of the road from Matthra to Ujjain across Central India. This is described as a place, twenty-one days' march from Tankal. It seems to be the place marked Kanhur which may answer well the itinerary, twenty-one days' march from Tankal on the Jumna, which must have been somewhere near Muttra. From here the further march to Gurgam took seventeen days according to Amir Khusru. If the identification of Gurgam with Kharegam should prove correct this may be the place that is meant by Amir Khusru. The actual importance of the identification of these three places consists in our gaining an idea of the road actually taken, which, in this present instance, appears to have followed more or less, the modern road leading from Muttra and going through Bharatpur and Kotta to Ujjain, and thence down to Māndhāta on the Narbada, and across south-eastwards to Elichpur.

17. *Kharababad.*—This was according to Amir Khusru the head-quarters of Paras Deo Dalvi, the commander-in-chief of Ram Deo of Deogir, which lay some considerable distance from Deogir and was reached by the army of Malik Kafur at the end of an arduous march and having crossed three rivers Sini, Godavari and Binhur (or Bhima). This seems to be a place set over against the south-eastern frontier of the dominions of the Raja of Deogir. If we could presume a little mixing up in the narrative of Amir Khusru, the identification suggested in the text for Kharababad, namely Bir, would be satisfactory. The difficulty in this is that Bir is not situated on the farther side of the

three rivers in the course of the march; otherwise Bir would serve the purpose well.

18. *Kāṭakadurgam.*—This means the fortress of the Kāṭaka or Kāḍava which was an alternative name of the Pallavas generally, and, in the period with which we are dealing, was applied in particular to the Pallava chieftains who had the country round Cuddalore for their possession and had for their capital Śēndamangalam, the fortress of which is referred to as Kāṭaka Durgam. The references in Pāṇḍaya inscriptions to the Kāṭakas are to this Kāḍava country, and should not for reasons given in the text, be taken to mean Cuttack up to which they do not appear to have ever extended their authority or influence. Kāṭaka is only popular Sanskritization of Kāḍava.

19. *Kīḻānilai.*—This is the famous fort quite on the frontier of Pudukoṭṭa, which in recent Pudukoṭṭa history had passed several times from hand to hand among the rulers of Tanjore, Ramnad and Pudukoṭṭa. In the twelfth and thirteenth centuries it was apparently on a road leading east and west from Arantāngi to Tiruppattūr and possibly Pon-Amarāvati. Parts of the old road could be seen even now. This is called Kīḻānilai as opposed to another village some miles to the north which is called Mēlānilai; there is a village between called Pudunilai.[1] In the days of the Nāyakas of Tanjore, Paṭṭukkoṭṭai, Arantāngi, Kīḻānilai and Tiruppattūr formed the four frontier forts well fortified and connected by a high road. In the days of the Ceylon war, Pon-Amarāvati, Kīḻānilai and Maṇamēlkkuḍi marked the uppermost northern boundary of the Pāṇḍya country.

20. *Kundāṇi.*—This is a place till recently unknown to fame in the Krishnagiri Taluka of the Salem district and on the frontier of Bangalore district. It seems to have been in early times a place of considerable importance and is on one of those military roads which were often made use of in the wars of the Carnatic. As a road from here passes through the Berigai Pāḷaiyam, Budikoṭṭa and thence to Bangalore, it was one of the capitals in the days of the last Hoysalas. (Mr. F. J. Richards' *Salem Gazetteer*, vol. i, part ii, p. 43).

[1] See map in Mr. Hemingway's *Gazetteer of Trichinopoly.*

21. *Kundukāla.*—This is the place to which the Ceylon army of invasion marched after taking possession of Rāmēśvaram, and having arrived at the place, the general found it convenient as a centre of operations. The Ceylon General therefore made fortifications of considerable strength in it and made it his head-quarters in the first stage of the war. It is described as having been midway between the seas, a description that would imply that it is a place from which one could sail south or north with equal facility. This place is said to have been attacked by Kulaśēkhara with a land army as well as a fleet of boats. This statement is quite in accordance with the local tradition, for which there is even some monumental evidence, that the narrow passage of the sea now bridged over was connected by land with the other shore. The very name Maṇḍapam, the railway station, is explained as having been given to the locality because of a pavilion to which the god of Rāmēśvaram used to be taken on occasions of an annual festival. They would not do so across the sea by means of boats. This is the place now called Kundugāl about two miles east of Pamban Railway Station, where there is a fairly good harbour, which the South Indian Railway Company make use of as their docks for repairs.

22. *Kurundangudi.*—There is a village of this name near Kālaiyār Kovil.

23. *Kham.*—The equivalent for this is suggested in Kaḍamba-vanam a city now in ruins, which must have been one of some considerable importance from the remains of its fortifications that one sees in the locality of Nārttāmalai about eleven miles from Pudukoṭṭa along the Trichinopoly road, and about a mile aside of it. The particular locality is called now-a-days Kaḍambar Malai and the god called Kaḍambavanēśvara. The city might have been Kaḍambavanam of which Kham would be a possible contraction. Further research may confirm this identification.

24. *Maṇamēlkkuḍi.*—There are two places of this name. Maṇamēlkuḍi proper is a little way to the south of the mouth of the river Veḷḷār which divides Pudukoṭṭa into two halves almost equally. There is a north Maṇamēlkuḍi a little way to the north of it. This seems to have been the limit of the advance of the

Ceylonese general although he claims to have destroyed the country for two leagues northward of it.

25. *Mānavīramadura*.—This seems apparently to stand for what is now, by contraction, called Mānamadura. The name was probably given from the title, it may be of a Pāṇḍya King, Mānavīra. This is a railway station on the Madura-Pamban line. It is on the Vaigai river and is a place of some importance. It is one of the alternative places proposed for the head-quarters of the Ramnad district now.

26. (1) *Mangalam*.—This is a common name of various places, and, in the course of the Ceylon war, this name occurs in various stages of the campaign. The first Mangalam, geographically speaking starting from Rāmēśvaram, is the place about fifteen or sixteen miles from the railway station Paramaguḍi on the road Paramaguḍi-Iḷaiyānguḍi-Kāḷaiyārkovil-Tiruppattūr road. This is called Vaḻudivāḷmangalam in old books in the locality. The present village is remarkable only for a Durga temple which is much sought after by the inhabitants of the locality. About a mile from the town towards the south, there are the remains of a temple, which contain a few broken inscriptions in characters which may be of the twelfth or thirteenth century. Just a little way from it is a pretty large bit of raised ground which is pointed out as the site of the old city which the Mahāvamśa account says was destroyed in the course of the Ceylon war. It is at a distance of about eight or nine miles by country road from Kāḷaiyār Kovil.

(2) There are two other Mangalams that figure in the campaign to which the Ceylon general had to go to meet the fugitive Vīra Pāṇḍya, the son of Vikrama Pāṇḍya who was put to death by his rival Kulaśēkhara. These are Kīḻamangalam and Mēlamangalam at the foot of the hills west of Madura, and very near the town of Periakuḷam. These are certainly places to which one in the position of Vīrā Pāṇḍya would naturally go for refuge, as access to the place for an army would be somewhat difficult, and a retreat for a fugitive into the Travancore country across the hills would be easy.

(3) There is a third Mangalam that figures in the course of the war in the campaigns in the Tinnevelly district after the

26

taking of Śrīvalliputtūr. The possibility is that it is the village Mangalam in the Śāttūr Taluk of the Ramnad district now. I do not know of any remains to make the place of any historical importance.

27. *Manjakkuḍi* is another village that figures in this campaign and is a village in the Tanjore district now, not very far from Maṇamēlkkuḍi.

28. *Mankul.*—The translator in Elliott's vol. iii suggests Namakkal as the equivalent of this which would be an impossible distance for a man from Madura to retire into for safety. Mankul is undoubtedly Mangalam. There are a number of these Mangalams about Madura. The Mangalam that is referred to here seems to be the two Kīḷa Mangalam and Mēla Mangalam near Periakuḷam in the western ghats. We have a historical precedent to justify this identification as that is the locality to which Vīra Pāṇḍya fled when his father's rival Kulaśēkhara had got the upper hand and assassinated the father and his family.

29. *Māvilangai.*—This would mean great Lanka. This is known to classical Tamil literature as old Māvilangai, and seems to refer to the country round Kānchīpuram and Vellore. A village of the Ramnad district (Paramaguḍi Taluk)[1] seems also to have been known by this designation. The former appears to be the territory referred to in Pāṇḍya inscriptions as northern Lanka, as opposed to Tēnnilankai, the Southern Lanka or Ceylon.

30. *Moṭupalli.*—This is one of the many ports at the mouth of the Krishna and was a port of great importance under the Kākatīyas, whose king Gaṇapati gave the charter embodied in the Moṭupalli inscription to the sea-going merchants of the place. This charter was renewed by the Reddi chief Anna Vema on another occasion. The so-called kingdom of Moṭupalli at the time of Marco Polo must have been the Kākatīya kingdom. It is marked on the Gazetteer Atlas of India some distance south of the mouth of the river Krishna. The ruler of the so-called kingdom of Moṭupalli, at the time that Marco Polo visited the coast must have been the Kākatīya king Paratāparudra. His

[1] No. 392 of 1914.

grandmother Rudramba, the daughter of king Gaṇapati, not wife, as Marco Polo says, had retired in his favour just a year or two before. This Pratāpa Rudra, the second of the name, ruled from 1292, or a little earlier, to 1328 when he died on his way to Delhi as prisoner of Muhammad bin Tughlak at Mantenna (Mantrakūṭa) on the Godaveri. It was his Brahman minister Kāṭama or Kāṭayya (Kattu of the Muhammadan historians) that became a convert to Islam, and was the chief minister under Sultan Firuz Tughlak (for authority see note above on p. 180). There seems to be little authority for regarding Moṭupalli as the same as Masulipatam, as Mr. Marsden gives Mosul as an alternative name, though it is just possible according to the inscription that Moṭupalli was itself on an island or near an island at the mouth of the Krishna.

31. *Muḍigonḍaśoḻapuram.*—This is otherwise called Gangaigonḍaśoḻapuram. That the two are names of the same place rests upon the following :—

(1) Muḍigonḍaśoḻa and Gangaigonḍaśoḻa are both of them titles of the great Chola Rājēndra I.

(2) Several inscriptions speak of the Pānḍyas crowning themselves in the capital of the Cholas at Muḍigonḍaśoḻapuram in the period of the Pānḍya invasions when the Chola capital was in Gangaigonḍaśoḻapuram.

(3) Reference was made in the text that Kulottunga I issued a royal order from his palace in Muḍigonḍaśoḻapuram; this Kulottunga's capital was Gangaigonḍaśoḻapuram, of course with other alternative capitals.

(4) Rājēndra Chola I himself issued the Tiruvālangāḍu plates from Muḍigonḍaśoḻapuram. These facts seem to establish the identity completely.

32. *Neṭṭūr.*—This is a place just five miles to the west of Iḷaiyānguḍi, and is supposed to mark the western fringe of the 'margossa forest' of this part of the forest country. It must have been a place of great importance in the twelfth century as several battles were fought in this place. It was here that Kulottunga III, the Chola King, defeated Vīra Pānḍya one of the rivals to the Pānḍya throne. Two battles were fought here before that by the Ceylonese general in his campaigns in favour

of this Vīra Pāṇḍya's father. It is about seven or eight miles north by west of Paramaguḍi Railway Station.

33. *Pāśa.*—This is called Pāśipaṭṭaṇam now, and is a port about ten or twelve miles north of Tonḍi and at the end of a great trunk road, passing through Palni, Dinḍigal, Tiruppattūr and Dēvakoṭṭa. It does not appear to have played any very important part except in this particular war.

34. *Pon-Amaravāti.*—This is the head-quarters of the division of Pudukoṭṭa now about twenty to twenty-two miles from Pudukoṭṭa and on a not particularly good road. It was the head-quarters of a division which was called Kaḍalaḍaiyādu-Ilankai-konḍa Śoḻavaḷanāḍu. It was a place of great consequence during the period of Pāṇḍya revival, and is described in the Mahāvamśa as having contained a royal palace of three stories. This is the place to which the Pāṇḍyas advanced whenever they made an effort to march upon the Chola country. There are vestiges of an old high road from Tiruppattūr to Pon-Amarāvati and full reasons are given in the text (104–7) for regarding that the old high road from Madura went by the way of Pon-Amarāvati, perhaps leaving aside the present day road from Pudukoṭṭa to Trichinopoly. According to the Mahāvamśa Pon-Amarāvati was on the northern most frontier of the Pāṇḍya country, the frontier line being marked by Pon-Amarāvati, Kiḻānilai and Maṇamēlkuḍi, a little to the south of the river southern Veḷḷār. This line marks the limit of the Ceylon invasions according to the Mahāvamśa itself.

35. *Ponparappi.*—This is a place in what is now the Salem district, on a tributary of the river South Pennar almost due west of Tirukkovilūr and at a distance of twelve or thirteen miles. It was the head-quarters of a principality under the Cholas, and was the division of the country referred to as Magadai Manḍalam or Magara Kingdom in inscriptions. It is this that had to be overcome before the Hoysalas could enter the Tamil country. Its territory appears to have extended north from that to threaten communications between Tiruvaṇṇāmalai and Krishnagiri.

36. *Puliyūr.*—Puliyūr and Perumparra Puliyūr, which occur in inscriptions are both of them alternative names of Chidam-

baram. The later Cholas as well as the Pāṇḍyas made it the fashion after the coronation of a new ruler in the royal capital Muḍigoṇḍaśoḷapuram, to have themselves anointed again in this place. This is identified for reasons given in the text with the Brahmastpuri of the Muhammadans.

37. *Santanēri.*—This is the form in which the word occurs in the Mahāvamśa account of the Ceylon campaign. It probably refers to what was known as Śāttalēri in Kīḻakkarai Taluk of the Ramnad district (No. 1 of 1912).

38. *Śarmali.*—There are two passes, named by Amir Khusru through which the Muhammadan army had to march before it could come into the country of Vīra Pāṇḍya. Of the two, Tabar is almost certainly Toppūr, but Śārmali is not clear, if we should expect to find it in any locality before the army reached the Kaveri. There seems again to be a mixing up of accounts. If we could take this statement of Amir Khusru to be a general statement as to the character of the route, it would be correct as any army had to pass through the pass of Toppūr once, and, if they marched straight upon Madura or the Pāṇḍya country proper, they would have had to march through another pass, one side of which was constituted by Śirumalai and the other side by Aḻagarmalai on the road to Madura. This is the pass known in modern Indian history, as the Nattam pass.

39. *Śiruvayal.*—There are two places of this name, one of them is a little to the north-west of Kāḷaiyār Kovil almost in the direction of Tiruppattūr; another one much farther north and quite close to the frontier of Pudukoṭṭa. In the description of the campaign of the Ceylonese general Śiruvayal seems to be closely associated with Śemponmāri; where it so occurs it is very likely that the Śiruvayal referred to is the farther one from Kāḷaiyār Kovil. It is very likely that both the places had to be separately conquered by the general.

40. *Śemponmāri.*—This is a place very near Kunnakkuḍi on the road from Kānāḍu Kāttān to Tiruppattūr. This is referred to in an inscription of the early thirteenth century as being in Talaiyūr Nāḍu in the Tiruppattūr Taluk (No. 129 of 1908). This is not very far from the more northern of the two Śiruvayals referred to under another head.

41. *Talabilla.*—This is described in the Mahāvamśa as the port of embarkation of the Ceylon army from the north-west of Ceylon. The army is said to have landed at a place of the same name on the opposite coast of Rāmēśvaram a journey of a night and day. There is, however, no Talabilla traceable on the coast of Rāmēśvaram, but from local enquiry it is found that a port east of Rāmēśvaram at a distance of about four miles was the port of landing in the following period. It is stated that it was there that the Kandyans landed the stone for the re-building of the Rāmēśvaram temple of which some are still left in the harbour at a place on the coast called Puḷiyaḍiśalai. That was probably what the Ceylonese called Talabilla. Other circumstances of this landing make it very probable that that was the place where the landing was effected. It should be noted here that it is about two miles straight from the building called Gandamādana where a pair of foot impressions is pointed out as Rama's feet. It was stated in the text that in all probability it was a Buddhist structure, possibly raised by Lankāpura on the occasion of his invasion.

42. *Tonḍi.*—Tonḍi is a port about twenty miles east from Kāḷaiyār Kovil and is on the road from Madura. This was known to classical Tamils as Śoḷan Tonḍi, and was a great centre of eastern trade including that of the Chinese in the days of classical Tamil literature. It seems to have retained some of its importance even in the centuries of the Muhammadan invasions. This was one of the places that the Ceylon general took after some considerable fighting.

43. *Tiruvēkambama.*—This is the form in which the word occurs in the account of the Ceylon campaigns. There is a place called Tiruvēganpaṭṭu a little to the south-east of Kāḷaiyār Kovil which would suit the details of the narrative.

44. *Tribhuvanam or Tiruppuvanam.*—This is a place in the Tanjore district about three miles or a little more from Kumbakonam and somewhat less than a mile from Tiruviḍaimarudūr. This ought not to be confounded with the Tiruppūvaṇam in the Madura district on the Madura-Ramnad line of the South Indian Railway. It is popularly known by the Tamil name Tiruppuvanam, and is given a fanciful origin that it was so called

because, as the story has it, Varaguṇa Pāṇḍyan, whom the ghost of a Brahmaṇ he put to death was always haunting, turned back there to see whether it was still following him after leaving the shrine at Tiruvaḍaimarudūr. The duplicate of inscriptions in the temple of the Chola emperor, Kulottunga III puts it beyond doubt that the place was called Tribhuvana-Virēśvara from one of his titles Tribhuvanavīra, which has been contracted into Tribhuvanam with its Tamil equivalent Tiruppuvanam; the name at any rate has nothing whatever to do with the story.

45. *Vēdāḷai.*—Toṇitturai, Marakkāyarpaṭṭaṇam, Vēdāḷai are all havens alongside of one another on the southern side of the Pēninsula of Manḍapam and set over against the island of Rāmēśvaram in a well sheltered part of the Gulf of Mannar. Being at the head of the gulf, it was apparently a starting point for the ships and boats getting ready to go for pearl fishing. (See under Battelar).

46. *Vēlanguḍi.*—There are two Vēlanguḍis, one of them about four miles from Kānāḍukāttān. That is not the Vēlanguḍi referred to in the Ceylonese campaign. On the road between Tiruppattūr and Pon-Amarāvati, of which a part over ten to twelve miles is traceable now, there is this village Vēlanguḍi eight miles or so, south of Pon-Amarāvati. The taking of Vēlanguḍi naturally led on to the capture of Pon-Amarāvati as well in the campaign. The road actually branches off a little less than a mile from Tiruppattūr on the Tiruppattūr-Tirumeyyam road, and one has to get to Kanḍavarāyampaṭṭi by a pathway. Then begins the road passing through Vēlanguḍi-Pūvālankurichi and Pon-Amarāvati, and shows even some of the old culverts.

APPENDIX A

(i) *Tirukkōḷūr*

At the back of the sanctum of the Vishṇu temple of the twentieth year Māravarman Sundara Pāṇḍya I.

(See Lecture II, pp. 44–45.)

(1) ஸ்வஸ்தி ஸ்ரீ :—
பூமருவிய திருமடந்தையும் புவிமடந்தையும் புயத்திருப்ப
நாமருவிய கலைம(ட)ந்தையுஞ் செயமடந்தையு நலஞ்சிறப்ப
கோள(ார்)ந்த சினப்புலியுங் கொடி(யு)ஞ் சிலையுங் குலந்தொ(ளி)ப்ப
வாளார்ந்த பொற்கிரிமேல் வரிக்கயல்கள் விளையாட
விருங்கடல் வலையத்தி னிதறம் பெருக
கருங்கலி கடிந்து செங்கோல் நடப்ப
(2) ஒருதுடை நீழ லிருநிலங் குளிர
மூவகைத் தமிழு முறைமையில் விளங்க
நால்வகை வேதமும் நவின வடனவழா [ன்றுடன் வளர]
ஐவ[வ]கை வேள்வியுஞ் செய்வினை யியற்ற
அறுவகைச் சமயமு மழகுடன் திகழ
வேழ்வகைப் பாடலு மியலுடன் பரவ
எண்டிசை யளவுஞ் சக்கரஞ் செல்லக்
கொங்கணர் கலிங்கர் கோ(3)சல மாளுவர்
சிங்களர் தெலிங்கர் சீன(ர்) குச்சரர்
வில்லவர் மகதர் விக்கலர் செம்பியர்
பல்லவர் முதலிய பார்த்திவ ரெல்லா
முறைவிட மருளென் றொருவர்மு னொருவர்
முறை(ெ)கட வத்(தி)–(?) [1]திறைகு (கொ)[2]ணர்த்திறைஞ்ச
இலங்கொளி மணிமுடி இந்திரன் பூட்டிய
பொலங்கதிரா ரமார் பினிற் பொலியப்
பனிமலர்ப்(த்) தாமரைத் திசைமுகன் படைத்த
மனுநெறி தழைப்ப (4)மணிமுடி சூடிப்
பொன்னிசூழ் நாட்டுப் புலியாவண போயகலக்

[1]முறைகடவித்தந் · [2]கொணர்

கண்ணிசூழ் நாட்டுக் கயலாவணை கைவளர
வெஞ்சின விவுளியும் வேழமும் பரப்பித்
தஞ்சையு முறந்தையுஞ் செந்தழல் கொளுத்திக்
காவியு நீலமு நின்று கவினிழக்க(ற்ற)
வாவியு மாறு மணிநீர் நலனழித்துக்
கூடமு மாமதிளுங் கோபுரமு மாடரங்கு
மாடமு மாளிகையும் மண்டபமும் பலவிடித்துக்
தொழுது வந்தடை(5)யா நிருபர்த் [நடுத கையா(2)].[1]
அழுத கண்ணும் [நிராவப பநிக்?][2]
கழுதை கொடுழுது கவடி விச்சச்
செம்பியனைச் சினமிரியப் பொருதுசுரம் புகவோட்டிப்
பைம்பொன் முடிதரித்துப் பாணனுக்குக் கொடுத்தருளிப்
பாடருஞ் சிறப்பிற் பரு(வி)திவான் றேயு
மாடகப் புரிசை யாயிரத் தளியிற்
சேரு வளவ னபிஷேக மண்டபத்து
வீராபிஷேகம் செய்து புகழ் விரித்து
நாடும் பரராச நாமத் தலைப்பிடுங்(6)கி
மூடுந் தருகண் மத(சர)யானை மேல்கொண்டு
நீராழி வைய முழுதும் பொதுவொழித்த
கூராழியுஞ் செய்ய தோளுமே கொண்டு
[பொ-ஜெய்யப்படர்த(?)][3] வருமறைசே ரந்தணர் வாழ்
தெய்வப் புலியூர்த் திருவெல்லை யிற்புக்கு
பொன்னம் பலம்பொலிய [ஆடுவா முலைவ(மை)][4]யொடு
மன்னும் திருமேனி கண்டு மனம்களித்து
கோலமலர் மேலயனும் குளிர் துழாய்
மாலும்(7) அறியா மலர்ச்சேவடி வணங்கி
வாங்குசிறை யன்னர் துயிலொழிய [உண்டெழப்பு?][5]
[மழுங்கமல வாவிகும்][6] பொன்னமரர் பதியு
ளொத்து(க்)கனந் தங்குமக மேருவைக் கொணர்ந்து
வைத்தனைய சோதிமணி மண்டபத் திருந்து
சோலைமலி பழநற் கொண்டு தான்மு(ச்சோறுடு முன்னிழ)ந்த
மாலைமுடியுந் தான(மவன்?) பு(4)கவென்(8) றழைப்ப
[மாந்தலை குலைய வாழ்கா(?)]க[7] கப்புறத்து(ப்)
போன வளவனுரிமை யொடுந்தான் புகுந்து
பெற்றபுதல்வனை நின்பே (ரெ) றென்று முன்காட்டி

1 திருபர்தந்தொகையர்   2 நீருவிப் பணிக்கக்(?)   3 போர்செயப்படாத ?
4 ஆடுவானுமையோடு.   5 வண்டெழுப்பும்.   6 பூங்கமலவாவிசூழ்.
7 மானந்தலைகுலையவாழ் நகர்

வெற்றியரியணைக் கீழ்வீழ்ந்து தொழுதிரப்பக்
காஞேடிமுன்னிழந்த வெம்மையெலாம் கையகலத்
தாஞேதகம்பண்ணி தண்டர்(9)ர் முடியுட்டெ(சூட்டி)[1]
விட்டபுகலிடந்தனமரா வேளைக்குத்தரிய[2](?)
மிட்டபடிக்கென்றுமிது பிடிபாடாகவெனப்
பொங்குதரை ஞாலத்துப் பூபாலர் கோவிளங்குஞ்
செங்கயல் கொண்டிநறுந் திருமுகமும் பண்டி(மு)ழந்த
சோழபதி யென்னு நாம்மும் தொன்னகரும்
மீள வழங்கி விடைகொடுத்து விட்டரு(10)ளி
ஒதக் கடற்பாரில் வேந்தர் கிளைக்குற்ற
வேதங் ளதிர்க்குங் (தவிர்க்குங்) கடவுளிவ னென்றுஎண்ணிக்
களையுற் [றிடையாதார தண்ட விடையின(?)][3]
கிளையுற் றனமுழுதுங் கேட்டருளென் றேத்தி
வணங்கும் வடகொங்கன் சிறைமீள வண்டின்
கணங்கொ(ள்) திருத்தோள் மாலைகழித் [தெலவழ(ங்)கி][4]
[அயபின் மற்ஞெருரு நாபற்றர்(?)][5]
முழங்கு முரச(க) கடற்றுனை முன்புகுந்தே
கண்கள்போலுங் கிளைதழைத்த தென்றனைக் கீழ்த்
தென்கொங்கன் வந்திட்ட தெண்டனுக்குமின்(?) (மீன்)பொங்கச்
சாத்திய வாபரணந் தக்கதென வழங்கி
ஆர்த்த பெருநண்பின் சிரையு மிட்டுத்
திருமாலும் நான்முகனும் சேவிப்ப செங்கட்
கருமால் களிற்றி(12)ல் வருமுக்கட் கடவுளென
மாட மதுரையிற்றும் போந்து பவனியிலே
கூடவிரு கொங்கரையுங் கும்பீடுகொண்டு அவர்தந்த
தொல்லைப் புவிக்குப் பிணங்காமற் ருன்சொன்ன
எல்லைக் கண்சிற்ப இசைவுதிமேற் பக்கொண்டு
இவ்வாறு செய்யா தொழியில் யமனுக்கு
வெவ்வேல் விருந்[து கருது][6]ம்மையென விட்டருள
முன்ன நமக்கு முடிவழங்குஞ் சேவடிச்[கழ
ன்னம்வழிடுவ[7] மென்ஞது பின்னொருநாள்
காவு லெனதுபொன் நாடெனுங் களியா(ல்)
ஏவல் எதிர்கொள்ளா திரைமறுத்த சென்னிவிடுத்த
தூசியும் பேரணியு மொக்கச் சுருண்டொதுங்க
வாசியும் வாரணமுந் [தெழுமதற்கு வக்][8] (தேருமடற்கருவிக்)

[1] தண்டார்முடியூட்டி(சூட்டி).
[2] தன் அமர் ஆவேளைக்குத் தரியம்.
[3] றிடையா நார்தண்ட.விடையின் (?)
[4] தளஸ்வழங்கி.
[5] ஆயபின் மற்ஞெருநாள் பற்றூர்.
[6] விருந்தாக்குதுமும்மையென
[7] கீழ்இன்னம் வழிபடுவ.
[8] தேருமதற்குடைக்.

காலாளும் வெட்டுண்ணக் கண்டுபயங் கைக்கொ(14)ண்டு
வேலா வலயத்து வீழ்ந்தவன்போய் மெய்யொடுங்க
அம்பருந்து ம்மாகத்து தடல்[ம அக்களத்தில்][1]
யானையின் வெண்மருப்புங் கையுங் குறைத்துளங்கள்
மீனவர்க்குப் பாகுடமா மென்றுதம் வீரர்கொள
மாகமு கடுதடவி மழை தடுக்குங்
காகநெடும் பந்தர்க் கவந்தத்தி னூடலுங்
கூகையின்பாடலுங் கண்டுங் கேட்டுங் களித்திட்
டேலக்கரு(15)ங் கூந்தல் வேள்வியிற்றுச் செய்வாய்ப்பொற்
சூலக்கை வல்லிபலி கொள்ள வாழ்த்தி
வென்று பகையின் மிலைகயொழிய வேக்தலறக்
கொன்றும் சினந்தணியாக் கொற்றநெடு வாளூரி
செங்குருதி நாரற் றெளிசெய்து தெஃபுலத்து
வெண்கவடி வித்தி வீரமுழு தெடுத்துப்
பாடும் பரணி[தாரி][2] வேந்தர் கேட்பிக்க
ஆடும் திருமஞ் சனநீரில் மண்குளிர
வாங்கவன(16) கட்டணத்துக் கற்புட்ட மக்காண
வோங்கு முரிமைக் குழாம்மொருங்குக் கைக்கொண்டு
மூரிமணிப் பட்ட(ங்) கட்டி (ரமுடி)சூட்டி
மார்பில்அணைத்து வளவன்முதற் தேதி(வி) யெனப்
பேர்கொடுத்த வஞ்சிமுத லாயபெய் வளையார்
யோ(பொ)ங்கு புனற்கும்ப முதலாப் புலவர்புகழ்
மங்கலங்க ளெட்டும் மணிக்கைத் தலத்தேந்திக்
கொடிகொண்ட நெற்றிட்டி(ற்ற) கோபுரஞ்(17) சூழ்
முடிகொண்ட சோழபுரி மண்டபத்துப் புக்குத்
திசைதொறுஞ் செம்பொற் செ(ய்)ற்ற(த்த)ம்ப நாட்டி
விஜையாபிஷேகம் பண்ணி யருள் செய்து
வாகைக் கதிர்வேல் வடவேந்தர் தம்பாத
மேற்ற தலையலைய வீரக் கழலணிந்து
விளங்கியல் மணியணி வீரஸிம்ஹாஸந(த்)து
வனங்கெழு கவரி யிருமருங் கசைப்ப
கடலென முழங்குங் கவிகலி யா(18)னை
வடகுல வேந்தர்த மணிப்புயம் பிரியா
திலகுகுழை அரிவையர் தொழுதுகின் றேத்து
முலக முழுதுடையா ரோடும்வீற் றிருந்தருளி(ய)
சீகோமாறபன்மரான த்ரி புவனசக்கரவ(ர்)த்திகள் சோணாடு கொண்டுமுடி

[1] மறவாககளத்தில். [2] தாரி.

கொண்ட சோழபுரத்து வீராஹிஷேகம் பண்ணி யருளிய ஸ்ரீஸுந்தரபாண்டிய தேவர்(க்)கு யாண்டு உய்-ாது (நாள் ?) கூயிளுல் மதுரோதய வளநாட்டு மாடக் குளக்கீழ்மதுரைக் கோயில்பள்ளியறை(க்) கூடத்துப் பள்ளிப்பீடம் மழவராயனில் எழுந்தருளி யிருந்து.[1]

TRANSLATION

MAY PROSPERITY EVER ATTEND,

While the goddess of wealth whose habitation is the lotus, and the goddess of earth rest upon his arms; while the goddess of learning whose habitation is the tongue, and the goddess of victory flourish in all their glory; while the destructive tiger and the evil-inflicting bow become alike in their decadence; while the fishes twain with lines of beauty play upon the brilliant gold mountain (Mēru); while good (dharma) increases in this sea-girt earth; while righteous rule prevails beating down the evil-producing dark-age (Kali); while the great earth is cool under the shadow of a single umbrella; while the three kinds[2] of Tamil flourish in their order; while the four Vedas continue to be chanted in the accustomed manner; while the five sacrifices are conducted according to the authorized rites; while the six systems of religion prosper in all their beauty; while the seven kinds of music flourished each in its mode; while the wheel of authority rolls unobstructed to the eight cardinal points; while the Konkaṇas, Kalingas, Kosalas, Māḷavas, the Chēras (Villavar), Māgadhas, Chāḷukyas (Vikkalar ?), Cholas (Śembiyar), Pallavas and all others, bringing each their tribute make their obeisance, pressing each party their petition, one before the other, where they are to live; while the garland, which Indra of the dazzling crown had put on his neck, shone over his breast; he had himself crowned in order that the path of Manu created by the cool-lotus-seated Brahma may prosper on earth. Getting

[1] The text of this inscription is taken from that published on pages 346–50 of vol. xii. of the Sen Tamil by Pundit A. M. Saṭāgoparāmānujāchāriar by the courteous permission of the Madura Tamil Sangam.

[2] 1. Iyal—natural or spoken or prose,
2. Iśai—verse and
3. Nāṭakam—dramatic—conventional, containing both the above with other distinguishing characteristics.

the land of the Kāvēri (Ponni) rid of the authority under the tiger-seal, and making the orders under the fish-emblem of the land of Kumāri (Kanni) prevail, he spread round his army of angry steeds and elephants, and gave over to red-fire the cities of Tanjore (Tanjai) and Uraiyūr (Uṛandai). While umbrellas and canopies spread their red and blue, he spoiled the beauty of the blue-water in tanks and streams, destroyed the country, ramparts, towers, and dining halls, terraces, and pavilions ; while the eyes of the ladies of those that would not render to him respectful submission filled with water, he had their territory ploughed with asses, and sown with cowries. He fought against the angry Chola till he lost his anger, and turned him into the desert for shelter. He then assumed the (Chola's) crown and made gifts to his minstrels. He then spread his fame by celebrating the anointment of heroes in 'the coronation hall of thousand pillars', of the hostile Chola, the golden walls of which reached up to the skies and defied being praised in song. Pulling out by the head the name 'other-king' (pararāja) that existed, he got rid of the community of property in the earth by mounting his war-elephant, of cruel look, which was in the habit of shutting its eyes, carrying with him his own broad shoulders and sharp weapons (described above). Passing the boundaries of the holy Puliyūr (Chidambaram), the residence of the Veda-chanting Brahmans against whom war is unthinkable, he delighted his eyes by the sight of the radiant form of the god with Umā in the 'golden-hall', refulgent with the divine dance. Laying his head in worship at the God's glorious feet, unknown alike to the beautiful lotus-seated Brahma and of the cool-basil-garlanded Vishṇu, he seated himself in the pavilion (maṇḍapa) effulgent like the golden Mēru in the city of the gods, near the beautiful lotus-pond where the sleeping swans are awakened by the humming of the bees. There then entered the Chola king, on the assurance being given that he would be restored the crown, the garland and the fertile kingdom he had lost—the Chola king who abandoned not long before both his honour and his capital alike on the field of battle. Pushing forward his own son and stating that he was the gift of the Pāṇḍya, the Chola threw himself at the foot of the throne of the victor, a suppliant for favour. He (the Victorious Pāṇḍya) then made a gift by pouring of water which, putting an end to all the heat in the hand of the Chola brought on by his wandering in the jungles, crowned him and offered to make over his kingdom as soon as the war in which he was engaged should be over. In execution of this, his promise, the ruler of all the rulers of the earth, issued a royal rescript with the royal sign-manual of the fishes, conferring, at the same time, the title Śoḻapati that he had lost before and the old city upon him again and dismissed him with pleasure. Among the kings who oppressed with the obstruction caused by their own kinsfolk, supplicated him as the god who alone could remove the afflictions to which the monarchs of this earth were liable, was the king of North Kongu who humbly petitioned for a hearing of all the harm that his own relatives had done him. Giving him a patient hearing, he sent him back to his quarters in the evening, presenting him with a garland which he had on, the sweet smell of which was the attraction to swarms of bees. Sometime after this, one day there came to him at the head of a vast army, whose great drums sounded like the ocean itself, the king of South (*ten*) Kongu. He prostrated in front of the throne saying 'all those near and dear to me are quite well (by your royal favour)'. The great king thought it fitting to present him some of the brilliant jewels that he himself had put on, and appointed him suitable apartments as a mark of great friendship. Like the three-eyed Śiva on the back of an elephant receiving the worship of Vishṇu (Tirumāl) and the four-faced Brahma (Nānmukan), he made a state entry (pavani) with the two kings of Kongu paying him homage. Not agreeing to their proposal for cession of territory, he imposed his own terms under penalty of death in case they should not be accepted, and dismissed them (to their kingdoms). Without considering that the right course was for him to continue to worship the feet of him that bestowed the crown on him the Chola, on a later occasion, declined to render the duty and the tribute due to his suzerain, under the delusion that his own fertile country was his security. The smaller and the larger divisions of the army sent by the Chola were rolled back upon themselves, the horses, elephants and chariots, and their complement of men were cut down till, overcome with fear, the Chola monarch rolled on the sea-girt earth shaking with fear. In that field of battle filled with warriors whose broad chests carried the arrows shot into them, the warriors of the Pāṇḍya ruler cut off the tusks and trunks of war-elephants to make tributes of them to their sovereign; the tuncated bodies of warriors who fell in battle danced under the canopy formed by crows (hovering over the field) which was high enough to reach the sky and seemed designed to shelter the field from rain; and all over the field was heard the 'song' of vultures; pleased with the sight and sound thus presented he caused the praise of the goddess of the golden trident (Durga in her aspect as the goddess of the battle-field) with sweet-scented hair and red lips to be sung to invoke acceptance of the offering. Having drawn his sword and killed vast multitudes so that enemy kings cried in distress, his anger did not subside; he irrigated in consequence the land of enemy kings with red-blood and sowed them with cowries, thus exhibiting his valour in full. Enemy kings thus making him hear the war songs (*paraṇi*) of poets, the earth cooling with the water of his bath, he took in the attack the whole body of the enemy's women folk. He then proceeded to Muḍigonḍaśoḻapuram, whose tall gates of entry (*gōpuras*) carried flags on their tops, preceded by the chief queen of the vanquished Chola and other distinguished ladies of the palace carrying 'the eight auspicious objects'[1] beginning with the water jar. He then anointed himself hero, having planted pillars of victory in all directions. Putting on then the 'anklet of heroes,' the wearing of which made the chains on the ankles of the victorious weapon-wielding northern monarchs stir, he took his seat upon the jewel-bedecked throne of heroes, while the fly-whisks gently wafted on either side of him. Seated along with him was the

[1] These are (1) Fly-whisk. (2) full water pot. (3) mirror. (4) Elephant goad. (5) Drum. (6) lamp. (7) banner. (8) pair of fishes.

Slightly different however are :—
mṛgarājō vṛshō nāgaḥ kalaśō vyajanam tathā | vaijayantī tathā bhēri dīpa ityashṭamangaḷam || —lion, bull, elephant, water-pot, flywhisk, banner, drum and lamp.

queen Ulagamuḻuduḍaiyāḷ (the queen of the world) deferentially praised by the most esteemed ladies of the northern monarchs whose elephant hordes trumpeted like the ocean itself.

In the twentieth year of Śrī Kō Māravarman Tribhuvanachakravarti Śrī Sundara Pāṇḍya Dēva who anointed himself a hero at Muḍigoṇḍaśoḻapuram after taking the Chola country—on the hundred thousand thirtieth (miswritten figure for 130) day seated in the couch Māḻavarayan in the hall in front of the bed-chamber, in the palace to the east of Māḍakkuḷam at Madura in Madurōdaya vaḷanāḍu—issued a royal order.

(ii) *Praśasti* (*Meykkīrti*) *of Jāṭāvarman Sundarapāṇḍya I* (*Text of Mr. T. A. Gopinatha Rao, M.A.*)

(See Lecture II, pp. 46–54.)

பூமலர் வளர்திகழ் திருமகள் புகழாகம் புணர்ந்திருப்ப
நாமலர் வளர்கலை வஞ்சி நலமிகுமா மணத்துறையச்
சிமையவரைத் திறன்மடந்தை திருத்தோளின் மிசைவாழ
விமையவர் கோனன்றிட்ட வெழிலாரங் கழுத்திலங்கப்
பகீரதிபோல் துய்யபுகட் படர்வல்லி கொழுந்தொட்டத்
திகிரிவரைக் கப்புறத்துச் செழுந்திகிரி சென்றுலவத்
தண்டா(ர்ம)......ணிக்கவிதை(க)தெண்டிரைசூழ் பார்நிழற்ற
வெங்கோபக் கலிகடிந்து செங்கோலெண் டிசைநடப்பச்
செம்முரசின் முகில்முழங்கச் சிலையகன்று விசும்படைய
திறற்புலிபோய் வனமடையக்
கயலிரண்டு நெடுஞ்சிகரக் கனவரையில் விளையாட
ஒருமைமனத் திருபிறப்பின் முத்தீயின் நால்வேதத்
தருமறையோ ரைவ்வேள்வி யாறங்க முடன்சிறப்ப
வருந்தமிழு மாரியமு மறுசமயத் தறநெறியுந்
திருந்துகின்ற மனுநெறியுந் திரம்பாது தழைத்தோங்கக்
குச்சரரு மாரியரும் கோசலருங் கொங்கணரும்
வச்சிரருங் காசியமோத் தாரு...மனருஞ் சோனகரும
வந்தியரு முதலாய விருநிலமா முடிவேந்த ரிறைஞ்சிநின்று திறைகாட்ட
(வ)டிநெடு வாளும் வயப்பெரும் புரவியுந்
தொடிநெடுந் தோளுமே துணையெனச் சென்று
சேரனுந் தானையுஞ் செருக்களத் தொழிய
வார சும்புலரா மலைநாடு நூறிப்
பருமா மரபிற் பொருதிறல் மிக்க
சென்னியைத் திரைகொண்டு திண்டோள் வலியிற

பொன்னி நாட்டுப் போசலத் தரைசர்
கலைப்புரி......டைத்துப் பொங்கு வீரப் புரவியுஞ்
செருவிரல் ஆண்மை சிங்கணன் முதலாய
தண்டத் தலைவருந் தானையு மழியடத்
துண்டித் தளவில் சோரி வெங்கலிப்
பெரும்பிணக் குன்ற மிருங்கன் னிறைத்துப்
டருந்துங் காகமும் பாறுங்........
அமரந்து மகிழ்ந்தால் அமர்கள மெடுப்பக்
கம்......னையுங்கனைப் புரவியுஞ் செம்பொற்
குவையுந் திகழ்கதிர் மணியு மடந்தைய
ராரம ரர்பு முடன் கவர்ந்தருளி
முதுகிடு போசளன் றன்னொடு முனையுமது
தவறென்னை பொற் பொற்றி நட......து
போனுட் பகையாய் நின்ற
சேரனைக் கொன்று சின......னிந் தருளிப்
நண்ணுதல் பிறரு லெண்ணுதற் கரிய
கண்ணனூர்க் கொப்பத்தைக் கைக்கொண்டருளிப்
பொன்னி சூழ் செல்வப் புனனாட்டைக்
கன்னி நாடெனக் காத்தருள் செய்யப்
பெருவரை யானிற் பின்னகருக் காக்கிய
கருநட ராஜனைக் களிறு திறைகொண்டு
துலங்கொளி மணியுஞ் சூழ் வேழமு
மிலங்கை காவலனை யிறைகொண் டருளி
வருதிறை மறுத்தங் கவனைப் பிடித்துக்
கருமுகில் நிகளங் காலிற் சேர்த்து
வேந்தர் கண்டறியா விற்றிண் புரிசைச்
செந்த மங்கலச் செழும்பதி முற்றிப்
பல்லவ னடுங்கப் பலபோ ராடி
நெல்விளை நாடு நெடும்பெரும் பொன்னும்
பருமை யானையும் பரியு முதலிய
வரசுரிமை கைக்கொண் டரசவற் களித்துத்
தில்லையம் பலத்துத் திருநடம் பயிலுந்
தொல்லை யிறைவர் தனைக்கழல் வழங்கிக்
குளிர்பொழில் புடைசூழ் கோழிமான் காளி
செறி வேம்பி னணிமலர் கலந்த
தொங்கல் வாகைத் தொடைகள் சூட்டித்
திங்களுயர் மரபு திகழவன் திருந்த
தன்............சையா னன்னிலை விசையம்
பிண்ண........ன்னக்கலை தேரின்மொழிப் பாவலர்
மண்ணின் மேலூழி வாழ்கென வாழ்த்தக்

கண்டவர் மனமுங் கண்ணுங் களிப்ப
வெண்டி ரைமகர வேலையி னெடுவரை
யாயிரம் பணைப்பணைத்த நந்தன் மீமிசைப்
பாயல் கொள்ளும் பரமஞ்.........கத்
தொருபெருங் கடவு ளுவந்தினி துறையு
மீபெருங் காவிரி யிடைநிலத் திலங்குந்
திருவரங் கம்பெருஞ் செல்வம் சிறப்ப
பன்முறை மணிதுலா பார மேறிப்
பொன்மலை யென்னப் பொலிந்து தோன்றவும்
பொன்மேய்ந் தருளிய செம்பொற் கோயிலுள்
வளர் திகழ்மா ளுதய வெற்பனைத்
திருவளர் குலமணி சிங்கா சனமிசை
ம.........த கலையென மகிழ்ந்தினி தெறித்தி
நகரோ தயமெனச் செழுங்கதிர் சொரியும்
கனகமா முடி கவின்பெறச் சூடிப்
பாராள வேந்த ருரிமைய ரிவைய
ரிருமருங்கு நின்று விரிபெருங் கவரியின்
மந்த வாடையு மலையத் தென்றலு
மந்தளிர்க் கரங்கொண் டசைய வீச
வொருபொழுதும் விடா துடனிருந்து மகிழும்
திருமக ளென்னத் திருத்தோள் மேவி
யொத்த முடிசூடி யுயர்பே ராணை
திக்கெட்டும் நடப்ப செழுந்தவஞ் செய்த
விவன்போ லுலகிலே வீரன் பலபத்திர மதிமுகத்தவணிமாம
களிலகு கொடி காதல்மு சூழ்ந்து நின்றேத்து முலகு முழுதுமு
டையாளோடும் வீற்றிருந்தருளிய ஸ்ரீகோச்சடைப்ப
ன்மரான திரிபுவனச் சக்கரவத்திகள் ஸ்ரீசுந்தரபாண்
டிய தேவற்கு யாண்டு.

(Taken with the courteous permission of the Madura Tamil Śangam from the Śen Tamil, vol. iv, pp. 514–16).

TRANSLATION

While the flower-born goddess (Lakshmī or Prosperity) resided in his glorious chest, while the Lady Learning who flourishes in the tongue, took her residence in his mind, while Lady Valour whose seat is the high mountain found her place on his broad shoulders, while the garland placed by Indra upon the Pāṇḍya's neck long ago is still beautifying his neck; while his fame, pure as the Bhagīrathi (Ganges), keeps to him like a creeper twining round his body, while the wheel of his ever-growing authority rolled beyond the mountain Chakravāḷa (the legendary mountain round the earth), while the cool pearl-like umbrella of his,[1] cast its shadow over the sea-surrounded earth; while his righteous authority prevailed in all directions beating down the angry Kali (the dark age); while the big well-girt drum sounded like the clouds, while *the bow flew to the skies, while the valiant tiger fled to the forests* and while *the twin-fish played high upon the big Mountain.*[2]

While the Brahmaṇas, of a single mind, of two-births, of the three fires, of the four Vedas, of the five sacrifices and of the six auxiliary sciences, flourished, while the invaluable learning in Tamil and Sanskrit, the righteous path of the six systems of religion, and the path of rectitude set up by Manu flourished without swerving in the least; the *Gūrjaras*, the *Āryas*, the *Kosalas*, the *Konkaṇas*, the *Vajras*, the *Kāśis*—the *Śonagas*, the *Avantis* and other kings of the great earth presented their tributes after making profound obeisance. The Pāṇḍya then marched forth with his long sharp sword, his strong big horse and his amuletted long arms, as his only companions. Leaving the Chēra and his army dead on the field of battle, he destroyed the Malai Nāḍu (mountain country) or Malabar, where the earth never dries up.[3] He then compelled the payment of tribute by the Chola who came of a great dynasty of rulers and possessed great fighting strength. He then attacked, as an act of his own strength, the Hoysalas in the Chola country. Breaking through their beautiful citadel, and destroying their cavalry of rising strength and valiant generals, like Singaṇa with their army, he filled the battlefield with hills of dead bodies with gurgling floods of blood, and made kites, crows, vultures and other birds of prey celebrate the battle by their noisy rejoicing. He captured

[1] Reading the text தண்டாரமணிக்கவிகை.

[2] In this passage the bow stands for the Chēra and implies his death; the tiger stands for the Chola and indicates his defeat and flight; and the twin-fish stands for the Pāṇḍya and exhibits the prevalence of his authority up to the Himalayas.

[3] Reading the last word of line 22: நாறி instead of நாற.

the enemy's rutting elephants, neighing horses, heaps of gold and jewels, and innumerable women then and there ; but disisted from pursuing the fleeing Hoysala in the conviction that it was unfair to do so. Putting to death the Chēra, who, while pretending to conduct himself towards him with an affection exceeding that of a mother, was actually inimical at heart and proved the traitor, he captured Kaṇṇanur-Koppam, merely approaching which would be impossible to conceive of for others, and brought the Chola country of Ponni (Kāvēri) as much under his protection as the land of Kanni (Kanyākumārī). He then put under a tribute of elephants the Hoysala (Karunaḍa Rāja) who fled for protection to his city protected by hill-like elephants [1] and accepted graciously the tribute of jewels and elephants from the king of Īḷam (Ceylon). Declining the tribute similarly sent by the Pallava chieftain, he captured him and, putting him in chains, laid siege to the flourishing city of Śēnda-mangalam. Fighting many a battle round the place which struck terror into the heart of the Pallava, he took possession of his fertile country, his reserves of gold, big elephants, horses and other items of royal wealth, and then restored the Pallava to his kingdom. He then entered the great temple at Chidambaram where, having worshipped at the feet of the dancing Śiva of immeasurable antiquity, he wore the garland of victory (வாகை) along with garlands of margossa brought from the groves round the temple of Kāḷi in Uṛaiyūr, while learned poets in sweet words sang the praises of the victorious king who adorned the royal family descended from the moon, and wished for his long life and prosperity. That great 'Self-Luminous One' who habitually lies in sleep upon the thousand-headed Ananta, like a big hill in the midst of the sea of high white waves, the home of the monster crocodile (makara), to the delight alike of the mind and eyes of those that saw Him, lies, in his great mercy, in the island of the great Kāvēri, Śrīrangam, as the sole God of this sea-girt earth. There, that this Śrīrangam may prosper in great wealth, he ascended the scales many times against jewels and pearls showing himself like a golden hill. In that gold-roofed

[1] Reading l. 44 பருவரை யாளிற் பின்னை கருக்கசக்கிய.

temple, on a luxuriously jewelled throne, shining like the growing dawn upon the Eastern hill, he wore the gold crown 'Nagarōdaya', shedding glorious light like the full-grown moon.[1] Alongside of him was seated Ulagamuḻuduḍaiyāḷ, who was attended on either side by the queens of other kings, wafting with the chauris (fly-whisks) the gentle breeze of the spring and the southern breeze of Malaya hill at once, while others of beautiful moon-like face and great affection sang her praise: 'Like the goddess Lakshmi in never separating, wearing a crown exactly like her husband and exercising similar authority to the points of the compass, who is there on earth like this great warrior unless it be Balabhadra.'[2]

In this wise seated with the queen Ulagamuḻuḍaiyāḷ, Śrī Kochchaḍaipanmar (Jaṭāvarman) Tribhuvanachchakravartigaḷ Śrī Sundara Pāṇḍya Dēva, in his year, etc.

(iii) *Inscription of the fourth year of Kō. Māravarman Kulaśēkhara Dēva*[3] *in Aḻvār Tirunagari.*

(See Lecture II, pp. 54–59.)

ஸ்வஸ்தி ஸ்ரீ

திருவ.. ......பாலலதுற் திருமகள் புணரவும்
சார்போல் கூ(2)ந்தற் கலைமகள் கலப்பவும்
பாரமக[4]மனத்தப் பாங்குட னிருப்பவுஞ்
செங்கோ னடப்பவும் வெண்குடை நிழ(3)ற்றவுங்
கருங்கலி முருங்கவும் பெரும்புகழ் விளங்கவுங்
கானஞ் செம்பியன் கடும்புலி யாளவு
மீனம் பொனவரை மீமிசை யொங்கவு
முத்தமிட பனுவலு நான்மறை முழுவது
மெத்த[5] வைச் சமயமு மினிதுடன் விளங்கவுஞ்
சிங்களங் கலிங்கக் தெலிங்கஞ் செதிபம்
கொங்கணங் குக்கிரங் கோசலங் குச(6)சர
முறைமை யிலாளு முதலில வேந்தர
திறை காட்டிச் செவடி வணங்க
மன்னர மாதர பொன்னணி கவரியு

1 Reading the first part of line 77. மதிநிறைந்த.

2 The construction of this part is very obscure.

3 Taken by courteous permission of the Madura Tamil Sangam from the Sen Tamil, ix. 357–58.

4 பார்மகள்மன.

5 மெய்த்த.

ளி(7)ருப்புடை மருகினு மொருபடி யிரட்டப்
பழுதரு சிறப்பிற் "செழுவை காவலன்"
வீர ஸிம்ஹாஸநதொராங் கிருத்தி
யாரு(8)ம் வெம்புமணி யிதட புடையிற
தாருஞ் சூழ்ந்த தடமணி மகுடம்
பன்னூ றாழி தொன்னிலம் புரந்து
வாழ்(9)கென சூட்ட மகிழ்ந்துட னஞ்சூடி
அலரமகரு முதலா வரிவை யாபா.
"வுலகமுழுதுடையா" ரொடுவீற்றிருந்தரு(10)ளிய
கொமுதற ஸ்ரீ கோட்டாற பனமரான திரிபுவனச்ச
க்ரவரத்திகள் ஸ்ரீ குலசெகர தெவற்கு யாண்டுநாலு

காளிரு நூற்றெட்டினால் செயங்கொண்ட சொழபுரத்தில் தெற்கில் தொப்பிற கொயிற்பள்ளியறைக் கூடத்துப்பள்ளிப்பீடம் காலிங்கராயனில் எழுந்தருளியிருந்து :—

TRANSLATION

MAY PROSPERITY ATTEND,

. . . While the goddess of prosperity was in his embraces, while the dark-haired goddess of learning was in intimate contact with him, while the goddess of the earth took her happy residence in his mind, his righteous authority prevailed and his white umbrella cast its protecting shadow, in order that the evil-working dark Kali may be crushed and that his great fame may shed its glorious lustre, in order that the tiger-banner of the Chola may have the rule of the forests and the fish emblem of the Pāṇḍya may be emblazoned on the heights of the golden hill (Mēru). In his reign prospered alike the three kinds of Tamil in verse, all the four branches of the esoteric Veda and the five true [1] systems of religion. All the kings of this old earth who had a character for righteous rule, from Simhaḷa (Ceylon), Kalinga, Telinga, Chēdi (Bundlekand), Konkaṇa, Kukkira (Kukkuṭa), Kosala and Kuchchara (Gurjara), presented their tribute and prostrated at his feet. While the queens of other kings, with gold-chased fly-whisks, were fanning uniformly on either side, the Queen Ulagamuḷududaiyāḷ was seated on one side of the king of

[1] The usual number is six, but the adjuuct true seems to make an alteration which is not clear.

Śeḻuvai [1] upon the throne of heroes. She was there crowned with the glorious crown of jewels, beautified with garlands of flowers varied with the leaves of ātti (ār, bauhinia racemosa) and neem, while the women led by the flowerborn goddess (Lakshmī) sang the blessing that both the king and queen may live for many hundred years protecting this long-lived earth. While being thus seated on the throne with the queen, the first among kings, Śrī Kō Māravarman Tribhuvanachchakravartigaḷ Śrī Kulaiśēkhara Dēva, in his fourth year, on the 208th day, being seated on the throne Kālingarāyan, in the hall in front of the bed chamber, *in the palace in the garden on the south side of Jayangondaśoḻapuram*.

(*iv*) *Note on the Muhammadan Conquest of the South.*

The two inscriptions of which the text and translation follow are records relating to Muhammadan rule and are dated in the Hijira years 761 and 771 respectively. The first of them at Tirukkolakkuḍi in the Tiruppattūr Taluk of the Ramnad District is noticed by the Epigraphist in his Report, and as there is no actual indication of the era of the date 761 it is referred to the Kollam era of Malabar beginning with the year A.D. 825. On this basis the two inscriptions would be respectively of dates A.D. 1586 and 1596. This would be a period with which the substance of the inscriptions would hardly agree. That was the period of the Vijayanagar emperor Venkaṭapati Rāya in whose time the authority of Vijayanagar was acknowledged in the south, and there were no powerful Muhammadan potentates whose authority could have been acknowledged in the same region. But the matter is now put beyond a doubt that these refer to the Hijira era by the name of the month in the second inscription which apparently was not known to the epigraphist at the time that that report was issued. It refers to the year 771 of a Rājādhirāja Sakalanṛpakulakkōn. This gives us no lead except the suspicion that that the 771 might be a Hijira date.

1 'Seḻuvai Kāvalan' is unusual. Literally it would mean king of Śeḻuvai, a city, country or something like it. Śeḻiyan is a common name for Pāṇḍya. Though from the same root Śeḻuvai is unusual, perhaps not altogether un-understandable.

But the month given Iravilādān could be none other than the Tamil version of Rabi-ul-Sāni, or Dhāni as the S and the DH interchanged. That the Hijira date was in use here and that these do refer to the Muhammadan times we have evidence of in other records of which, as was pointed out above, one of them refers to the ninth year of Mahārājā Mahamadi Surattān, at Panaiyūr in the Tirumeyyam Taluk in the Pudukoṭṭa State. Another record at Rāngiyam (Rājaśingamangalam) in the same Taluk of the State refers itself to the year 732 of Ādi Surattān (Sultan). All these taken together leave no doubt that the era referred to is the Hijira, and the time to which the records refer is the period of the Muhammadan occupation of the south.

Coming to the subject-matter of the two inscriptions, the records are in quaint Tamil, and the literal rendering may not make the sense clear. The first record relates to an expedition sent by the Muhammadan Sultan of the south under a number of generals to destroy the Kaḷḷar settlement of Śūraikkuḍi the place known as Vanniyan Śūraikkuḍi, which had sometime before been taken possession of by a family of Kaḷḷars. This place later on became the head-quarters of the chiefs, who called themselves Araiyan Viśayālaya Dēva, as a general title with distinguishing names. The expedition was sent apparently to destroy this village which must have become very troublesome to its neighbours. The people most troubled apparently were those of Viraiyāchilai about four miles west by south of Tirumeyyam, and Tirukkoṭṭiyur, six miles south of Tirupputtūr. The inhabitants of these towns and the villages dependent on them were placed by the Muhammadan general (encamped at Māttūrkoḷam) under the protection of the inhabitants of Pon-Amarāvati, a place of considerable importance in the neighbourhood immediately to the west, and on the high road from Trichinopoly to Madura, an arrangement which probably involved what is called Pāḍikkāval (guardianship of the rural tract).

The second record relates to the territory round Dēvakoṭṭa, which apparently was under Muhammadan Government for sometime. Apart from the mere embellishments of the record and the somewhat quaint oaths and assurances, apparently popular in the locality, the document merely records that the citizens of Kanḍadēvi, which was a head township of the country round, agreed among themselves :

(1) to provide the usual service by way of men required for personal attendance upon the governor, those required for carrying on his administrative work and those required for conducting the administration in a lower capacity ;

(2) they agreed, in case the sending of a royal contingent be infeasible, to a levy on mass on hearing of any occurrence of decoity in the locality by the people of the neighbourhood, such as the Kāttūrkoṭṭai, a place I am not able to identify. The records state that the inhabitants of Arantāngi were their natural enemies. The record thus shows an arrangement come to by the people among themselves to provide for the necessary protection under countenance of the Government for the time being against disturbers of the peace.

(a) *Inscription of Hijira* 761.

(From a copy of the inscription taken by Mr. N. P. Swaminatha Aiyar, B.A., Archæologist, Pudukoṭṭa, who kindly placed the copy at my disposal.)

At Tirukkoḷakkuḍi, Tiruppattūr Taluk, Ramnad District (in the east wall of the front Manḍapa of the rock-cut shrine of Tirukkoḷanātha Temple). (*Vide* pp. 153 and 164–65, above Lecture VI.)

ஸ்வஸ்தி ஸ்ரீ இராசராச இராசாதிராச சகல நிருவ குல(க்):கோனை காலம். இராசாக்கள் தம்பிரானுற்க்கு ௭௱௬௰௧ (761)ஸு பங்குனிமீ 5உ பொன்னமராபதி நாட்டு நாட்டவரோம் விரையாச்சிலை உள்இட்ட ஊரா வருக்கும் கொட்டியூர் உள்இட்ட ஊரவருக்கும் பிடிபாடு பண்ணிக்குடுத்த பரி சாவது.

இராசாக்கள் தம்பிரானார் சூரைக்குடி அழியச்செய்வதாக மஞ்சிலிசு எலிசு காவண, ஆசம் காத்தாவண முவாசம் கான்காவண இராசாத்தி க(ர)னுடனே பரிகரம் ஏவப்பட்டு சூரைக்குடியும் அழியச் செயிது மாத்தூர்(க்)குளத்திலே விடுதியா விரையாச்சிலை கோட்டியூர் ஊரவர்களை(க்) காணச்சொல்லி அருளிச் செய்தபடியாலே இவ்வடிகள் கண் அளிவுக்கு இராசாக்கள் தம்பிரானார் தோனது கானுக்கும் எங்களுக்கும் பிரமாணம் வரக்காட்டி அருளினபடி முன்னாள் நம் முடபாராய் நமக்கு இறுத்துப் போந்த விரையாச்சிலை உள்ளிட்ட ஊரும் கோட்டியூர் உள்ளிட்ட ஊரும் தங்கள் நாட்டுடனே கூட்டி தங்கள் மரயாதி

கடமை இருக்கக்கடவர்களென்றும் ஒன்றுபட நடத்திப் போதக்கடவர்களென்றும் இச்சேதிக்குத் திருக்கோளக்குடி நாயினார் கோயில் திருமலையிலே கல்வெட்டிக் குடுப்பதென்று பிரமாணம் வந்தபடியாலே நாங்களும் நாட்டுடனே கூட்டி எங்கள் மரியாதிகடமை இறுப்பதாக சந்திராதித்தவரை செல்வதாகக் கல்வெட்டிக் குடுத்தோம் பொன்னமராபதி நாட்டு நாட்டவரோம் விரையாச்சிலை யுள்ளிட்ட ஊரவருக்கும் கோட்டியூருள்ளிட்ட ஊரவருக்கும்.

இப்படிக்குப் பொன்னமராபதி நாட்டுறு

TRANSLATION

May prosperity attend. The reign of the king of (Sakalanṛpa-kulak-kōn) the family of kings (Rājarāja), great King of kings. (Rājādhirāja) king of the whole group of kings. In the year 761 of the lord of kings (Rājākkaḷtambirān), in the month of Panguni (March-April), on the fifth day, we the citizens of Pon-Amarāvati [1] (Nāṭṭavar), executed a deed of agreement to the residents of Virayāchchilai and the (attached) villages, and to those of Kōṭṭiyūr and attached villages on the terms hereunder set forth:— The lord of kings (above referred to) ordered the destruction of Śūraikkuḍi [2] by sending forward at the head of their troops Manjilis Elis Khan, Az-am Khan, Muazam Khan under the command of Rājātti Khan. Having destroyed Śuraikkuḍi these had encamped in Māttūr Kuḷam[3] to which they summoned the inhabitants of Virayāchchilai and Koṭṭiyūr. As a consequence, since the said lord of kings charged both Dhunad Khan and ourselves with the protection of these subjects (of his) under proper assurance, we agreed that the people of Virayāchchilai[4] and those of Koṭṭiyūr,[5] having assembled in their nāḍu (assembly of townsmen), do pay us what is due to us as a matter of longstanding custom; and that they do so, united as one body. It was further

1 Pon-Amarāvati, head-quarters of a division twenty-two miles south-west of Pudukoṭṭa.

2 Śūraikkuḍi seems to be what is now called Vanniyan Śūraikkuḍi on the road from Kānāḍukāttān to Tiruppattūr, about five miles from the former place.

3 Māttūr Kuḷam is a little town eight miles from Trichinopoly on the road to Pudukoṭṭa from Trichinopoly.

4 Virayāchchilai in Pudukoṭṭa State about four miles from Tirumeyyam aside of the road to Tiruppattūr.

5 Koṭṭiyūr obviously Tirukkoshṭiyūr, six miles South of Tiruppattūr on the road to Sivaganga from Tiruppattūr.

agreed that the deed of agreement be incised in the rock containing the temple of Tirukkōḷakkuḍi Nāyanār (the god at the rock-cut temple in the place). In consequence thereof, meeting in our own assembly, we got this inscription cut out, agreeing to discharge the duty to which we are liable, as long as the sun and the moon should last; we of the Pon-Amarāvati nāḍu to the inhabitants of Virayāchchilai and attached villages, and to those of Koṭṭiyūr and attached villages.

(b) *Inscription of Hijira* 771.[1]

(On a stone planted under the Pipal tree in front of the Zamindar's bungalow at *Kanḍadēvi*, a mile and a half from *Devakoṭṭa*. The stone is said to have originally been at the corner of the tank nearest to this spot.)

Ref.: same as above.

South face.

ஸ்வஸ்தி ஸ்ரீ ராசாதிராச ராசா
திராச சகல நிருப குல(க்)
கோ ந(ன்) காலம். இராசாக்
கள் தம்பிரானார்(க்)
குயாண்டு எழுநூ(ற்)
ற்று எழுபத்தொன்று
வது இரவிலாதரந்
எ[illegible] ஆன கார்த்திகை
மீ உ நாள் இராசாக்
கள் தம்பிரானார் ஸ்ரீபா
தத்துக்கு அணை நா
டு மீதாக்கண்ட பெரு
மாள் வேலைக்காரர்
ஆன காரணவரும் இ(நா?)
ந்தார்களும் ப்ரத்தி
யம் பண்ணிக்குடுத்
தபடிக்குக் கல்லு வெட்
டி நாட்டினபடி தே
சத்தில் உள்ள வன்னிய
ரும் கள்ளர் கரும(ர்)புற
த்தார் பட்டர் வித்து
வான்கள் பாடகர்
எங்களுக்குச் சத்து
ருவான அறந்தாங்கி
யார் மறவ(ரு)ம் உள்ளம
ணித்தர் எல்லார் முன்
பாக நாங்கள் பண்ணி
ன ப்ரத்யத்தில் ஒன்று
தப்புதலானார்களுக்கு

[1]From an eye copy taken by me with the good offices and active assistance of the late Mr. C. S. Anantarama Ayyar, B.A., Divisional Officer, whose interest in such work was genuine. He died within a fortnight of my visit to him and I inscribe, as a very faint token of my esteem and affection for him, this last piece of work of his in collaboration.

East face.

(ம் இண)ங்குவரா யிருக்கிற
வர்களுடனே எங்க
ள் ஆயுஸ்உள்ள அளவு
ம் உறவாருதல் ஊரு
ண்டாக நடத்திப் (போ)
(க்) குக இராசாக்கள் தம்
பிரானார்க்குப் பர்தம் வி
டாமல் திருவுள்ளத்துக்
குப் பொருந்தன் நாட்டுக்
கு வேண்டுங் காரண"
வரும் சேவிக்க வேண்
டும் பரிகாரமு ங் கொ
ண்டு வந்து சேவியா
மல் இதிலெ சிலதா
ழ்வு ஆகுதல் இது நமிர்
து யாதொரு பொ
ழுது அருளிப்பாடெற
இராசாக்கள் தம்பி
ரானார் சிபாதத்தில்
நிர்ணயமான ஆளும்
திருமுகமும் வந்தால்
ஆயுத மெடுக்க வல்ல
மனித்தரில் ஒருத்
தர் நில்லாம ல (று) தியாக
த் தேற நாங்கள் விடை
கொண்டு வாராமல்
இருக்குதல் எங்கள் வகுப்
பாராகா ம (ல்) ஆக்கிக்
கொண்டருளின இ
த்தாலே காத்தூர்

North face.

கோட்டைடயார் மற்(று)
முள்ளவர்கள் இராசாக்க(ள்)
தம்பிரா னார்க்கு இராச்
சயத்திலெ சிலசில
களவு செய்யும் அள
வுக்கு இவர்களை அழி
யக் செய்ய இராசபரிகா
ம் வரவேணு மென வ(ரு)
காமல் ஆன ஆளும் திரு
முகமும் வந்த நாழிகை
யிலே இவர்களை அழி
யச் செய்யாம லிருக்
குதலைச் செய்யாமல் இரா
சாக்கள் தம்பிரானார் சிபா
தத்தைத் தப்பி னோமாகில்
எங்களுக்கு ச்சத்துரு
ஆன மனிதர்க்கு மீசை
சிறைத்து இவர்களுக்கு
நாங்கள் குடும்பமாக
இருக்கக்கட வோமெனவும்
எங்களுடைய பெண்
டுகளை எங்களுக்குச் சத்
துரு வான மனிதர்க்கு
வித்துவான்கள் பாட
கர் பாணர் புலவர் இவர்
கள் பிடித்துக்கொண்
டு போய் தானப் பொறி
பொறித்துத் தங்கள் (சிறு)
பசகளுக்குக் குடுக்கக்க
டவர்களென்றும் செக
டியும் அடித்து ஆறோ
டியிலே ஏழு பிராமண
ரை இருத்(தி) இவர்களை
பிதக் கணமாகவந்து

West face.

இந்தப் பிராமணரை(க்)
கங்கைக் கரையிலே
கொன்ற பாபியாய்
மஹா பாபம் செய்த அ
வர்கள் கிடக்கும் நரக
த்திலே கிடக்கக் கட
வோம் எனவும் எங்
கள் உருவத்தைப் பெண
உருவமாக வகுத்து பி(பா)
ணர் புலையர் பள்ளர்
பறைடர் மற்றும் உள்ளகீழ்
சாதிகளும் எங்களுடை
ய இந்த உருவத்தை எழுதி
நாங்கள் இருந்த தேசத்திலும்
மற்றும் உள்ள தேசத்தி
லும் இவர்கள் சிறுபசுக
ள் காலிலே கட்டி இழுக்
சக் கொண்டு திரியக்கட
வர் களெனவும் இப்படிக்
கலைமந்து எங்கள் நா
ட்டுக்குத் தாயூரான
இதிலே மணத் தோர
ணமுங் கட்டிக் கல்லு
ம் வெட்டி நாட்டினோ
ம் ஆனை நாட்டில்
காரண வரும் இளாத (?)
தார்களும் இவ்வ
ளைவரோம்.

TRANSLATION

May prosperity attend. In the time of the 'Great king of kings,' 'Great king of the family of kings' 'king of the whole group of kings'; in the year 771 of the 'lord of kings', on the 7th day of Iraviladhan (Rabi-ul-Sani), which is the 11th day of Kārttigai: in the territory subject to the authority of the said 'lord of kings' the temple management, who are the servants of Kanḍaperumāḷ[1] and the Inamdars (holders of free gifts), made the deed of assurance and got it transcribed on stone on the following terms:—If we fail in any one detail, in this deed of assurance executed by us, in the presence of the inhabitants of this (part of the) country such as the Vanniyar, Kaḷḷar, Karumār (artisans apparently), citizens, Bhaṭṭas (Brahmans), learned men, musicians, our enemies who are the residents of Arantāngi and all other men, we agree that you see to it that we are put out of relationship for life with those that act up to it. Among (such details are) failure to bring to the 'lord of kings' those required for his continuous personal service,[2] those that

[1] Seems to stand for the God in the Śiva temple at Kanḍadēvi.
[2] Reading line 38க்குப் பேரும், meaning the number of people.

may be required for the carrying out of the administration of his territory, and those that are required for service (in the capacity of peons), or providing these in insufficient number; besides this,[1] whenever 'the lord of kings' should send his orders, by his servants appointed for the purpose, our failure to muster together all those among us capable of bearing arms, without letting a single one stay behind, and take his orders as to the service required of us. Further by this deed by which we have brought into one party even those that are not of us, we agree that in case the inhabitants of Kāttūr Koṭṭai and others,[2] should commit robbery in the territory of 'our lord of kings', if the king's troops could not come to destroy them for any reason, the moment we receive royal orders sent by the appointed orderly officer, it would be failure in us if we did not destroy those robbers. If we fail in any of these particulars of our duty to 'the lord of kings', we agree that our mustaches be shaved and that we be regarded as the wives of our enemies. More than this we agree that our women folk be taken to our enemies by men of learning, musicians, minstrels, poets and be made over to their own boys, after putting on them the mark of gift.[3] We further agree that we suffer in the hell of those who, having assembled by beat of the bronze cymbal, seven Brahmaṇas on the ghat of a running river, and having gone round them by the right, kill them on the banks of the Ganges. Further again we agree that we be depicted as women, and that low caste people, like pinar ? (perhaps pāṇar), pulayas, paḷḷas paraiyas and other such, may tie up such pictures of ours to the feet of their children so that they may roam about with these in this, our own country, and the country round this. Having thus agreed, we the officials and Iladars[4] and others of this territory under the authority (of the 'lord of kings'), put up festoons of marriage and set up this stone in this the mother city of our nādu (country or our peoples).

1 Reading in line 44. இறுதலிர்ந்து for நலிந்து
2 Reading the last word of line 60, மற்று instead of மற
3 Meaning that these be obtained in gift and made over in servitude.
4 Seems meant for Inamdars.

APPENDIX B

IBN BATUTA IN SOUTH INDIA [1]

The mountain of Serendil (Adam's Peak), Ceylon.
(Lecture VI, pp. 175)

It is one of the highest mountains in the world and can be seen from the open sea even at a distance of nine days' journey from it. As we climb the peak, its lower slopes are hidden from view by clouds. There are on this summit, many trees that never shed their leaves, flowers of different colours, and a red rose as large as the palm of one's hand. It is said that on the petals of this rose is an inscription containing the name of the Almighty God and the name of his Prophet. Two mountain roads lead to the foot of Adam: Father's road, and Mother's road, otherwise called Adam and Eve. Mother's road is an easy road by which pilgrims return. But those who take it going there are not considered to have made the pilgrimage. Father's road is rough and difficult. Near the gate at the foot of the mountain is a grotto called Iskander (Alexander), and a spring of water.

The ancients have hewn in the rock a sort of step by which one ascends the mountain. They have also planted iron spikes and suspended chains on to them to which one holds while making the ascent. Those chains are ten in number; two near the gate at the foot of the mountain; after these seven others which are linked one on to the other; then the tenth, 'the

[1] A summary account of this part of Ibn Batuta's work appeared in the *Madras Journal of Literature and Science* for 1888-89 rendered from the French by Mrs. L. Fletcher (pp. 37-60). I am indebted for this translation to Miss Ida Gunther, B.A., L.T., Lecturer, Queen Mary's College for Women, Madras. This is translated from vol. iv. of the French edition of Ibn Batuta by Messrs. C. Defremery and B. L. Sanguinettie.

chain of the profession of faith' (Mussalman), so called because the person who reaches it and looks down below will be seized with hallucination and fear of falling, and he will repeat the words: 'I declare that there is no other god but God, and that Mahomet is his Prophet'. When you have got beyond this tenth chain, you come to a road kept in bad repair. The cavern of Nadir is seven miles from the tenth chain. It stands in a spacious place near a spring, also called khidhr, full of fish. Nobody catches fish there. Near by are two basins hewn in the rocks on either side of the road. In the khidhr grotto, pilgrims leave their belongings and then go another two miles up to the summit of the mountain where they find the foot.

Description of the Foot

The noble foot mark—that of our father Adam—is to be seen in a black high rock standing in an open place. The foot print on the stone is deeply impressed; it is eleven spans long. Formerly the people of China used to go there, they cut out of the rock the impression of the big toe and the one next to it, and deposited this fragment in a temple in the town of Leitoun (Tseuthoung) to which they go from distant places. In the rock bearing the foot print three hollows have been dug in which idolatrous pilgrims deposit gold and precious stones and pearls. Fakirs who arrive at the grotto of khidhr, try to outbeat one another in finding what lies in these hollows. As for us, we found only a few small stones and a little gold which we gave to our guide. It is usual for pilgrims to spend three days in the cavern of khidhr, and during that period to visit the foot morning and evening. We did the same.

At the end of three days, we returned by 'Mother's Road', and encamped near the grotto of Cheim, which is the same as Seth, son of Adam. We afterwards stayed near the bay full of fish, and the villages of *Cormolah*, of *Djbercavern*, of *Diedineouch* and of *Atkalendjeh.* It is in this last named place that the sheik Abon'abd Allah, son of the Khafif, spent the winter. All these villages and stations are situated on the mountain. Near the foot of the latter, on this same road, stands 'dirakht rewan,' 'the walking tree', an ancient tree that does not lose a single leaf. I have not met any one who has seen its leaves. It is given the prefix 'walking' because the person who looks at it from the mountain top, thinks it stands far away at the foot of the mountain, whilst he who looks at it from below, believes it to be in quite the opposite place. I met a troop of *Yogees* who never leave the foot of the mountain but are waiting for the leaves of this tree to fall. It stands in an absolutely inaccessible spot. Idolators say: 'whosoever eats the leaves of this tree, recovers his youth, even though he be an old man.' But this is false, another of their lies.

Beneath this mountain is the great bay containing precious stones. Its waters are extremely blue. From here we marched for two days as far as the large town of Dinewar, near the sea, inhabited by merchants. Dinewar (Dinēśvara) contains, a large temple, with an idol that bears the name of the town. In this temple there are about 1,000 Brahmans and *Yogees*, and about 500 women, born of idolatrous fathers, who sing and dance the whole night before the god. The town and its revenues are the particular property of the idol; and those who live in the temple and those who visit it, are fed on that money. The idol is made of gold, the size of a man. It has two large rubies in place of eyes, which, I am told, shine like lanterns during the night.

We left Dinewar for the little town of Kaly (Galle) six parasangs (about thirty-six miles or so) distant. A Mussalman, the coxswain of the boat Ibrahim, whom we met there, entertained us at his house. Then we set out for Calenbou (Colombo), one of the largest and most beautiful towns in the island of Serendib. Djalesty, the Vezir prince of the sea, lives there with about 500 Abyssinians. Three days after leaving Colombo, we arrived at Batthalah, already mentioned, and visited the Sultan spoken above. I met the coxswain of the boat Ibrahim and we set out for the country of Ma'bar. The wind was strong and the water was on the point of entering the vessel. Without a skilled captain, we drifted near certain rocks and the ship was all but wrecked; then we entered shallow water, the vessel grounded and we were face to face with death. The passengers threw their belongings into the sea and bade farewell to all. We cut down the mast of the ship and threw it into the sea. The sailors made a raft with the plank. We were two parasangs distant from the shore. I wanted to go down on to the raft, but I had with me two concubines and two friends, and the latter said to me: 'Will you go down and leave us?' I liked them better than myself, and said 'Go down both of you, as well as the young girl whom I love.' The other young girl said: 'I know to swim well. I will tie myself with a cord to the little boat and swim with those people.' My two comrades descended; one of them was Mohamed, son of Ferhan Attaouzery, and the other, an Egyptian. One of the young girls was with them, the second swam. The sailors made a raft with the help of which they swam. I gave them all the valuables I possessed, personal property, jewels and amber. They got to land safe and well, for the wind helped them. I remained on the vessel, the master of which reached the shore on a plank. The sailors set to work to construct four rafts, but the night before they were finished, the sea broke upon us. Then, several idolaters came in one of their boats to fetch us. We went ashore with them to the land of Ma'bar, and told them we were friends of their Sultan to whom they paid tribute. They wrote to inform him of this. The sovereign was engaged in a war with the infidels at a distance of two days' march; I sent him a letter telling him what had happened to me. The idolaters in question led us into a large wood, and brought us a fruit resembling the water-melon; it grows on the dwarf palm tree. Inside this fruit is a kind of down (or cotton) containing a honied substance which is extracted and made into a sort of pastry called 'tell' just like sugar. They served us with excellent fish. We remained there for three days, at the end of which an amir named Kamar-ud-din, accompanied by a detachment of horse and foot soldiers arrived from the Sultan. They brought one palanquin and six horses. I mounted a horse, so did my friend, the master of the ship, and one of the two young girls; the other was carried in the palanquin. We reached the fort of Arcot (Hercatou) where we spent the night. There I left the young girls, a party of my slaves and my companions. The second day we reached the camp of the Sultan.

THE SULTAN OF MA'BAR

He was Ghiyath eddin Addameghany (Ghiyazu-d-din Dhāmaghani) originally a horseman in the service of Malic Modjir, son of Abourredidja, one of the officers of Sultan Mohamed; then he served the Amir Hadjy, son of the Sayyid Sultan Djelal eddin (Jalalu-d-din). At last, he was invested with royalty. Before this he was called Siradj eddin; but after his accession he took the name of Ghiyath eddin. Formerly, the country of Ma'bar had submitted to the authority of Sultan Mohammed, king of Dihly (Delhi). A revolt was stirred up amongst his followers by my father-in-law, the Sheriff Djelal eddin Ahsan Shah (Sharif Jalalu-d-din Ahsan Shah), who reigned there for five years, after which he was killed and replaced by one of his amirs, Alauddin Odeidjy (Alau-d-din Udauji), who governed for one year. At the end of this time he set out to conquer the infidels; he took a considerable amount of riches and ample spoils from them, and returned to his own state. The following year, he led a second expedition against the idolaters, routed them and massacred a large number. The same day on which he inflicted this disaster upon them, it happened that he took off his helmet in order to drink; an arrow shot by an unknown hand struck him and he died on the field. His son-in-law Kothb-eddin (Qutbu-d-din Firoz) was placed upon the throne; but as his conduct was generally disapproved of, he was killed at the end of forty days. The Sultan Ghiyath-eddin was invested with authority; he married the daughter of the Sultan and Sheriff Djelal eddin. It is the sister of this same girl that I had married at Dihly (Delhi).

MY ARRIVAL AT THE (COURT OF) SULTAN GHIYATH EDDIN.

When we approached the neighbourhood of his camp, he sent one of his chamberlains to meet us. The Sultan was seated in a wooden tower. . . . It is the custom throughout India, for nobody to enter the presence of the Sovereign bare-footed. Now, I had no boots, but an idolater gave me a pair, though there were a certain number of Mussalmans in this place. I was surprised that idolaters showed greater generosity than they (Mussalmans). I then presented myself before the Sultan who ordered me to sit down, sent for the kadhi (Kazi) and pilgrim *Sadr Azzeman Behaeddin* (Sadru-l-Zaman Bahau-d-din) and lodged me in three tents pitched in the neighbourhood of his. The people of this country called these tents 'Khiyam' (plural of 'Khaimah'). The Sultan sent me carpets as well as the viands used in the country, that is to say, rice and meat (curry). The custom in this country, as in our own, is to serve sour milk after the meal.

After all that, I had an interview with the Sultan. I proposed that he should send an army to the Maldive islands. He agreed to this proposal and ordered some ships to be got ready. He also resolved to send a present to the Sultan of the Maldives, some robes of honour and gifts to the amirs and viziers. He entrusted me with the drawing up of a marriage contract with the Sultan's sister; finally he ordered three vessels to be filled with alms for the poor of the island and said to me: 'You will return at the end of five days.' The admiral Khodjah Serlec said to him: 'It is not possible to sail for the Maldives until three months hence.' Then the Sultan said to me: 'Since this is the case, come to *Fattan* (Paṭṭaṇam) in order that we might end this expedition and return to our capital of Moutrah (Madura). It is from there that they will set out.' I went and stayed there with him, and, whilst waiting, sent for my concubines and my friends.

The March of the Sultan, and His Shameful Conduct in Killing Women and Children

The country we had to traverse was a wood formed of trees and reeds, so overgrown, that nobody could penetrate it. The Sultan ordered every army man, great or small, to carry a hatchet and cut down these obstacles. When the camp had been arranged, he set out on horseback to the forest, accompanied by soldiers. They cut down trees from morning till midday. Then food was served for everybody; after that they began hewing till evening. Every infidel found in the forest was taken prisoner. They sharpened stakes at both ends and made their captives carry them on their shoulders. Each was accompanied by his wife and children and they were thus led to the camp. It is the custom of these people to surround their camp with a palisade having four gates. They call it *catcar* round the habitation of the king. Outside the principal boundary, they erected a platform about a half *brasse* high and lighted a fire on it during the night. Slaves and sentinels spent the night there holding a fagot of very slender reeds in their hands. When infidels approached to attack the camp during the night, they lighted the fagots. The brightness of the flames converted night into day, and the horsemen set out in pursuit of the infidel.

The next morning, the Hindu prisoners were divided into four sections and taken to each of the four gates of the great *catcar*. There, on the stakes they had carried, the prisoners were impaled. Afterwards their wives were killed and tied by their hair to these pales. Little children were massacred on the bosoms of their mothers and their corpses left there. Then, the camp was raised, and they started cutting down the trees of another forest. In the same manner did they treat their later Hindu prisoners. This is shameful conduct such as I have not known any other sovereign guilty of. It is for this that God hastened the death of Ghiyath-eddin (Ghiyazu-d-din).

One day whilst the Kadhi (Kazi) and I were having our food with (Ghiyazu-d-din), the Kazi to his right and I to his left, an infidel was brought before him accompanied by his wife and son aged seven years. The Sultan made a sign with his hand to the executioners to cut off the head of this man; then he said to them in Arabic: 'and the son and the wife.' They cut off their heads and I turned my eyes away. When I looked again, I saw their heads lying on the ground.

I was another time with the Sultan Ghiyath-eddin (Ghiyazu-d-din) when a Hindu was brought into his presence. He uttered words I did not understand, and immediately several of his followers drew their daggers. I rose hurriedly, and he said to me; 'Where are you going'? I replied: 'I am going to say my afternoon (4 o'clock) prayers.' He understood my reason, smiled, and ordered the hands and feet of the idolater to be cut off. On my return I found the unfortunate swimming in his blood.

The Victory that Ghiyath-eddin won over the infidel which is one of the greatest successes of Islam

In the neighbourhood of his territory was an infidel sovereign named Belal Deo (Baḷḷāḷa Dēva), who was one of the principal Hindu Kings. His army exceeded hundred thousand men, and he had besides, twenty thousand Mussalmans formed of criminals and slaves. This monarch thought it expedient to go against the Coromandel Coast where the Mussalman army numbered but six thousand soldiers, the half of whom were excellent troops and the remainder were worth absolutely nothing. The Muhammadans fought a battle with him near the town of Cobban (Koppam); he routed them, and they retired to Moutrah (Madura) the capital of the country. The infidel sovereign encamped near Cobban (Koppam) which is one of the grandest and strongest places that the Mussalmans possess. He laid siege to it for ten months, and at the end of this time, the garrison had provisions only for fourteen days. Belal Deo (Baḷḷāḷa Dēva) sent a proposal to the besieged to retire with safe-conduct, and to abandon the town to him; but they replied, 'we must refer this question to our Sultan.' He then promised them a truce, which was to last for fourteen days, and they wrote to Sultan Ghiyath-eddin (Ghiyazu-d-din) telling him how they were situated. The prince read their letter to the people the following Friday. The faithful wept and said: 'We will sacrifice our lives to God. If the idolater takes that town, he will next lay siege to us: we prefer to die by the sword.' They then undertook to expose themselves to death, and set out marching the next day, placing their turbans on the neck of their horses, which showed that they were seeking death. The bravest and most courageous of them, 300 in number were posted to the vanguard; the right wing was under Seif-eddin Behadur (Seifu-d-din Bahadur), the hero, who was a pious and brave lawyer; and the left wing was under, Almelic Mohamed 'assilahdar' (armiger). The Sultan remained in the centre with three thousand men, and the rear-guard was formed by the remaining 3,000 under the command of Assad-eddin Keikhosrew

Alfaricy. In this order the Mussalmans set out, at the siesta hour, towards the infidel camp. Their horses were sent out to graze. They fell upon the encampment; the infidels, imagining the assailants were but robbers, went in disorder to meet them and fought with them. In the midst of all this, the Sultan Ghiyath-eddin arrived, and the Hindus sustained the worst of all defeats. Their king tried to mount his horse although he was eighty years of age. Nasir-eddin (Nasiru-d-din) nephew and successor of the Sultan overtook the old man and wanted to kill him, for he did not know who he was. But one of his slaves said: 'He is the Hindu King.' He then took him a prisoner to his uncle who treated him with apparent consideration and promised to release him. But when he had extorted from him his wealth, elephants and horses and all his property, he had him killed and flayed; his skin was stuffed with straw and hung up on the wall of Moutrah (Madura) where I saw it suspended.

But let us return to our point. I left the camp and went to the grand and beautiful town of *Faṭṭan*, on the seashore. It has an admirable harbour with a wooden pavilion raised on stout posts. Leading to this pavilion is a pathway made of planks covered over with a roof. When an enemy arrives, all the ships in port are fastened to this pavilion; foot soldiers and archers go up there and the assailant has no means of hurting any one. This town contains a beautiful mosque built of stone where you find many grapes and excellent pomegranates. There I met the pious Sheik Mohammad Annciçaboury, one of those fakirs with hair hanging over his shoulders, whose spirit is troubled. He was accompanied by a lion tamed by him; the animal eats with the fakirs and lies down beside them. The Sheik had with him about thirty fakirs, one of whom had a gazelle that lived in the same place as the lion and the latter did it no harm. I tarried in the town of Fattan.

In the meantime, a *Yogee* had prepared for the Sultan Ghiyath-eddin some pills amongst the ingredients of which were iron filings. The Sultan took a larger dose of them than was necessary for him and fell ill. In this state he reached Fattan; I went out to meet him and offered him a present. When he had settled down in the town, he sent for the admiral Khodjah

Sorour and said to him : 'Attend to nothing besides those vessels that are to go to the Maldives.' He wanted to return to me the price of the present I had made him. I refused, but repented of it afterwards, for Ghiyath-eddin (Ghiyazu-d-din) died and I got nothing. The Sultan remained for half a month at Fattan, then he left for his capital ; I remained yet a fortnight longer and then set out for his residence, which is Madura, a grand town with wide roads. The first prince who made that town his capital was my father-in-law the Sultan Sheriff Djelal-eddin Ahsan Shah (Jalalu-d-din Ahsan Shah), who modelled it on Delhi and built it carefully.

When I arrived at Madura, there was a contagious disease prevalent there which killed people in a short time. Those who were attacked succumbed in two or three days. If their end was delayed, it was only until the fourth day. On leaving my dwelling, I saw people either sick or dead. In this town I bought a young slave who, I was assured, was healthy ; but she died the following day. A woman, whose husband had been one of the viziers of the Sultan Ahsan Shah (Ahsan-Shah) came to me one day with her son aged eight years, a child full of spirit, and I gave both her and her son some money. They were both healthy and strong ; but the next day the mother returned to ask a shroud for her son, for he died suddenly. In the Sultan's audience hall, at the time of his death, there were certain women servants brought to boil rice for the people. These women got ill and were thrown on the earth, exposed to the sun's rays.

When Ghiyath-eddin (Ghiyazu-d-din) entered Madura, he found his mother, his wife and son a prey to the disease. He remained three days in the town, then he went to a river, one parasang away, on the shore of which stands an infidel temple. I went to see him on a Thursday, and he ordered me to stay with the Khadi (Kazi). When tents had been pitched for me, I saw people hurrying along, pushing one against the other. One of them said, 'the Sultan is dead ; ' the other was sure that it was his son that was dead. We found out the truth and knew that the son was dead. He was the Sultan's only son ; his death was one of the causes that made the father's malady worse and killed him. The following Thursday the Sultan's mother died.

THE DEATH OF THE SULTAN. THE ACCESSION OF HIS BROTHER'S SON, AND MY DEPARTURE FROM THE NEW PRINCE'S COURT.

The third Thursday, Ghiyath-eddin (Ghiyazu-d-din) died. I heard the news and hastened to return to town, fearing a tumult. I met Nasir-eddin (Nasiru-d-din), the nephew and successor of the deceased, who was sent for to the camp as the Sultan left no son. He asked me to retrace my steps to the camp with him; but I refused, and this refusal left an impression on his mind. This Nasir-eddin (Nasiru-d-din) was a domestic servant at Delhi before his uncle came to the throne. When Ghiyath-eddin (Ghiyazu-d-din) became king, the nephew fled to him in the garb of a fakir, and fate willed it that he should reign after him. When they had sworn allegiance to Nasir-eddin (Nasiru-d-din) poets recited his praises in verse, and they gave him magnificent gifts. The first who rose to recite verses was the Khadi Sadrazzeman (Kazi Sadru-s-Zaman), to whom he gave 500 pieces of gold and a robe of honour; then came the vizir named Alkadhi (the judge) whom the Sultan gratified with two thousand pieces of silver. As for me, he made a present of 300 pieces of gold and a robe of honour. He distributed alms among fakirs and the poor. When the preacher gave his first sermon in which he mentioned the name of the new sovereign, they loaded him with drachmas and dinars placed in gold and silver basins. The funeral of Ghiyath-eddin (Ghiyazu-d-din) was celebrated with great pomp. Each day the *Koran* was read beside the tomb. Then, those whose business it was to read the tenth part of the holy book, delivered a lecture, after which food was served and the public ate; finally, silver pieces were given to each individual according to his rank. This went on for forty days. The ceremony was renewed annually on the anniversary of the death of the deceased.

The first step taken by Nasir-eddin (Nasiru-d-din) was to ruin his uncle's vizir by extorting sums of money from him. He made Melic Bedr-eddin (Malik Badru-d-din) vizir, the same man whom his uncle had sent to meet me when I was at Fattan. He died very soon; and the Sultan nominated as his successor, Khodjah Sorour, the admiral, with the title of Khodjah Djihan (Khwaja-i-Jehan) similar to the vizir of Delhi. Whoever addressed the vizier by any other title, had to pay a fine of a certain number of gold pieces. Then the Sultan Nasir-eddin killed the son of his paternal aunt, who was married to the daughter of Ghiyath-eddin (the late Sultan), and afterwards married his widow. He was told that Melic Maç-oud (Malik-Masud) had visited his cousin in prison before he was put to death; so he killed him as well as Melic Behadour (Malik Bahadur), who was a generous and virtuous hero. He ordered that I should be provided with all the ships that his uncle had sanctioned for my expedition to the Maldives. But I was attacked with the deadly fever, and thought I would die. God inspired me to have recourse to the tamarind which is very plentiful in this place. I took about a pound of it and soaked it in water, then drank this beverage which made me better in three days, and with God's help I was cured. Being disgusted with the town of Madura, I asked the Sultan's permission to go on my voyage. He said to me, 'How will you go? There is only one month for the Maldive expedition to be got ready. Stay then until we give you all that the master of the world (the late Sultan) ordered for you.' I refused and he wrote to Fattan giving me leave to sail in any vessel I pleased. I found there were eight vessels sailing for Yaman from Fattan and embarked on one of them. We met three war ships, which fought with us for a time and then retired. After that we arrived at Caoulem (Quilon). As I was free from all illness, I remained in this town for three months and then set sail in order to find the Sultan Djemal-eddin Alhinaoury (Jamalud-din of Honawar) but infidels attacked us between Hinaour (Honawar) and Facanaour.

How we were despoiled by the Hindus

When we reached the little island situated between Hinaour (Honawar) and Facannaour, infidels attacked us with ten men-of-war, and after a lively engagement defeated us. They took verything I possessed—the store I held in reserve for a rainy day—pearls, precious stones given me by the king of Ceylon, clothes and provisions given me by wealthy men and holy persons. They left me no garment but a pair of drawers. They also seized all that belonged to every passenger and sailor, and made us go ashore. I returned to Calicut and entered one of the mosques. A lawyer sent me a dress, the Kadhi (Kazi) a turban, and a certain merchant another dress. Here I had news of the marriage of the vizir Abd Allah (Abdulla) with the Sultana Khadidjah, after the death of the vizir Djemal-eddin (Jamalu-d-din), and I also heard that the woman I left behind had given birth to a boy. I thought of going to the Maldive islands, but I remembered the enmity which had existed between me and the vizir Abd Allah. In consequence, I opened the Koran and these words came before my eyes 'Angels will descend and say to them "fear not and be not sad."' I implored the blessings of God, and set sail. After ten days I arrived at the Maldives and landed on the isle of Cannalous. The Governor of this isle, Abd Al'aziz Almakdachaouy, welcomed me kindly, treated me and gave me a boat fully equipped. I afterwards arrived at Hololy, the island where the Sultana and her sisters go for a holiday and for bathing. The natives call these amusements 'tetdjer', and indulge in these games on their ships. The viziers and chiefs sent the Sultana presents and gifts whilst she remained on the isle. I met the sister of the Sultana there, her husband, the preacher Muhammad, son of the vizier Djemaled-din, and his mother who had been my wife. The preacher visited me and had food with me.

In the meanwhile, some of the inhabitants of the island went to the vizier Abd Allah and announced my arrival to him. He questioned me regarding my position and the persons who had accompanied me. I then informed him that I had come in order to fetch my son, aged about two years. The mother of the child went to the vizier to complain to him about my intention; but he said to her: 'I will not prevent him from taking his son.' He forced me to go to the island (of Mahal) and lodged me in a house opposite the tower of his palace in order to know all about me. He sent me a full robe, betel, and rose water according to their custom. I took him two pieces of silk in order to throw them before him the moment I saluted him. They were accepted and the vizier did not come to entertain me that day. They introduced my son to me and it struck me that his stay with the islanders had done him much good. I then sent him back again to them and remained five days in the island. It seemed to me I ought to hasten my departure and I asked leave to do so. The vizier having called me, I went to him. They brought me the two pieces of stuff they had taken from me, and I threw them down while saluting the vizier as is the custom. He made me sit beside him and put me questions regarding myself. I ate in his company and washed my hands in the same basin with him—this is what he does with nobody. Afterwards betel was brought and I returned. The vizier sent me cotton drawers and hundreds of thousands of cowries, and behaved perfectly.

In the meanwhile I departed. We were forty-three days on sea after which we reached Bengal, a large country producing an abundance of rice. I have not seen any place in the world where goods are cheaper than here; but it is a foggy country and people coming there from Khorasan call it 'douzakhas pouri ni met' which means, in Arabic, 'a hell full of good things.'

ADDITIONAL SPECIAL NOTE

Nationality of the Khiljis

ON page 75 above, I have said, following the authority of Major Raverty and Elphinstone, the Historian, that the Khiljis were 'a people who were Turks, but having been long staying in Afghanistan first round Herat and then Eastwards they became so assimilated to the populations of the locality that they were taken to be more Afghans than Turks.' That position is supported by Beale in his *Oriental Biographical Dictionary* The late. Dr. Vincent Smith states on page 230 of the *Oxford History of India.* 'Although the Khalij or the Khilji tribe is reckoned by Raverty among the Turks, the contemporary author Ziau-d-din Barani, who must have known the fact states that 'Jalalu-d-din came of a race different from the Turks,' and that by the death of Sultan Kaikobad, 'the Turks lost the Empire.' In regard to this point I append a letter very obligingly written by Dr. A. Suhrawardy of the Calcutta University in answer to an enquiry I made on the point at issue. I publish the letter with grateful acknowledgments to the learned doctor for his courtesy in spite of personal inconvenience.

'With reference to your question regarding the origin of Jalalu-d-din and Alau-d-din, the Khilji sovereigns, I beg to say that in 'Tazikhi-Feroz Shahi of Zayau-d-din Barni,' Jalalu-d-din is not considered as belonging to the race of the Turks; nor is it clearly laid down in it that he came of an Afghan race. This fact will be clear from Mr. Elliotts' *History of India* (Vol. iii, page 34), in which the author has given the translation of a portion of Feroz Shahi, which runs as follows :—

'At the same time, Jalalu-d-din who was Ariz-i-Mamalik (Muster Master-General), had gone to Baharpur, attended by a body of his relations and friends. Here he held a muster and inspection of the forces. He came of a race different from that of the Turks; so he had no confidence in them, nor would the Turks own him as belonging to the number of his friends.'

I fail to understand how Mr. Vincent Smith considers him an Afghan.

According to 'Tazikh-i-Ferishta by Abdul Casim,' Jalalu-d-din is considered as belonging to the race of the Turks, as it will be apparent from the following lines from the translation of Tarikhi Ferishta by John Briggs (pp. 285–7). Vol. I :—

'Nizamu-d-din Ahmed relates, that he has seen, in some respectable works, that the tribe of Khalich or Kalij, is descended from Khalich Khan, a son-in-law of Chengiz Khan, and that his history is this :—Kalij Khan and his wife constantly disagreed, but he was afraid of throwing her off on account of the power of his father-in-law. At length when Chengiz Khan, having pursued Jalalu-d-din Khwarazm Shah to the banks of Indus, was on his return towards Iiran and Turan, Kalij Khan, being well acquainted with the mountainous country of Ghur and Jurjistan, watched his opportunity to throw off his allegiance to Changiz Khan, and remained with his tribe, amounting to 30,000 families, in those hills. Upon the death of Chengiz Khan, none of his descendants thought fit to persecute Kalij Khan, who remained ever since in those hills ; and as the race of Ghur was now seated on the throne of India, the Khiljis, on account of their vicinity, went to Delhi in parties, and remained there. Jalalu-d-din Khilji of Delhi ; and Sultan Mahmud Khilji of Mandu, are both descended from Kalij Khan, vulgurly called Khalij Khan, and from him the tribe is called Khilji. But, according to the author of Saljuqnāma, Turk, the son of Japhet, the son of Noah, had eleven children, one of whom was called Khulich ; and from him are descended the Khilichis or Khiljis. I conceive this account the most probable of the two, because the Khiljis are often mentioned in the histories of the kings of Ghazni, particularly in the reigns of Subukhigin and Sultan Mahmud ; and it is certain, that they existed anterior to the time of Chengiz Khan ; but it is possible that Kalij Khan might be of the tribe of Khalji, and that the father of Jalalu-d-din, and the ancestor of Sultan Mahmud of Malwa, may have both been descended in a direct line for him.'

I have gone through the Persian text of both Feroz-i Shahi and Tarikhi-i-Ferishta and found that the translations so far given here are correct.

An *Oriental Biographical Dictionary*, by T. W. Beale, page 137.

'It is mentioned in the above-named book that Feroz Shah surnamed Jalalu-d-din was the first Sultan of the second branch of the Turks-Afghan dynasty called Khilji.'

In conclusion, I beg to say that no sound inference can be drawn from the materials now before me that they were Afghans, nor can these be the basis of our conclusion that they were Turks. In my opinion, the conclusion arrived at by T. W. Beale is to some extent satisfactory.

INDEX

The following abbreviations are used in the Index :—

K.	= King	Dy.	= Dynasty
Cap.	= Capital	Rds.	= Roads
Feud.	= Feudatory	Hoys.	= Hoysala
Sur. n.	= Surname.	Inscn.	= Inscription
Vill.	= Village.	Dt.	= District.